Appalachian Trail Guide to
SHENANDOAH NATIONAL PARK
with side trails

2012
Fourteenth Edition

THE POTOMAC APPALACHIAN TRAIL CLUB
118 Park St., S.E.
Vienna, Virginia 22180
www.patc.net

Fourteenth Edition
Edited
by
John Hedrick

Printing History

The area covered in this Guide was originally part of a more comprehensive publication known as *Guide to Paths in the Blue Ridge*. The first version was issued in 1931, and referred to Virginia only. In a second edition in 1934, the area covered was extended to include Pennsylvania and Maryland; supplements were issued in 1935 and 1937. The third edition was published in 1941 and the fourth in 1950. In 1959, the comprehensive guidebook was divided into three sections, one of which covered the area represented by this Guide. Subsequent editions were published in 1967, 1973, 1977, 1986, 1991, 1994, 1999 and 2009.

Library of Congress Cataloging-in-Publication Data
Hedrick, John.
Appalachian Trail guide to Shenandoah National Park : with side trails / John Hedrick.—Fourteenth ed.
p. cm.
ISBN 978-0-915746-64-4
1. Hiking--Appalachian Trail--Guidebooks. 2. Hiking—Virginia—Shenandoah National Park—Guidebooks. 3. Appalachian Trail—Guidebooks. 4. Shenandoah National Park (Va.)—Guidebooks. I. Title.
GV199.42.A68H44 2012
917.55'9--dc23
2011045315

Appreciation

This edition has been made possible with the help of many dedicated people, including:

Shenandoah National Park:
John Buchheit and Melissa Rudacille

and

PATC: Dave Pierce, Shirley Schulz and Andy Zipser.

Front cover photo by Rob and Ann Simpson,
www.snphotos.com.

Back cover photo, of Overall Run Falls in the winter,
by Lee Sheaffer

In a guide of this size, it is inevitable that errors, both typographical and factual, will occur. Please report any you find to *publications@patc.net*, so that they may be corrected in future editions.

Introduction

Bill Bryson, in his best-selling book *A Walk in the Woods*, declares that Shenandoah National Park is "my favorite part of the Appalachian Trail." Hikers have varying tastes, of course, but there are strong reasons for the appeal of the 101 miles of the Appalachian National Scenic Trail (the *AT*) within Shenandoah National Park.

For one thing, because the *AT* here is along the crests of the Blue Ridge Mountains, the climbs and descents are gentle. Then too, because of the height of the trail, hikers again and again emerge from forest to rocky outcrops offering stunning vistas to east or west. Of course, wildlife abounds in Shenandoah, from black bears and deer to wild turkeys and many species of birds, and wildflowers crowd the trailsides in spring.

A special treat for Bryson and other hikers: the *AT* crosses Skyline Drive, the sky-high and historic roadway through the park, some 28 times! The proximity of the *AT* to Skyline Drive is a real boon to hikers who are not thru-hikers (those hiking the entire 2,175 miles of the *AT*). Hikers choosing to walk just a section and visitors anxious to step onto the *AT* for just a mile or two—all have a starting-off spot every few miles.

The *AT* in Shenandoah National Park is full of wonders and surprises. Moving from south to north, in early June you'll stand amidst an ocean of mountain laurel in bloom just before the Sawmill Run Overlook: on both sides of you, as far as your eyes can see, cascades of pink and white. You'll circle Blackrock, an immense pile of quartzite rocks encrusted with black rock tripe (hence the name). On Loft Mountain you'll have a panoramic view of mountains to the west, peak upon peak. We guarantee you'll rest a while here! In season, you'll still find Milam apples from the old apple trees at Milam Gap. Between Fishers Gap and Spitler Knoll Overlook, a series of wonderful rock ledges invites you to rest or lunch as you gaze westward. Farther north, the trail's many other vistas include those from Hogback, Little Hogback, and North and South Marshall.

As you gaze east or west along the *AT*, Wilderness spreads below you—Wilderness designated by Congress that encompasses 40% of Shenandoah, preserving the natural world. The *AT* in Shenandoah witnesses the human story as well, in a family cemetery, in an old homesite grown over with trees, in a former orchard or pasture. There is human history, too, in rock retaining walls built by the Civilian Conservation Corps, in waterbars kept clear by the PATC, in the trail itself with its thousands of footsteps.

Welcome to Shenandoah National Park! The world along the *AT*, set apart from everyday life, is a world that refreshes and renews. And here are three very special places in that world in Shenandoah, one from each District of the park. On the *AT* near Jenkins Gap in the North District, if you listen quietly, birdsongs from dozens of birds will sound all around you. In the South District, just north of Loft Mountain, you can sit beside a cool and lovely stream. Yes, as high as the *AT* is in the park, at this point it touches Ivy Creek. Finally, in the Central District just north of Swift Run Gap, there's a brooding, dark stretch of trail that some thru-hikers have said they love. You won't have far-flung views on the *AT* here—just silence, and peace, and tall, tall yellow poplars.

Martha Bogle
Superintendent
Shenandoah National Park

ABBREVIATIONS

AT	Appalachian Trail
mi	mile or miles
PATC	Potomac Appalachian Trail Club
SNP	Shenandoah National Park
SDMP	Skyline Drive Milepost
USGS	United States Geological Survey
SR	State Route
RWMA	Rapidan Wildlife Management Area

USE OF MILEAGE NUMBERS

In the section titled "Side Trails," wherever two series of mileages are given (example: 0.0-9.2), the left-hand figures are the mileages in the direction as described, the figures to the right are the mileages in the reverse direction.

Springs
The purity of water from natural sources found along trails cannot be guaranteed. All water from natural sources should be treated before use.

The Potomac Appalachian Trail Club expressly denies any liability for any accident or injury to persons using these trails.

TABLE OF CONTENTS

Welcome sign

Photo by Lee Sheaffer

USE OF GUIDE AND TRAIL

This guide is one of a series of guidebooks covering the entire Appalachian Trail (*AT*) from Maine to Georgia. The Potomac Appalachian Trail Club is responsible for preparing this guide, and another covering the area extending north from SNP to the Maryland-Pennsylvania border.

Format of Guidebook

Shenandoah National Park falls naturally into three districts, North, Central and South, each defined by a major road crossing of the Blue Ridge and an entrance station to Skyline Drive. The Trail data are divided into 9 sections, demarcated by Blue Ridge gaps and numbered from north to south. The North District includes Sections 1 and 2; the Central District includes Sections 3, 4, and 5; the South District includes Sections 6, 7, 8, and 9. At the beginning of each District is an overall sketch map of the entire District. Within each section, the Trail Description is given first from north to south, followed by the same information given from south to north:

• Each section begins with a profile map showing elevation change along the route of the Trail.

• For each section, both general information and detailed Trail data are provided.

• The general information includes a brief description of the overall route and notes features of particular scenic or historic interest; it lists side trails, trail approaches, accommodations (huts and cabins), and appropriate PATC or USGS maps.

• The detailed data are designated for on-the-Trail use by hikers. They briefly describe the beginning and end of each Trail section, outline geographical features and useful mileages, and note precise location of accommodations (huts and cabins), water, and side trails.

The Trails

This guide provides information on 107.1 miles of the Appalachian Trail and over 500 miles of side trails of various types.

Trail Markings

Trail markings in SNP take one of two forms. At trail intersections and other key points along the *AT* and side trails, the Park Service has erected concrete posts that provide trail information. The data are stamped on metal bands ringing the posts. Along the length of each trail and many woods roads are colored blazes painted on trees. Blazes are typically 2" by 6." A single blaze painted at regular intervals marks the general direction of the trail or woods road. A double blaze (two blazes, one placed above the other) is placed to warn hikers to "take notice." It may indicate an intersection with another trail, an obscure turn or a change in direction which otherwise might not be noticed. The color of the blaze identifies the type of trail being hiked:

• The *AT* is marked by white blazes and is for foot travel only. The *AT* was relocated, in part, and improved by the Civilian Conservation Corps in the 1930s as a three- to four-foot-wide path running the length of SNP. The footway is obvious and easily followed. The Potomac Appalachian Trail Club maintains the entire length of the *AT* in SNP.

• Side trails are marked by blue blazes and are for foot travel only. Blue-blazed side trails are more rustic trails maintained at more rugged standards than the *AT*. The trail width is typically three feet or less, and blazes may be spaced farther apart. The Potomac Appalachian Trail Club maintains approximately 80% of the blue-blazed trails in SNP.

• Yellow-blazed trails are for both horses and foot travelers. Yellow-blazed trails are typically three feet wide, and the footway may be rougher than that experienced on blue-blazed trails. SNP crews maintain most of the yellow-blazed trails. Most Park fire roads are also yellow-blazed. Horses are limited to trails and fire roads that are yellow-blazed.

Trail Use

Those using the *AT* or side trails should be careful not to damage property or to litter. Park regulations forbid the use of any motorized vehicle on trails. Fire and camping regulations are listed in detail. Cutting of any standing tree, dead or alive, is prohibited. Flowers should not be picked. All forms of wildlife are protected and hunting is prohibited. Old homesites, cemeteries, and walls are protected resources, as are their associated artifacts. Do not disturb, remove or camp in their vicinity.

Some of the side trails have their lower ends outside the Park on private land. Owners can and sometimes do close them to hikers—usually after some unfortunate event. *Respect for private property rights is extremely important.* Many of these closed trailheads are clearly marked on PATC trail maps. However, maps are only as current as their date of publication. If you are unsure about the status of boundary access on private land, check with SNP. If your trailhead starts on private property, please stay on the trail and respect the rights of the property owner.

Due to gypsy moth damage and other blights affecting the forest, trail users should plan for the possibility of difficult going on some trails due to downed trees and excessive herbaceous growth. The lack of tree cover provides ideal growing conditions for field grasses, wildflowers, ferns, stinging nettles, thorny blackberry, and many other non-woody plants. In selected cases, this growth can close in on a trail, making hiking extremely difficult. Hikers should also be prepared for extended stretches of hiking in full sun on the higher ridges in the Park. Sunscreen, a hat, and extra water are recommended if hiking is anticipated in these areas.

From early November to early January during hunting season, Skyline Drive is gated and locked at night due to excessive wildlife poaching. Gates are closed and locked at dusk and re-opened at 8 a.m. the following morning. Hikers have several options to determine when and where these closures will occur. The Park maintains a non-emergency phone number that can provide this information (540-999-3500) and has it listed on its web site (*www.nps.gov/shen*). In the event that you are locked in the Park, there are instructions on the back of the closed gate that will tell you where to go and who to call for assistance. The Park also maintains a 24-hour emergency phone number, (800-732-0911). For locations of public telephones, see "Public Telephones."

Bicycles

None of the trails or woods roads within the boundaries of SNP are open to bicycle use. Bikes are allowed on any paved surface within the Park. This would include all of Skyline Drive and any other paved service road inside the Park. There is also a paved walkway between Big Meadows Campground and the Byrd Visitor Center where bikes are allowed. Hikers should report any unauthorized use of hiking trails, horse trails, or woods roads to SNP at 800-732-0911.

Responsibility for Safety

It is extremely important to plan your hike, especially in places where water is scarce. Purify water drawn from any source. Water purity cannot be guaranteed. The Appalachian Trail Conservancy and the various maintaining clubs attempt to locate good sources of water along the Trail but have no control over these sources and cannot, in any sense, be responsible for the quality of the water at any given time. You must determine the safety of all water you use.

Certain risks are inherent in any *AT* hike. Each *AT* user must accept personal responsibility for his or her safety while on the Trail. The Appalachian Trail Conservancy and its member maintaining clubs cannot ensure the safety of any hiker on the Trail, and, when undertaking a hike on the Trail, each user thereby assumes the risk for any accident, illness, or injury that might occur on the Trail.

Enjoy your hike, but please take all appropriate precautions for your safety and well being.

Although criminal acts are probably less common on the Appalachian Trail than in most other human environments, they do occur. Crimes of violence, including murder and rape, have been committed over the years. It should be noted, however, that serious crimes on the *AT* have a frequency rate on the order of fewer than one per year or less, on a trail that enjoys three to four million visitors in the same period. Even if such events are less common on the Trail than elsewhere, criminals can be more difficult to deal with because of the remoteness of most of the Trail. When hiking, you must assume the need for at least the same level of prudence as you would exercise if walking the streets of a strange city or an unknown neighborhood.

A few elementary suggestions can be noted. It is best not to hike alone, but do not assume safety just because you are hiking with a partner. Be cautious of strangers. Be sure that family and/or friends know your planned itinerary and timetable. If you customarily use a "Trail name," your home contacts should know what it is. Although telephones are rarely handy along the Trail, if you can reach one, dial 911 or ask the operator to connect you to the state police if you are the victim of, or a witness to, a crime.

The carrying of firearms is not recommended. The risks of accidental injury or death far outweigh any self-defense value that might result from arming oneself.

Be prudent and cautious. Trust your gut.

Trail Maps

Detailed maps of the *AT* are available for the entire area covered by this Guide. Their use is highly recommended.

The maps have been prepared by the Maps Committee of PATC based on terrain and road information extracted from USGS maps. These 6-color, topographic maps indicate the route of the *AT* highlighted in contrasting color, side trails, shelters, cabins, highways, all SNP facilities, and major geographical features. Three PATC maps cover the *AT* in SNP:

Map #	Scale/Currency	Area Covered
9	1:62,500 Edition 18 (2009)	North District SNP (Front Royal to US-211)
10	1:62,500 Edition 21 (2008)	Central District SNP (US-211 to US-33)
11	1:63,360 Edition 16 (2009)	South District SNP (US-33 to I-64)

ATC maps are available from the PATC Sales Office in Vienna, Va., at *www.patc.net* and at various other distributors. These maps, like the Guide, are periodically revised. The edition information, shown above, is current with publication of this Guide. These maps are considered the best for hiker use.

The relevant USGS 7.5 min. by 7.5 min. quadrangles (1:24,000 scale) are also indicated under "Maps" for each District of SNP. These may be purchased at the Maps Sales Office at USGS Headquarters in Reston, Va.; or by mail from "Map Distribution, US Geological Survey, Box 25286 Federal Center, Denver, CO 80225." Since relocations in SNP have been minor, these maps do portray the *AT* in a satisfactory manner; however, in most cases they do not reliably show the many blue-blazed side trails open to the public. The USGS maps are primarily helpful to those wishing to study the detailed terrain and hydrological features of the area.

Phone Numbers/Websites

Listed are phone numbers and web pages for the three organizations responsible for the trails listed in this Guide. General information is most easily obtained by going to the website; however, useful telephone numbers and addresses have also been listed.

Appalachian Trail Conservancy
Website: *www.appalachiantrail.org*
Telephone: 304-535-6331
Address: Washington St. & Storer College Place
                 P.O. Box 807
                 Harpers Ferry, WV 25425

Potomac Appalachian Trail Club
Website: *www.patc.net*
Telephone: *General Information:* 703-242-0315
                 Office hours for the above number are:
                      Monday-Thursday, 7-9 p.m.
                      Thurs. and Friday, noon to 2p.m.
Fax: 703-242-0968 (available 24-hours/day)
Address: 118 Park Street, SE
                 Vienna, VA 22180-4609

Shenandoah National Park
Website: *www.nps.gov/shen*
Telephone: 540-999-3500 (recorded information)
                 800-732-0911 (emergency only)
                 800-828-1120 (TDD)
Address: 3655 US Highway 211 East
                 Luray, VA 22835-9036

ARAMARK: Lodging inside Shenandoah National Park
Address: P.O. Box 727
                 Luray, VA 22835

Reservations: 800-999-4714
FAX: 540-743-7883
Web Site: *www.visitshenandoah.com*

Shenandoah National Park Association

A non-profit organization devoted to supporting the interpretive and educational programs of Shenandoah National Park:

Address: 3655 US HWY 211E
Luray, VA 22835
Phone: 540-999-3582
Fax: 540-999-3583
Web Site: *www.snpbooks.org*

Camping Reservations
Phone: 1-877-444-6777
Web Site: *www.recreation.gov*

Trail Relocations

Always follow the marked Trail. If it differs from the guidebook's Trail description, it is because the Trail recently was relocated in the area, probably to avoid a hazard or undesirable feature or to remove it from private property. If you use the old Trail, you may be trespassing and generating ill will toward the Trail community.

Information on Trail relocations between guidebook revisions often is available from the ATC information department. Every effort has been made in this guide to alert you to relocations that may occur. Do not follow new trails that are not blazed, because they may not be open to the public yet.

Trail Ethics

Treat the land with care to preserve the beauty of the Trail environment and ensure the Trail's integrity. Improper use can endanger the continuity of the Trail. Private landowners may order hikers off their property and close the route. Vandalism, camping and fires where prohibited, and other abuse can result in Trail closure. Please follow a few basic guidelines:

• Do not cut, deface, or destroy trees, flowers, or any other natural or constructed feature.

• Do not damage fences or leave gates open.

• Do not litter. Carry out all trash. Do not bury garbage for animals or others to uncover.

• Be careful with fire. Extinguish all burning material; a forest fire can start more easily than many realize.

• In short: Take nothing but pictures, leave nothing but footprints, kill nothing but time.

Dogs are often a nuisance to other hikers and to property owners. Landowners complain of dogs running loose and soiling yards. The territorial instincts of dogs often result in fights with other dogs. Dogs also frighten some hikers and chase wildlife. If a pet cannot be controlled, it should be left at home; otherwise, it will generate ill-will toward the AT and its users. Also, many at-home pets' muscles, footpads, and sleeping habits are not adaptable to the rigors of AT hiking. A dog on any Park trail must be on a leash. Dogs are prohibited on some trails.

Ask for water and seek directions and information from homes along the Trail only in an emergency. Some residents receive more hiker visitors than they enjoy. Respect the privacy of people living near the Park boundary.

Keep to the defined Trail. Cutting across switchbacks, particularly on graded trails, disfigures the Trail, complicates route finding and causes erosion. The savings in time or distance is minimal; the damage is great. In areas where log walkways, steps, or rock treadway indicate special trail construction, take pains to use them. Those have been installed to reduce trail widening and erosion.

Park Regulations — General

1. Dogs (except for trained guide and work dogs) must be on a leash while within Park boundaries. They are prohibited on the following trails:

- Fox Hollow Trail
- Traces Trail
- Stony Man Trail
- Limberlost Trail
- Old Rag Ridge Trail
- Old Rag Saddle Trail
- Dark Hollow Trail
- Story of the Forest Trail
- Bearfence Mountain Loop Trail
- Frazier Discovery Trail

2. No open wood or charcoal fires may be kindled except in fireplaces provided at trailside huts and those provided in established picnic grounds and campgrounds.

3. No lighted cigarette, cigar, pipe heel, match or other burning material shall be thrown from any vehicle or saddle horse, or dropped into any grass, leaves, twigs or other combustible or flammable material. Smoking within the Park may be prohibited or limited by the superintendent when, in his or her judgment, a current fire hazard makes such action prudent.

4. The use of fireworks or firecrackers in the Park is prohibited.

5. Hunting is prohibited in the Park.

6. The feeding of wildlife is *strictly* prohibited by law. The food harms the animal, and the animal can harm YOU.

7. Visitors must take home any trash they generate in the Park.

Camping Regulations

1. Permits are required for backcountry camping. See Backcountry Camping Regulations (next section).

2. At public campgrounds, the regular fireplaces con-

structed for the convenience of visitors must be used. Firewood is sold at Park waysides during the summer travel season. Do not transport firewood from outside of the Park into the Park.

3. No person, party or organization is permitted to camp in any public camping area in the Park for more than 30 days in any calendar year.

4. The installation of permanent camping facilities by visitors is prohibited. The digging or leveling of the ground in any campsite is prohibited.

5. Campers may not leave their camps unattended for more than 24 hours without special permission obtained in advance from the superintendent. Camping equipment left unattended in any public camping area for more than 24 hours will be subject to removal by order of the superintendent. The expense of such removal will be paid by the person or persons leaving such equipment.

6. The superintendent may establish hours during which quiet must be maintained at any camp, and prohibit the running of motors at or near a camp during such hours.

7. At all campsites, food or similar material (including toothpaste, shampoo, and other sweet-smelling substances) must be either: (1) completely sealed in a vehicle or trailer that is constructed of solid, nonpliable material; or (2) suspended at least ten (10) feet above the ground and four (4) feet horizontally from any post, tree trunk or branch. **Note:** Do not damage trees in this process.

Backcountry Camping Regulations
Definition of Terms

"Backcountry" in Shenandoah National Park is defined as the primitive, undeveloped portions of the Park managed primarily for natural conditions and processes. Facilities and/or cultural resources surrounded by backcountry are part of the backcountry. The Skyline Drive historic zone and associated developed zones are specifically excluded.

Backcountry Permits

No person or group of persons traveling together may camp without a *valid backcountry camping permit*. You <u>must</u> have a valid backcountry permit in order to camp in the backcountry overnight. Permits may be denied when it is necessary to protect Park resources or Park visitors, or to regulate levels of visitor use in legislatively designated wilderness areas. Permits are presently available without charge. At the Park, permits will be issued only between the hours of sunrise and one hour before sunset. For backcountry camping and permit information visit web site *www.nps.gov/shen*. Backcountry permits may be obtained at the following locations:

• Dickey Ridge Visitor Center, located in the North District at SDMP 4.6

• Byrd Visitor Center, located in the Central District at SDMP 51.0

• Park Headquarters, located on the western boundary of the Park on US 211

• The entrance stations located at Front Royal, Thornton Gap, Swift Run Gap, and Rockfish Gap

• At self-registration backcountry permit booths at the following locations:

    1. North District—*AT* at Park Entrance at Possums Rest
    2. Central District—Weakley Hollow near the start of the Old Rag Ridge Trail at Old Rag fee station
    3. Big Meadows Campground, near the camp–ground office
    4. South District—Loft Mountain Information Center
    5. South District—on *AT* near Rockfish Gap

Permits can also be requested by mail and should be accompanied by the camper's name, address, phone number, number in party, entry and exit dates of trip, description of vehicle (make, model, color and tag number) and trip itinerary, including where you will park and trail areas in which you will camp. Permit requests should be sent to: Shenandoah National Park Headquarters, 3655 US Hwy 211 East, Luray, Virginia, 22835.

Leave No Trace

The National Park Service and other federal land management agencies have adopted the "Leave No Trace" (LNT) outdoor skills and ethics education program developed by the National Outdoor Leadership School (NOLS). This is a national educational program whose mission is to educate wildland user groups, federal agencies and the public about minimum-impact camping and hiking The program is not meant to provide a set of rules and regulations, but is intended as principles and practices that help the backcountry or wilderness visitor to make better decisions "based on an abiding respect for and appreciation of wild places and their inhabitants." NOLS provides the LNT Skills and Ethics Series of educational publications that are directed to LNT practices for specific geographical regions of the country or to specific forms of outdoor recreation. The LNT Southeastern States booklet provides recommended LNT practices for the region including SNP. SNP and the PATC support and teach LNT within the Park and in public outreach programs.

The principles of Leave No Trace are:
1. Plan ahead and prepare
2. Travel and camp on durable surfaces
3. Properly dispose of waste
4. Leave what you find
5. Minimize campfire impacts
6. Respect wildlife
7. Be considerate of other visitors

The practice of LNT techniques by SNP backcountry visitors is strongly encouraged and can assure the Park backcountry regulations, which are based in the same recreation ecology science as the LNT program, are understood and adhered to by backcountry visitors to preserve and improve backcountry conditions. A brochure that provides Park backcountry camping regulations information and recommended backcountry use practices is available at the Park contact stations, by mail, or at the Park's web site.

Group Size

Group size is limited to 10 people to camp. Divide a larger group into smaller parties. Parties larger than 10 people should camp in separate groups out of sight of each party.

Location of Camp

No person or group may backcountry camp:

(1) Within one-quarter mile of a paved road, Park boundary, or Park facilities such as a campground, picnic area, visitor center, lodge, wayside, or restaurant.

(2) Within 100 yds. of a hut, cabin, or day-use shelter. Camping may occur in Park-constructed, designated campsites.

(3) Within 10 yds. of a stream or other natural water source.

(4) Within 20 yds. of a Park trail or fire road.

(5) Within 50 yds. of standing buildings or ruins, including stone foundations, chimneys, and log walls.

(6) Within 50 yds. of another camping party or a "no camping" post.

Backcountry campers should check their sites carefully before pitching a tent. A large number of dead trees now exist within the Park boundary due to gypsy moth-killed trees and other forest blights. Campers should be on the lookout for standing dead trees or dead limbs, which could fall unexpectedly. Campers should be especially careful during windy or icy conditions.

Camping Selection

When selecting an area to camp, look for and try to camp on pre-existing campsites out of sight of trails and roads.

1. Pre-existing campsites: are established by prior visitor use and are not posted or signed.

    a. Do not camp more than two consecutive nights in the same location.

2. Dispersed camping: may occur on a previously undisturbed area. Please use "pristine site camping" Leave No Trace practices.

    a. Limit your stay to one night.

    b. Get out of sight of Park trails.

3. Designated camping: campsites are Park-constructed and posted to concentrate backcountry camping at high-use sites.

    a. Only provided at *AT* huts to accommodate overflow camping.

    b. Camping may not exceed two nights in one campsite location

4. No-camping areas. The following areas are closed to backcountry camping to preserve special resource conditions and values.

    a. Limberlost Trail Area (bounded by Whiteoak Canyon Fire Road, the Skyland-Big Meadows Horse Trail, and Skyline Drive).

    b. Hawksbill Mountain summit (above 3,600 ft.).

    c. Whiteoak Canyon (between the Skyland-Big Meadows Horse Trail and Cedar Run Link Trail.

    d. Old Rag Mountain Summit (above 2,800 ft.).

    e. Big Meadows (Big Meadows Clearing area within view of Skyline Drive).

    f. Rapidan Camp (no camping within 1/2 mi of buildings).

Fires

No open wood or charcoal fires may be kindled in backcountry areas except in fireplaces provided at trailside huts. The use of small gasoline, propane or solid fuel camping stoves is recommended. Fires at trailside huts must not be left unattended and should be completely extinguished.

Water

Although the Park may have sources of clean, potable water, any water source could become polluted. Most water sources along the trails (with the exception of public campgrounds) are unprotected and susceptible to contamination. All water should be treated to remove bacteria, protozoa and virus. Bringing water to a rolling boil will remove these germs, according to William W. Forgey, MD. (CDC recommends boiling for two minutes.) Filters with a pore size under 1 micron will remove all but viruses. Iodine or chlorine will remove viruses and giardia cysts, but are ineffective against cryptosporidium, another common protozoa. Avoid contaminating the water supply and the surrounding area. Dishes, clothes and hands should never be washed in the water supply. Washing should be done well away from the water supply.

Pets

Pets must be on a leash at all times and are prohibited on posted trails. See "General Regulations" for a list of these trails.

Food Storage

At all backcountry campsites, food (including toothpaste, shampoo, suntan lotion, creams and any other aromatic substance) must be stored in one or more of the following three ways so that wildlife cannot have access to it:

1) Hang food in a tree at least ten feet above the ground and four feet horizontally from the tree trunk.
2) Hang food on a food storage pole provided at some backcountry facilities.

3) Store food within an agency-approved bear-proof storage container. For a list of approved storage containers, go to *www.sierrawild.gov/bears/allowed-bear-cannisters*.

Sanitation
- All trash must be packed out of the backcountry and properly disposed of in appropriate refuse containers.
- No bathing or washing of food, clothing, dishes, or other property at public water outlets, fixtures or pools, except at those designated for such purpose.
- No polluting or contaminating of Park area waters—springs, streams, etc. Biodegradable soaps and shampoos are considered to be pollutants and should be used well away from water sources.
- In developed areas, human body waste should be disposed at designated locations or in fixtures provided for that purpose. In non-developed areas, human body waste should be disposed at a distance of 20 yds. or more from streams, trails, or roads. Solid waste must be buried in a hole at least three inches deep.

Other
- The cutting of green boughs for beds is prohibited.
- Any article likely to frighten horses should not be hung near a road or trail used by horses.
- Hunting is prohibited inside the Park boundary. No camp may be established in the Park and used as a base for hunting outside the Park.

Fines

Rangers in Shenandoah National Park have a responsibility to protect Park resources for future generations. Hand-in-hand with this responsibility is the need to issue citations to individuals who do not follow the regulations for using this federal property. Depending on the nature of the violation, fines can run from $50 for minor infractions (such as camping in the backcountry without a permit), up to $5,000 for major infractions (such as hunting wildlife). Rangers can, at their own discretion, also fine each individual member of a party in violation of the regulations. Rangers also have the right to impound animals/pets that are running loose in the Park, or on hiking trails. Individuals interested in visiting Shenandoah National Park should acquaint themselves with the regulations before they enter the Park. Familiarity with the rules will ensure that your visit to Shenandoah will be an enjoyable one.

Shelters, Huts and Cabins

Shelters

Four three-sided day-use trail shelters are located in the Park. Trail shelters are to be used for picnics and for temporary shelter from storms. *Overnight stays are not allowed* in these shelters. Trail shelters can be found at the following locations:

• Byrds Nest #1, southwest of the Old Rag summit, on the Saddle Trail

• Byrds Nest #2, on the Hawksbill summit

• Byrds Nest #4, south of Elkwallow Wayside, off the *AT*

• Old Rag Shelter, 1/2-mile southwest of Old Rag summit, on the Saddle Trail

Huts

Nine three-sided shelters along the *AT* have been designated "huts"—Gravel Springs and Pass Mtn. huts in the North District, Rock Spring, Bearfence Mtn. and Byrds Nest #3 in the Central District, and Hightop, Pinefield, Blackrock huts and Calf Mountain Shelter in the South District. These nine huts may be used for overnight stays by overnight backpackers with a valid backcountry camping permit. To prevent overuse or improper use, huts are monitored by SNP Park Rangers, PATC hut overseers, the PATC Trail Patrol Ridgerunners, and other volunteers during seasons of heavy use. Huts are to be used on a first-come, first-served basis. The designated campsites near each hut are for overnight backpackers who prefer to use a tent instead of the hut.

AT distances between huts and shelters, listed north to south (parentheses indicate distance off trail):

From US 522 to Tom Floyd Wayside	**2.9**
Tom Floyd Wayside to Gravel Springs Hut (0.2 mi.)	**10.4**
Gravel Springs Hut (0.2 mi.) to Pass Mtn. Hut (0.2 mi.)	**13.1**
Pass Mtn. Hut (0.2 mi.) to Byrds Nest #3 Hut	**4.4**
Rock Spring Hut (0.2 mi.) to Bearfence Hut (0.2 mi.)	**10.9**
Bearfence Hut (0.2 mi.) to Hightop Hut (0.1 mi.)	**12.4**
Hightop Hut (0.1 mi.) to Pinefield Hut (0.1 mi.)	**8.2**
Pinefield Hut (0.1 mi.) to Blackrock Hut (0.2 m)	**13.2**
Blackrock Hut (0.2 mi.) to Calf Mtn. Shelter (0.3 mi.)	**13.0**
Calf Mtn. Shelter (0.3 mi.) to US 250 at Rockfish Gap	**7.0**

Cabins

A total of six historic rustic backcountry cabins are located inside the Park boundaries. Cabins are operated and maintained by the PATC as a concessionaire to the Park and are available for rent to the public and club members on a first-come, first-served basis. Two are the original cabins built by mountain families before the Park was established, and one (Corbin Cabin) is on the National Register of Historic Places. The remainder were built by the PATC or CCC.

Cabins are equipped with all necessary items except food, personal bedding, lights and firewood. There is a natural water source at each cabin (spring or stream); however, these sources are not tested and the purity of the water cannot be guaranteed. Boiling is recommended. There is a wood stove and/or fireplace for cooking inside, plus all necessary pots, pans, plates, cutlery, cups, saucers, glasses, etc. A propane stove is also available. Bunks, mattresses and blankets (one per occupant) up to stated capacity of the cabin are also provided. It is advisable to bring one's own sleeping bag, lanterns and fuel. A broom, ax, saw, first aid kit and other items necessary for good housekeeping are provided. Cabins are available at the following locations:

• North District—Range View Cabin, just off the *AT* east of Elkwallow Wayside

• Central District—Corbin Cabin, along the Nicholson Hollow Trail or at the end of Corbin Cabin Cutoff Trail

• Central District—Jones Mountain Cabin, along the Jones Mountain Trail

• Central District—Rock Spring Cabin, off the *AT* south of Hawksbill Mountain

• Central District—Pocosin Cabin, along the Pocosin Fire Road

• South District—Doyles River Cabin, off the Doyles River Trail

Fees for overnight stays vary from cabin to cabin; however most are significantly less than the amount charged for "front-country" accommodations. There is no vehicular access to these rustic cabins—they must be reached by foot travel or horseback on trails designated for that purpose. Winter access can be further complicated by Skyline Drive closure. Check with the Park (540-999-3500) for information on Skyline Drive closures. Wheeled conveyances used to transport coolers and other supplies are not allowed on Park fire roads or trails. See *www.patc.net* for cabin information.

The PATC also maintains a number of cabins just outside the Park boundary. A complete guide with photos describing all the cabins in the PATC system, both inside and outside the Park boundaries, is available from the PATC for a small fee and can be ordered at *www.patc.net*. Individuals wishing to rent cabins should call PATC between 7 p.m. and 9 p.m., Monday-Thursday, or noon to 2 p.m. Thursday or Friday, at 703-242-0315. These are the **only** hours during which club members and the public can make cabin reservations. Reservations may be made two calendar months prior to the date of use. Cabin availability may be checked online, at *www.patc.net*, or by calling PATC at the times listed above.

Campgrounds

A total of four campgrounds is located inside the Park at the following locations:

- North District, Mathews Arm Campground—179 sites
- Central District, Big Meadows Campground—217 sites
- Central District, Lewis Mt. Campground—32 sites
- South District, Loft Mountain Campground—219 sites

Campground availability and opening/closing dates may vary from year to year. Campgrounds typically open in the spring and close after the fall color season (late October). Of the campgrounds listed above, only one, Big Meadows, accepts reservations. Reservations can be made by calling 877-444-6777, or online at *www.recreation.gov*. All other campsites are available on a first-come, first-served basis.

Camp Stores

There are four camp stores inside the Park boundaries. All are easily accessible from Skyline Drive or the *AT*. Camp stores are available at the following locations:

- South District—Loft Mountain Campground near the Registration Office (SDMP 79.8)
- Central District—Big Meadows, next to the Byrd Visitor Center (SDMP 51.2)
- Central District—Lewis Mountain Campstore (SDMP 57.5)
- North District—Elkwallow Wayside (SDMP 24.1)

Snack food is also available at the gift shops located inside the Park. These include:

- South District—Loft Mountain Wayside (SDMP 79.5)
- Central District—Big Meadows Wayside (SDMP 51.2)
- Central District—Skyland Lodge (SDMP 41.7)
- North District—Elkwallow Wayside (SDMP 24.1)

Camp stores and gift shops are typically open from mid-

May thru October, depending on campground opening dates, which vary from year to year. Backpackers are required to leave their packs outside these facilities, due to limited space inside the facilities.

Restaurants

Five places for food are located inside the Park, at the following locations:

• South District—Loft Mountain Wayside: snack bar (SDMP 79.5)

• Central District—Big Meadows Lodge: dining room/tap room and Big Meadows Wayside (SDMP 51.3)

• Central District—Skyland: dining room/taproom (SDMP 41.7)

• North District—Elkwallow Wayside: snack bar (SDMP 24.1)

Restaurants are typically open from mid-May into October at varying times. Hours are extended during times of peak tourist activity. Backpackers are required to leave their packs outside these facilities, due to limited dining space.

Accommodations

Lodging is available at three locations in the Central District of the Park. Skyland was originally established as a resort by George Freeman Pollock. A number of permanent cabins were built on the site and were refurbished when the Park was established. Today, these cabins are available as part of the Skyland complex, in addition to more modern lodging. A total of 179 rooms is available at Skyland.

Also in the Central District is Big Meadows Lodge, which was built in 1939 shortly after establishment of the Park. The lodge features rustic cabins hidden among the trees, along with several multi-room units. The dining room is finished in native American chestnut from local chestnut trees killed by the blight.

More rustic accommodations are available at Lewis

Mountain, which includes the comfort of a furnished cottage with bathroom, lights, heat, towels and linen with the economy of an outdoor concrete cooking area with overhead shelter, fireplace, storage cabinet and picnic area. Food and other supplies are available at the camp store.

None of the rooms, cabins, or cottages have telephones, and some non-smoking rooms are available. Advance reservations for the following year are taken starting on June 1 of the current year. For more information, call ARAMARK at 800-999-4714.

Visitor Centers

Two visitor centers and one information center provide publications, displays, audio-visual programs, and rangers to answer questions. The visitor and information center can also provide Park information, backcountry permits, Junior Ranger information, and passport cancellations. Books and other interpretive materials are also sold by the Shenandoah National Park Association at all visitor and information centers. Dickey Ridge Visitor Center is located on Skyline Drive at SDMP 4.6 and Byrd Visitor Center at SDMP 51.0 (Big Meadows). The latter is close to the *AT*. Loft Mountain Information Center is on Skyline Drive at SDMP 79.5 and is open weekends from May through October. Visitor centers are generally open from April through November.

Contacting a Park Ranger

Ranger stations generally are not open to the public.

In an emergency, the best way to locate a ranger is to use one of the public telephones listed in the next section and call the main Park switchboard, which is staffed 24-hours a day (800-732-0911). During normal business hours, your best chance of speaking to a ranger in person is to stop at one of the visitor centers located in the previous section, or at a Park entrance station. Rangers at the visitor centers are specifically available to the public at these locations and can spend the necessary time to help you plan a hike or answer any questions you may have. During non-business hours, visitor centers and ranger stations are closed, and the number above is the only number available to field emergencies.

Public Telephones

A number of public telephones are available in the Park. They can be used at the following locations (Note: "restricted" means only local, collect or credit card calls may be made):

• <u>Park Headquarters</u> on US 211 on the western edge of the Park (exterior)

• <u>North District</u>
—Front Royal Entrance Station (emergency)
—Dickey Ridge Visitor Center (exterior/restricted)
—Mathews Arm Campground (emergency)
—Elkwallow Wayside (exterior)

• <u>Central District</u>
—Panorama parking area adjacent to restrooms (exterior)
—Big Meadows Campground (exterior)
—Big Meadows Lodge (exterior)
—Lewis Mountain Campground (emergency)
—Old Rag Park boundary fee station (emergency)
—Swift Run Entrance Station (exterior)
—Whiteoak Canyon Park boundary fee station (emergency)

• <u>South District</u>
—Loft Mountain Information Center (emergency)
—Loft Mountain Campground (restricted)
—Rockfish Gap Entrance Station (emergency)

Skyline Drive Closures and Inclement Weather

Skyline Drive may be closed for a variety of reasons, most relating to inclement weather, but on occasion for other reasons as well. The Park Service maintains a non-emergency phone number (540-999-3500) with information on the status of Skyline Drive

In the event that you are locked inside the Park after a closure, you should follow the instructions printed on the back of the closed gate. This information will tell you who and where to call for assistance. The Park also maintains a 24-hour emergency phone (800-732-0911) which can assist you during any emergency and help to get you out of the Park.

Clothing, Equipment, and Weather

Hikers should keep in mind that temperatures are often colder along the Blue Ridge crest than at low elevations, especially in winter. The average low temperature at Big Meadows (elevation 3,530 ft.) during the month of January is 17°F, while at Park Headquarters (elevation 1,100 ft.), it is 21°F. The average lowest temperature at Big Meadows is 4°F, and the record low temperature is -26°F in 1994.

Snow accumulates sooner and lasts much longer in the Park than it does in the Washington area. The first measurable snows typically appear during the month of November and continue through April. The average snow depth at Big Meadows during the winter months is 6.3 inches, with January being the snowiest month. Hikers should also keep in mind, when hiking along exposed ridges in windy weather, that wind chill exacerbates the danger already posed by low temperatures.

During summer months, long pants offer considerable protection from snakes, poison ivy, ticks and nettles; however, the warmer months may make wearing long pants a challenge. At Park Headquarters (elevation 1,100 ft.), the average temperature during June is 92°F, while at Big

Meadows (elevation 3,530 ft.) it is 72°F. The average maximum temperatures at lower elevations typically occur in July at 96.1°F, and the record high temperature is 105°F in July 1988.

In rainy weather, waterproof jackets or ponchos are advisable and it is wise to have a set of dry clothes to change into. The Park typically receives an average rainfall of 53.69 inches per year at Big Meadows, and 37.25 inches per year at Park Headquarters. November is the rainiest month and, therefore, the time of year when hypothermia poses the greatest threat to hikers and backpackers.

Good shoes or boots are important if one is hiking very far. Special attention should be given to obtaining comfortable shoes with non-slip soles.

The amount of equipment needed will vary with the length of hike and season. In general, it is good advice to carry at least a compass, a first aid kit, a whistle, a flashlight, and a small canteen (or a large canteen in hot weather).

Do not depend on springs or small streams for water during hot, dry weather. Carry enough water for your needs. Backcountry users are encouraged to purify all unprotected surface water.

GPS and Cellular Phones

Recently there has been a profusion of cellular phones and global positioning systems (GPS) on the market. While these are useful tools, they have limitations in the backcountry. Both these devices rely on radio waves to operate and must be in line-of-sight of a cellular tower or, in the case of GPS, of at least three satellites to perform properly. Because of the hilly terrain and deep hollows of the Park, cellular phones can be unreliable. If you are unable to obtain a signal on your cellular phone, moving to higher ground might solve this problem. The same problem may be experienced with GPS.

While both of these devices are useful, they do not take

the place of a map, a compass and common sense. Do not start your hike using solely GPS. GPS will tell you exactly where you are, but it may not be able to tell you where to go or what trail to take. The media, of late, have been full of stories of people who became lost because they had a GPS and a cell phone but no map. GPS is not a substitute for a good trail map and should not be used as one.

Being Lost

Stop, if you have walked more than a quarter-mile (roughly five minutes of hiking) without noticing a blaze or other trail indicator. If you find no indication of the trail, retrace your course until one appears. The major mistake many hikers make is insisting on continuing when the route seems obscure or uncertain. Haste, even in a desire to reach camp before dark, only complicates the difficulty. When in doubt, remain where you are to avoid straying farther from the route.

Hiking long distances alone should be avoided. If undertaken, it requires extra precautions. A lone hiker who suffers a serious accident or illness might be risking death if he has not planned for the remote chance of isolation. Your destinations and estimated times of arrival should be known to someone who will initiate inquiries or a search if you do not appear when expected.

A lone hiker who loses his or her way and chooses to bushwhack (hike off-trail) runs considerable risk if an accident occurs. If the hiker falls helpless away from a used trail, he or she might not be discovered for days or even weeks. Your pack should always contain enough food to sustain you until daylight, when a careful retracing of your steps might lead you back to a safe route.

If you are unable to pick up your trail and your trip plans are known to relatives, friends, or co-workers, stay where you are! The Park will initiate a search when its personnel have been notified of your disappearance. If you have not previously made your trip plans known to others outside the Park, start hiking towards the lowest elevation in your surroundings, and keep going. Sooner or later, you are bound to pick up a side stream that will lead to a major watershed in the Park, or civilization just outside the Park boundary. SNP is a narrow park, and civilization or another hiking trail or road often can be reached in a day by most hikers in average physical condition. In poor weather conditions, it may take longer. Don't panic!

If you should get lost while dayhiking during the colder weather and must stay in the woods overnight, rake together a large pile of leaves with your hands and burrow inside. If conditions are windy, leaves can be held in place with downed sticks or branches. A pile of leaves can provide some insulation and could help you survive a cold night in the woods. If snow is on the ground, try to locate shelter from the wind, such as a rock overhang or a hollow log. If food supplies are adequate, try jogging in place to stay warm and rub extremities (if not frostbitten) to promote circulation.

Distress Signals

An emergency call for distress consists of three short calls, audible or visible, repeated at regular intervals. A whistle is particularly good for audible signals. Visible signals may include a light flashed with a mirror in daytime or flashlight at night. (Do this only in a genuine emergency.)

Anyone recognizing such a signal should acknowledge it by a signal of two calls—if possible by the same method of signaling, then should go to the distressed hiker and determine the nature of the emergency. If more competent aid is needed, try to arrange it.

Emergencies

Report emergencies to a ranger or to any uniformed personnel at any entrance station or call the emergency number at 800-732-0911. When calling on a cellular phone within the

Park, be aware that because of the line-of-sight requirement of most cell phones, their use is limited. Sometimes moving to higher ground can solve this problem.

The Park Service would like to emphasize that these numbers are emergency phone numbers only and should be used as such. Emergency services take up a large part of the Park Service's already very tight budget. While the Park Service is there to assist in an emergency, in the past few years there has been an increase in the number of emergency calls that have turned out to be non-emergencies. Please use caution and common sense before calling for emergency assistance when no emergency actually exists.

Winter ice　　　　　　　　　　　　　*Photo by Lee Sheaffer*

FIRST AID ALONG THE TRAIL

By Robert Ohler, M.D., and the
Appalachian Trail Conservancy

Hikers encounter a wide variety of terrain and climatic conditions along the *AT*. Prepare for the possibility of injuries. Some of the more common Trail-related medical problems are briefly discussed below.

Preparation is key to a safe trip. If possible, every hiker should take the free courses in advanced first aid and cardiopulmonary-resuscitation (CPR) techniques offered in most communities by the American Red Cross.

Even without this training, you can be prepared for accidents. Emergency situations can develop. Analyses of serious accidents have shown that a substantial number originate at home, in the planning stage of the trip. Think about communications. Have you informed your relatives and friends about your expedition: locations, schedule, and time of return? Has all of your equipment been carefully checked? Considering the season and altitude, have you provided for water, food, and shelter?

While hiking, set your own comfortable pace. If you are injured or lost or a storm strikes, stop. Remember that your brain is your most important survival tool. Inattention can start a chain of events leading to disaster.

If an accident occurs, treat the injury first. If outside help is needed, at least one person should stay with the injured hiker. Two people should go for help and carry with them notes on the exact location of the accident, what has been done to aid the injured hiker, and what help is needed.

The injured will need encouragement, assurances of help, and confidence in your competence. Treat him or her gently. Keep the patient supine, warm, and quiet, protected from the weather with insulation above and below. Examine the patient carefully, noting all possible injuries.

General Emergencies

Back or neck injuries: Immobilize the victim's entire body, where he or she lies. Protect head and neck from movement if the neck is injured, and treat as a fracture. Transportation must be on a rigid frame, such as a litter or a door. The spinal cord could be severed by inexpert handling. This type of injury must be handled by a large group of experienced personnel. Obtain outside help.

Bleeding: Stop the flow of blood by using a method appropriate to the amount and type of bleeding. Exerting pressure over the wound with the fingers, with or without a dressing, may be sufficient. Minor arterial bleeding can be controlled with local pressure and bandaging. Major arterial bleeding might require compressing an artery against a bone to stop the flow of blood. Elevate the arm or legs above the heart. To stop bleeding from an artery in the leg, place a hand in the groin, and press toward the inside of the leg. Stop arterial bleeding from an arm by placing a hand between the armpit and elbow and pressing toward the inside of the arm.

Apply a tourniquet only if you are unable to control severe bleeding by pressure and elevation. *Warning: This method should be used only when the limb will be lost anyway.* Once applied, a tourniquet should only be removed by medical personnel equipped to stop the bleeding by other means and to restore lost blood. The tourniquet should be located between the wound and the heart. If there is a traumatic amputation (loss of hand, leg, or foot), place the tourniquet two inches above the amputation.

Blisters: Good boot fit, without points of irritation or pressure, should be proven before a hike. Always keep feet dry while hiking. Prevent blisters by responding early to any discomfort. Place adhesive tape or moleskin over areas of developing redness or soreness. If irritation can be relieved, allow blister fluid to be reabsorbed. If a blister forms and continued irritation makes draining it necessary, wash the area with soap and water, and prick the edge of the blister with a needle that has been sterilized by the flame of a match. Bandage with a sterile gauze pad and moleskin.

Dislocation of a leg or arm joint is extremely painful. Do not try to put it back in place. Immobilize the entire limb with splints in the position it is found.

Exhaustion is caused by inadequate food consumption, dehydration and salt deficiency, over-exertion, or all three. The victim may lose motivation, slow down, gasp for air, and complain of weakness, dizziness, nausea, or headache. Treat by feeding, especially carbohydrates. Slowly replace lost water (normal fluid intake should be two to four quarts per day). Give salt dissolved in water (one teaspoon per cup). In the case of over-exertion, rest is essential.

Fractures of legs, ankles, or arms must be splinted before moving the victim. After treating wounds, use any available materials that will offer firm support, such as tree branches or boards. Pad each side of the arm or leg with soft material, supporting and immobilizing the joints above and below the injury. Bind the splints together with strips of cloth.

Shock should be expected after all injuries. It is a potentially fatal depression of bodily functions that is made more critical with improper handling, cold, fatigue, and anxiety. Relieve the pain as quickly as possible. Do not administer aspirin if severe bleeding is present; Ibuprofen or other nonaspirin pain relievers are safe to give.

Look for nausea, paleness, trembling, sweating, or thirst. Lay the hiker flat on his or her back, and raise the feet slightly; or position the patient's body, if it can be moved safely, so the head is down-slope. Protect the patient from the wind and keep as warm as possible. A campfire will help.

Sprains: Look or feel for soreness or swelling. Bandage, and treat as a fracture. Cool and raise the joint.

Wounds (except eye wounds) should be cleaned with

soap and water. If possible, apply a clean dressing to protect the wound from further contamination.

Chilling and Freezing Emergencies

Every hiker should be familiar with the symptoms, treatment, and methods of preventing the common and sometimes fatal condition of *hypothermia*. Wind chill and/or body wetness, particularly aggravated by fatigue and hunger, can rapidly drain body heat to dangerously low levels. This often occurs at temperatures well above freezing. Shivering, lethargy, mental slowing, and confusion are early symptoms of hypothermia, which can begin without the victim's realizing it and, if untreated, can lead to death.

Always keep dry, spare clothing and a water-repellent windbreaker in your pack, and wear a hat in chilling weather. Wet clothing loses much of its insulating value, although wet wool is warmer than other wet fabrics. Always, when in chilling conditions, suspect the onset of hypothermia.

To treat this potentially fatal condition, immediately seek shelter, and warm the entire body, preferably by placing it in a sleeping bag and administering warm liquids to the victim. The close proximity of another person's body heat may aid in warming.

A sign of *frostbite* is grayish or waxy, yellow-white spots on the skin. The frozen area will be numb. To thaw, warm the frozen part by direct contact with bare flesh. When first frozen, a cheek, nose, or chin often can be thawed by covering it with a hand taken from a warm glove. Superficially frostbitten hands sometimes can be thawed by placing them under armpits, on the stomach, or between the thighs. With a partner, feet can be treated similarly. Do not rub frozen flesh.

Frozen layers of deeper tissue beneath the skin are characterized by a solid, "woody" feeling and an inability to move the flesh over bony prominences. Tissue loss is minimized by rapid rewarming of the area in water slightly below 105 degrees Fahrenheit (measure accurately with a thermometer).

Thawing of a frozen foot should not be attempted until the patient has been evacuated to a place where rapid, controlled thawing can take place. Walking on a frozen foot is entirely possible and does not cause increased damage. Walking after thawing is impossible.

Never rewarm over a stove or fire. This "cooks" flesh and results in extensive loss of tissue.

Treatment of a deep freezing injury after rewarming must be done in a hospital.

Heat Emergencies

Exposure to extremely high temperatures, high humidity, and direct sunlight can cause health problems.

Heat cramps are usually caused by strenuous activity in high heat and humidity, when sweating depletes salt levels in blood and tissues. Symptoms are intermittent cramps in legs and the abdominal wall and painful spasms of muscles. Pupils of eyes may dilate with each spasm. The skin becomes cold and clammy. Treat with rest and salt dissolved in water (one teaspoon of salt per glass).

Heat exhaustion, caused by physical exercise during prolonged exposure to heat, is a breakdown of the body's heat-regulating system. The circulatory system is disrupted, reducing the supply of blood to vital organs such as the brain, heart, and lungs. The victim can have heat cramps and sweat heavily; may have skin that is moist and cold; may have a face that is flushed, then pale; and may have a an unsteady pulse and low blood pressure. He or she may vomit and be delirious. Place the victim in shade, flat on his or her back, with feet 8 to 12 inches higher than the head. Give sips of salt water—half a glass every 15 minutes—for about an hour. Loosen clothes. Apply cold cloths.

Heat stroke and *sunstroke* are caused by the failure of the heat-regulating system to cool the body by sweating. These are emergency, life-threatening conditions. Body temperature can rise to 106 degrees or higher. Symptoms include weakness, nausea, headache, heat cramps, exhaustion, rapidly rising body temperature, pounding pulse, and high blood pressure. The victim may be delirious or comatose. Sweating will stop before heat stroke becomes apparent. Armpits may be dry and skin flushed and pink, then turning ashen or purple in later stages. Move victim to a cool place immediately. Cool the body in any way possible (e.g., sponging). Body temperature should be regulated artificially from outside the body until the heat-regulating system can be rebalanced. Be careful not to over-chill once temperature goes below 102 degrees.

Heat weakness causes fatigue, headache, mental and physical inefficiency, heavy sweating, high pulse rate, and general weakness. Drink plenty of water, find as cool a spot as possible, keep quiet, and replenish salt loss.

Sunburn causes redness of the skin, discoloration, swelling, and pain. It occurs rapidly and can be severe at higher elevations. It can be prevented by applying a commercial sunscreen; zinc oxide is the most effective. Protect from further exposure and cover the area with ointment and a dressing. Give the victim large amounts of fluids.

Artificial Respiration

Artificial respiration might be required when an obstruction constricts the air passages or after respiratory failure caused by air being depleted of oxygen, such as after electrocution, by drowning, or because of toxic gases in the air. Quick action is necessary if the victim's lips, fingernail beds, or tongue have become blue, if he or she is unconscious, or if the pupils become enlarged.

If food or a foreign body is lodged in the air passage and coughing is ineffective, try to remove it with the fingers. If the foreign body is inaccessible, grasp the victim from behind, and with one hand hold the opposite wrist just below the breastbone. Squeeze rapidly and firmly, expelling air forcibly from the lungs to expel the foreign body. Repeat this maneuver two to three times, if necessary.

If breathing stops, administer artificial respiration, since air can be forced around the obstruction into the lungs.

Poison Ivy

Poison ivy is the most common plant found along the Trail that irritates the skin. It is most often found as a vine trailing near the ground or climbing on fences or trees, sometimes up to 20 feet from the ground. A less common variety that is often unrecognized is an erect shrub, standing alone and unsupported, up to 10 feet tall.

The leaves are in clusters of three, the end leaf with a longer stalk and pointed tip, light green in spring but darkening as the weeks pass. The inconspicuous flowers are greenish; the berries, white or cream. The irritating oil is in all parts of the plant, even in dead plants, and is carried in the smoke of burning plants. Those who believe themselves immune may find that they are seriously susceptible if the concentration is great enough or the toxins are ingested.

If you have touched *poison ivy*, wash immediately with strong soap (but not with one containing added oil). If a rash develops in the next day or so, treat it with calamine lotion or Solarcaine. Do not scratch. If blisters become serious or the rash spreads to the eyes, see a doctor.

Lyme Disease

Lyme disease is contracted from bites of certain infected ticks. Hikers should be aware of the symptoms and monitor themselves and their partners for signs of the disease. When treated early, Lyme disease can usually be cured with antibiotics.

Inspect yourself for ticks and tick bites at the end of each day. The four types of ticks known to spread Lyme disease are smaller than the dog tick, about the size of a pinhead, and not easily seen. They are often called "deer ticks" because they feed during one stage of their life cycle on deer, a host for the disease.

The early signs of a tick bite infected with Lyme disease are a red spot with a white center that enlarges and spreads, severe fatigue, chills, headaches, muscle aches, fever, malaise, and a stiff neck. However, one-quarter of all people with an infected tick bite show none of the early symptoms.

Later effects of the disease, which may not appear for months or years, are severe fatigue, dizziness, shortness of breath, cardiac irregularities, memory and concentration problems, facial paralysis, meningitis, shooting pains in the arms and legs and other symptoms resembling multiple sclerosis, brain tumors, stroke, alcoholism, depression, Alzheimer's disease, and *anorexia nervosa*.

It is not believed people can build a lasting immunity to Lyme disease. A hiker who has contracted and been treated for the disease should still take precautions.

Hantavirus

Hantavirus is extremely rare and difficult to "catch." Prevention measures are relatively simple: Air out a closed, mice-infested structure for an hour before occupying it; don't pitch tents or place sleeping bags in areas in proximity to rodent droppings or burrows or near areas that may shelter rodents or provide food for them. Don't sleep on the bare ground, use a mat or tent with a floor or ground cloth; in shelters, ensure that the sleeping surface is at least 12 inches above the ground. Don't handle or play with any mice that show up at the campsite, even if they appear friendly; treat your water; wash your hands if you think you have handled droppings.

Lightning Strikes

Although the odds of being struck by lightning are low, 200 to 400 people a year are killed by lightning in the United States. Respect the force of lightning, and seek appropriate shelter during a storm.

Do not start a hike if thunderstorms are likely. If caught in a storm, immediately find shelter. Large buildings are best; tents offer no protection. When indoors, stay away from windows, open doors, fireplaces, and large metal objects. Do not hold a potential lightning rod, such as a fishing pole. Avoid tall structures, such as flagpoles, fire towers, powerline towers, and the tallest trees or hilltops. If you cannot enter a building, take shelter in a stand of smaller trees. Avoid clearings. If caught in the open, crouch down, or roll into a ball. If you are in water, get out. Spread out groups, so that everyone is not struck by a single bolt.

If a person is struck by lightning or splashed by a charge hitting a nearby object, the victim will probably be thrown, perhaps a great distance. Clothes can be burned or torn. Metal objects (such as belt buckles) may be hot, and shoes blown off. The victim often has severe muscle contractions (which can cause breathing difficulties), confusion, and temporary blindness or deafness. In more severe cases, the victim may have feathered or sunburst patterns of burns over the skin or ruptured eardrums. He or she may lose consciousness or breathe irregularly. Occasionally, victims stop breathing and suffer cardiac arrest.

If someone is struck by lightning, perform artificial respiration and CPR until emergency technicians arrive or you can transport the injured to a hospital. Lightning victims may be unable to breathe independently for 15 to 30 minutes but can recover quickly once they can breathe on their own. Do not give up early; a seemingly lifeless individual can be saved if you breathe for him promptly after the strike.

Assume that the victim was thrown a great distance;

protect the spine, treat other injuries, then transport him to the hospital.

Snakebites

Reports of bites are extremely rare, but hikers on the Appalachian Trail may encounter copperheads and rattlesnakes on their journeys. These are pit vipers, characterized by triangular heads, vertical elliptical pupils, two or fewer hinged fangs on the front part of the jaw (fangs are replaced every six to 10 weeks), heat-sensory facial pits on the sides of the head, and a single row of scales on the underbelly by the tail. Rattlesnakes have rattles on the tail.

The best way to avoid being bitten by snakes is to avoid their known habitats and reaching into dark areas (use a walking stick to move suspicious objects). Wear protective clothing, especially on feet and lower legs. Do not hike alone or at night in snake territory; always have a flashlight and walking stick. If you see a snake, walk away; you can outdistance it in three steps. Do not handle snakes. A dead snake can bite and envenomate you with a reflex action for 20 to 60 minutes after its death.

Not all *snakebites* result in envenomation, even if the snake is poisonous. The signs of envenomation are one or more fang marks (in addition to rows of teeth marks), burning pain, and swelling at the bite (swelling usually begins within five to 10 minutes of envenomation and can become very severe). Lips, face, and scalp may tingle and become numb 30 to 60 minutes after the bite. (If those symptoms are immediate and the victim is frightened and excited, then they are most likely due to hyperventilation or shock.) Thirty to 90 minutes after the bite, the victim's eyes and mouth may twitch, and he may have a rubbery or metallic taste in his mouth. He may sweat, experience weakness, nausea, and vomiting, or faint one to two hours after the bite. Bruising at the bite usually begins within two to three hours, and large blood blisters may develop within six to 10 hours. The victim may have difficulty breathing, have bloody urine, vomit blood, and collapse six to 12 hours after the bite.

If someone you are with has been bitten by a snake, act quickly. The definitive treatment for snake-venom poisoning is the proper administration of antivenom.

Keep the victim calm. Increased activity can spread the venom and the illness. Retreat out of snake's striking range, but try to identify it. Check for signs of envenomation. Immediately transport the victim to the nearest hospital. If possible, splint the body part that was bitten, to avoid unnecessary motion. If a limb was bitten, keep it at a level below the heart. *Do not apply ice directly to the wound.* If it will take longer than two hours to reach medical help, and the bite is on an arm or leg, place a 2 x 2 1/4"-thick cloth pad over the bite and firmly wrap the limb (ideally, with an elastic wrap) directly over the bite and six inches on either side, taking care to check for adequate circulation to the fingers and toes. This wrap may slow the spread of venom.

Do not use a snakebite kit or attempt to remove the poison. This is the advice of Maynard H. Cox, founder and director of the Worldwide Poison Bite Information Center. He advises medical personnel on the treatment of snakebites. If you hike in fear of snakebites, carry his number, 904-264-6512, and if you're bitten, give the number to the proper medical personnel. Your chances of being bitten by a poisonous snake are very, very slim. Do not kill the snake; in most Trail areas, it is a legally protected species.

First-Aid Kit

The following kit is suggested for those who have had no first aid or other medical training. It weighs about a pound and occupies about a 3" x 6" x 9" space.

Eight 4" x 4" gauze pads

Four 3" x 4" gauze pads

Five 2" bandages

Ten 1" bandages
Six alcohol prep pads
Ten large butterfly closures
One triangular bandage (40")
Two 3" rolls of gauze
Twenty tablets of aspirin-free pain killer
One 15' roll of 2" adhesive tape
One 3" Ace bandage
Twenty salt tablets
One 3" x 4" moleskin
Three safety pins
One small scissors
One tweezer
Personal medications

Georgia Tech students doing trail maintenance work.

Photo by Patrick Wilson

SHENANDOAH NATIONAL PARK

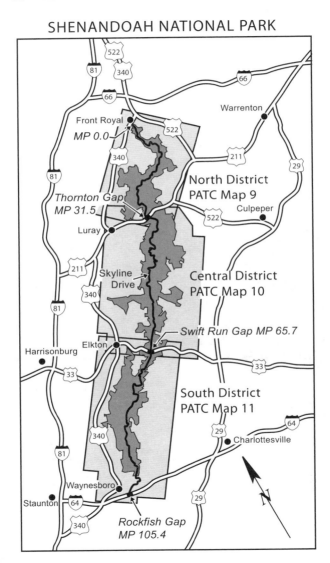

Warrenton

North District
PATC Map 9

Front Royal
MP 0.0

Thornton Gap
MP 31.5

Luray

Culpeper

Skyline
Drive

Central District
PATC Map 10

Swift Run Gap MP 65.7

Harrisonburg

Elkton

South District
PATC Map 11

Charlottesville

Waynesboro

Staunton

Rockfish Gap
MP 105.4

N

THE APPALACHIAN TRAIL

The Appalachian Trail (*AT*) is a continuous, marked footpath extending 2,178.3 miles from Katahdin, a granite monolith in the central Maine wilderness, south to Springer Mountain in Georgia along the crest of the Appalachian mountain range.

The Trail traverses mostly public land in 14 states. Virginia has the longest section, with 547 mi., while West Virginia has the shortest, almost 25 mi. along the Virginia-West Virginia boundary and a short swing into Harpers Ferry at the Maryland border. The highest elevation along the Trail is 6,643 ft. at Clingmans Dome in the Great Smoky Mountains. The Trail is only 124 ft. above sea level near its crossing of the Hudson River in New York.

Trail History

Credit for establishing the Trail belongs to three leaders and countless volunteers. The first Trail proposal to appear in print was an article by regional planner Benton MacKaye of Shirley, Massachusetts, entitled, "An Appalachian Trail, a Project in Regional Planning," in the October 1921 issue of the *Journal of the American Institute of Architects*. He envisioned a footpath along the Appalachian ridgeline where urban people could retreat to nature.

MacKaye's challenge kindled considerable interest, but at the time most of the outdoor organizations that could participate in constructing such a trail were east of the Hudson River. Four existing trail systems could be incorporated into an Appalachian Trail. The Appalachian Mountain Club (AMC) maintained an excellent series of trails in New England, but most ran north-south; the Trail could not cross New Hampshire until the chain of huts built and operated by the AMC permitted an east-west alignment. In Vermont, the southern 100 mi. of the Long

Trail, then being developed in the Green Mountains, were connected to the White Mountains by the trails of the Dartmouth Outing Club.

In 1923, a number of area hiking clubs that had formed the New York-New Jersey Trail Conference opened the first new section of the *AT*, in the Harriman-Bear Mountain section of Palisades Interstate Park.

The Appalachian Trail Conference, now the Appalachian Trail Conservancy, (ATC) was formed in 1925 to stimulate greater interest in MacKaye's idea and coordinate the clubs' work in choosing and building the route. The Conservancy remains a nonprofit educational organization of individuals and clubs of volunteers dedicated to maintaining, managing, and protecting the Appalachian Trail.

Although interest in the Trail spread to Pennsylvania and New England, little further work was done until 1926, when retired Judge Arthur Perkins of Hartford, Connecticut, began persuading groups to locate and cut the footpath through the wilderness. His enthusiasm provided the momentum that carried the Trail idea forward.

The southern states had few trails and even fewer clubs. The "skyline" route followed by the *AT* in the South was developed largely within the new national forests. A number of clubs were formed in various parts of the southern Appalachians to take responsibility for the Trail there.

Perkins interested Myron H. Avery, a former junior partner in his law firm then resident in Washington, D.C., in the Trail. Avery, who served as chairman of the Conference from 1931 to 1952, enlisted the aid and coordinated the work of hundreds of volunteers who completed the Trail by August 14, 1937, when a Civilian Conservation Corps crew opened the last section (on the ridge between Spaulding and Sugarloaf mountains in Maine). At the eighth meeting of the ATC, in June 1937, Conference member Edward B. Bullard proposed a plan for an "Appalachian Trailway" that would set apart an area on each side of the Trail, dedicated to the interests of those who travel on foot.

Steps taken to effect this long-range protection pro-gram culminated first in an October 15, 1938, agreement between the National Park Service and the U.S. Forest Service for the promotion of an Appalachian Trailway, through the relevant national parks and forests, extending one mile on each side of the Trail. Within this zone, no new parallel roads would be built or any other incompatible development allowed. Timber cutting would not be permitted within 200 feet of the Trail. Similar agreements, creating a zone one-quarter mile in width on state-owned lands, were signed with most states through which the Trail passes.

After World War II, the encroachments of highways, housing developments, and summer resorts caused many relocations, and the problem of maintaining the Trail's wilderness character became more severe.

In 1968, Congress established a national system of trails and designated the Appalachian Trail and the Pacific Crest Trail as the initial components. The National Trails System Act directs the Secretary of the Interior, in consultation with the Secretary of Agriculture, to administer the *AT* primarily as a footpath and protect the Trail against incompatible activities and the use of motorized vehicles. Provision was also made for acquiring rights-of-way for the Trail, both inside and outside the boundaries of federally-administered areas.

In 1970, supplemental agreements under the act— among the National Park Service, the U.S. Forest Service, and the Appalachian Trail Conference—established the specific responsibilities of these organizations for initial mapping, selection of rights-of-way, relocations, maintenance, development, acquisition of land, and protection of a permanent Trail. Agreements also were signed between the Park Service and the various states, encouraging them to acquire and protect a right-of-way for the Trail outside federal land.

Slow progress of federal efforts and lack of initiative by some states led Congress to strengthen the National Trails System Act. President Jimmy Carter signed the amendment, known as The Appalachian Trail Bill, on March 21, 1978. The new legislation emphasized the need for protecting the Trail, including acquiring a corridor, and authorized $90 million for that purpose. With 5.9 mi. unprotected as of 2011, this part of the project is expected to be completed by the end of this decade.

In 1984, the Interior Department formally delegated the responsibility of managing the *AT* corridor lands outside established parks and forests to the Appalachian Trail Conference. The ATC, with the member clubs as partners, retains primary responsibility for maintaining the footpath, too.

In 2005, the Appalachian Trail Conference changed its name to the Appalachian Trail Conservancy in order to recognize its broader mission of preserving the Trail experience. The Conservancy is governed by a volunteer board of directors, composed of 15 elected officers who serve two-year terms. ATC leadership committees also include a Stewardship Council (which recommends policies to the board) and four Regional Partnership committees that serve as direct organizational links to the Trail-maintaining clubs.

The Conservancy publishes information on constructing and maintaining hiking trails, selected official *AT* guides, and general information on hiking and trail use.

The Conservancy membership consists of organizations that maintain the *AT* or contribute to the Trail project, as well as individuals. ATC membership provides the individual with a subscription to *AT Journeys*.

Membership forms and a complete list of publications are available from the Appalachian Trail Conservancy, P.O. Box 807, Harpers Ferry, W. Va. 25425; 304-535-6331; or *www.appalachiantrail.org*. The ATC store is at 888-AT STORE (287-8673) or *www.atctrailstore.org*. The visitor center at ATC's central office is open 9 a.m. to 4:30 p.m.

(Eastern Time), seven days a week.

The *AT* inside Shenandoah National Park

The Potomac Appalachian Trail Club began work on the *AT* in the Blue Ridge within a month of its founding. Myron Avery and J. Frank Schairer began scouting for trail routes within the present boundaries of Shenandoah National Park in early 1928. Work continued with the assistance of other PATC members (notably Albert J. Jackman and Marvin Green) through the next decade. Dr. Halstead S. Hedges, an ophthalmologist living in Charlottesville and early PATC member, did much of the route location for the *AT* south of Swift Run Gap. The *AT* within the Park was built by the PATC between April 1928 and August 1930, and side trail construction continued through the next decade. The builders of Skyline Drive used much of the original *AT* route for the road, and new routes for the Trail were scouted by PATC members with construction assistance from the CCC. (The excellent rockwork seen on the *AT* and along Skyline Drive was constructed by the CCC.) The establishment of Shenandoah National Park in 1935 began a history of close cooperation between Park management and the PATC that continues to the present.

Potomac Appalachian Trail Club

The Potomac Appalachian Trail Club, founded in November 1927, is one of the 31 organizations maintaining the Appalachian Trail under the Appalachian Trail Conservancy. It is also the fourth largest in number of members (over 6,400), being surpassed only by the Appalachian Mountain Club in Boston, the Green Mountain Club in Vermont, and the New York/New Jersey Trail Clubs.

Altogether, the PATC is responsible for maintaining 239 miles of the Appalachian Trail and over 1,000 miles of other trails. Within SNP, this includes the entire length of the *AT*, and over 80% of the side trails. In 2011, the PATC contributed more than 81,000 hours of volunteer service (including trail work) to the public. This work was performed by over 600 volunteer trail, shelter and cabin overseers. During any given day of the year, it is likely that a PATC overseer is working somewhere inside the Park.

PATC maintains side trails in George Washington National Forest and has developed a 251-mile side trail known as the Tuscarora Trail running from the North District of SNP through Hancock, Maryland and reconnecting with the *AT* north of Carlisle, Pennsylvania (see the Tuscarora Trail). As noted earlier, PATC also maintains a network of shelters and cabins.

PATC publishes two guides for the *AT*—this guide, and the *Appalachian Trail Guide: Maryland and Northern Virginia, with Side Trails*. The guidebook for PATC's portion of the *AT* in Pennsylvania is covered in a guide published by the Keystone Trails Association (KTA), of which PATC is a member. PATC also publishes and maintains a guidebook for the Tuscarora Trail, which leaves the Park in the North District of SNP, and a book of circuit hikes within the Park (*Circuit Hikes in the Shenandoah National Park*).

PATC:

• maintains a network of shelters and cabins; 38 cabins are available for rent to PATC members

• publishes books about history of trail areas and trail-related books, in addition to the trail guides and maps

• provides training on topics such as first aid, backpacking and safe use of wilderness tools

• leads hiking and backpacking trips in the Mid-Atlantic region

• hosts AT through-hikers, weekend backpackers, and day-hikers at the Club's Blackburn and Bears Den Trail Centers

• has many volunteers and trail crews working on the

Appalachian Trail in Shenandoah National Park and many other trail areas, which offer educational and social opportunities and welcome new participants of all abilities

• manages land to protect trailheads and viewsheds and provides public trail shelters

The Club has an active **Mountaineering Section**, which offers assistance and training in rock climbing techniques, as well as more difficult climbing opportunities for the advanced climber.

The **Ski Touring Section** conducts workshops for beginners, participates in work trips to improve ski trails in local areas and organizes trips to local and distant ski areas.

The **Shenandoah Mountain Rescue Group** is a semi-professional group of volunteers dedicated to wilderness search and rescue and outdoor safety education. The group meets twice monthly at PATC Headquarters and conducts frequent training in the field.

A select group of members participates in PATC's **Trail Patrol**, which makes regular patrols in SNP and other parks. The patrol is available to assist backcountry hikers and backpackers and to provide information on trail routes and conditions.

PATC's website (*www.patc.net*) has comprehensive information about the Club and its activities. It provides a secure online order service for maps, guidebooks and other publications, as well as information about location and amenities of rental cabins, and is a wealth of information to enhance the outdoor experience. PATC membership provides the individual with a subscription to the monthly newsletter, the *Potomac Appalachian,* and discounts on publications, maps and cabin rentals.

More information about membership, publications, cabins and PATC activities is available from PATC Headquarters, 118 Park St., S.E., Vienna, VA 22180-4609; *www.patc.net;* or at 703-242-0315 between 7 p.m. and 9 p.m. Monday through Wednesday and noon-2 p.m. Thursday and Friday.

AT on Loft Mountain   *National Park Service photo*

SHENANDOAH NATIONAL PARK

Shenandoah National Park, in the Blue Ridge Mountains of Virginia between Front Royal and Waynesboro, is world-renowned for scenic views from its Skyline Drive and for the flora and fauna characteristic of the Appalachian Mountains. Its 306 square miles are rich in forest and wildlife and in crystal streams with cascades and waterfalls. The Park rises from 600 feet above sea level beside Shenandoah River near Front Royal to 4,050 feet at the summit of Hawksbill Mountain. More than fifty peaks, many with hiking trails, rise above 3,000 feet.

The Park has three contiguous sections. The North District extends from Front Royal south to US 211 in Thornton Gap, and the Central District from Thornton Gap to US 33 in Swift Run Gap. The South District, which originally reached from Swift Run Gap to Jarman Gap, now includes a section to Rockfish Gap that was once the Blue Ridge Parkway. In crossing over US 250 and Interstate 64, the Shenandoah Park's Skyline Drive becomes the Blue Ridge Parkway.

The 105.4-mile Skyline Drive, with parking overlooks at 75 viewpoints, extends the full length of the Park, with entrance stations at Front Royal, Thornton Gap, Swift Run Gap, and Rockfish Gap. A single-entry fee is charged for those not carrying a Golden Eagle Pass, Golden Age Pass, Shenandoah Annual Pass or Interagency Annual Pass. The Appalachian Trail comes into the Park from the north about five miles southeast of Front Royal and continues inside the Park all the way southward to Jarman Gap, after which it is mostly outside but near the Park boundary as far as Rockfish Gap.

Human History

Note: All cultural artifacts are protected and it is illegal to remove any artifact from the Park. Please leave any discovered artifact in the location and way you found it. If you discover that you have picked up a cultural artifact, return it to the same place and as nearly as possible in the same position that you found it.

First Americans

Arrowheads, spearpoints, and a variety of stone tools from the past are still occasionally seen by hikers in the Park. The oldest evidence shows that humans were here perhaps 10,000 years ago.

The higher mountains in those early days of human habitation would have been starting a forest where ice-age grassland and brushland had previously prevailed. Pollen studies indicate the earliest trees were mostly spruce, with some fir, hemlock, and pine. Early deciduous trees were cottonwood, aspen, birch, alder, ironwood, blue beech, and ash. Oaks and hickories came later but would rapidly increase.

Present archaeological digs inside the Park unearthed extensive evidence of Archaic-period people who hunted with spears and gathered nuts and other plant-produced foods and medicines in the Blue Ridge between 9,000 B.C. and 1,000 B.C. Dr. Michael A. Hoffman of the University of Virginia, a principal investigator, concluded the high point of Indian use on the parkland was from 2,500 B.C. to 1,000 B.C. The people had learned, as he put it, "primary forest efficiency," adapting to the character of the hardwood forest.

The first white explorers found Sioux-speaking natives living east of the Blue Ridge crest—Manahoacs in the Rappahannock River drainage, and Monacans where the small streams drain into the James River. Explorer John Lederer wrote that they worshiped "one God," and their leaders were eloquent in speaking, and skilled in governing. Resident Indians were gone from the Shenandoah Valley west of the Blue Ridge, though abundant village sites date into the 1500s. It's likely the powerful Iroquois from the north, bolstered by French and Dutch merchants paying guns and ammunition in return for furs, drove the natives out.

European-Americans

Evidence of white occupation and use of these mountains—stone walls and chimneys, for instance, or long-abandoned wagon roads—are easy for hikers to find, especially in seasons when the leaves are off the trees and bushes.

The northern half of the Park, as it turned out, was controversial ground. The region was supposedly administered by the Virginia colony, yet was legally proven by the Fifth Lord Fairfax to be part of his five-million-acre proprietary stemming from direct grants from British kings. Starting in 1710, Virginia Governor Alexander Spotswood and associated gentlemen stepped up the region-wide land rush. After crossing the Blue Ridge in 1716 with his "Knights of the Golden Horseshoe," Spotswood signed patents to vast territories to fellow Cavaliers. Some of these grantees sold land and got more. Others moved quickly to establish plantations, often including mountains for the available supply of timber and cleared mountain land for livestock pastures or tobacco fields. Many Spotswood patents overlapped the Fairfax proprietary, because in high court in London, the domain's boundary corner here (the headwaters of the Rappahannock) was moved fifty miles south to the Conway River near present-day Bootens Gap.

Early plantations could be vast. The Shirley brothers had holdings embracing 49,000 acres in Madison County in the Park's Central District, with adjoining land in Page County west of the Park. Thomas Marshall, a surveyor associated with George Washington for a time, had large holdings which included the north and south peaks of Mt. Marshall—the naming often associated with Thomas's son, John, the famous U.S. chief justice. Col. Isaac Overall (of Overall Run) had 28,000 acres of the parkland, and his heir later still held much of it when the national park was being established. The Brown brothers (Browns Gap) had several plantations in the Park's South District, including large territories both inside and outside the present Park boundary.

Timber was cut repeatedly, though never all the parkland. Iron was mined inside and alongside all three Park districts, and many thousands of acres of forest were cleared in charcoal-making for smelting the ore. (The stone parts of an iron furnace, active in the 1800s, remain as a massive ruin alongside Madison Run in the South District.) Manganese was also mined in impressive quantities. Copper was widely distributed, even atop Stony Man Mountain, but was not concentrated enough to sustain profitable mining operations.

When plantations became unprofitable from soil exhaustion and economic and political troubles, the descendants of English gentlemen sold the land. Much of the land was bought by Shenandoah Valley and Piedmont farmers of German-Irish descent who maintained thousands of acres of bluegrass sod (Big Meadows is an example) for grazing beef cattle from April to October.

Origins of the Mountain Residents

The mountain people, so well-known to George Freeman Pollock (founder of Skyland Resort) and Appalachian Trail/PATC pioneers such as J. Frank Schairer, grew out of better known strands of history. Recent research indicates that 70% of the mountain residents owned their land or had homes in the valley or Piedmont, and held mountain land for grazing or timber, or the hope of rich minerals.

Many owners, especially cattlemen, had tenant families living on their mountain lands when the Park was established in 1935. Many of the families had lived for generations on the same sites. Some of the ancestors were workers assigned to outlying plantation "quarters." A few families may have dated back still earlier, having been hunters/trappers/traders on the frontier and likely claiming land title as squatters. Squatters could earn legal ownership from the courts if beneficial use of the land was demonstrated and the true owner was distant and negligent in visiting and using his land. Still others bought or leased small tracts from Lord Fairfax, whose long aim was to populate his vast holdings with people who "almost" owned, but agreed to pay annual "quit rents" through the generations—a practice ended by the American Revolution. Some mountain folk were descended from Irish workers who fled the potato famine in their homeland and worked on railroads or turnpikes being built across the Blue Ridge in the nineteenth century. Other mountain people were English, German, or Scotch-Irish.

A hundred or more old cemeteries remain in the Park, some representing forgotten plantations and others representing generations of mountain folk. A few are still active and new burials are possible in accord with tradition. Some have occasional maintenance by kinfolk. Most are lost and hard to find, seldom rediscovered or visited. Two homes of mountain families have been saved and stabilized by the Potomac Appalachian Trail Club (Corbin Cabin and Jones Mountain Cabin) and are used as locked cabins by hikers (see Shelters, Huts and Cabins).

History of Park Establishment

Shenandoah National Park was established through a remarkable combination of efforts at the federal, state and local levels. In its annual report for the year 1923, the National Park Service suggested the need for a national park in the Appalachians. The Secretary of the Interior set up the Southern Appalachian National Park Committee to study possible sites. After thorough investigation, the Blue Ridge, stretching north and south from George Freeman Pollock's Skyland Resort, was recommended as a possible site, as were the Great Smoky Mountains in North Carolina and Tennessee. Congress passed a bill instructing Interior's committee to investigate the likely boundary and methods of acquiring the land. President Coolidge signed the bill in February 1925.

The next problem was the familiar one of financing. No federal funds could be made available. A volunteer Shenandoah National Park Association was formed to raise money, and, in a statewide campaign, got pledges adding up to $1,249,000. At the request of Governor Harry F. Byrd, the Virginia legislature approved a bill providing an additional $1 million. Congress passed a bill in May 1926 to authorize the Park—when and if title to suitable lands was donated to the federal government and accepted by the Secretary of the Interior.

Survey and appraisal of tracts within the maximum boundary were begun that same year by a newly created state agency authorized to acquire the needed acreage through county by county condemnation (eminent domain). Although 3,870 tracts were carefully appraised, only a third were acquired, due primarily to a shortage of funds. A contiguous block of land was eventually assembled, but with a distressingly irregular boundary.

The Park was formally established when Secretary Harold Ickes of Interior accepted the state's deeds to 176,430 acres in December 1935, after the U.S. Supreme Court had delayed the Park to consider a mountain man's challenge to the constitutionality of Virginia's land condemnation. Most of the 465 families still living within the boundary agreed in legal form to move out as soon as suitable housing was available outside the Park boundary. The diversity of these people was so great that any general description would be at least partly false. The number of families had been declining since the late 1800s, partly because of growing economic and educational privation. Some mountain families were prosperous, and some were in economic trouble. Many did not operate on a money economy. While many were hurt by the loss of the American chestnut to an oriental blight, and decline of the leather manufacturing market for chestnut-oak tanbark, the mountain families still felt they were living well on what they produced and gathered in the Blue Ridge.

President Franklin D. Roosevelt dedicated the Park in a ceremony at Big Meadows on July 3, 1936. By that time, Shenandoah was already surpassing the visitor count of the most popular national parks. Preparation for visitors had been vigorously launched in 1931 by President Herbert Hoover. Hoover had a fishing camp in the Park, the now famous Rapidan Camp, which the Hoovers donated to the Commonwealth of Virginia after he left office, to be included in the future Park. Hoover liked the views from the Blue Ridge crest and said they were "topnotch." He supported the construction of a road from Swift Run Gap to Panorama. The contractors were to hire local people who were suffering from drought and the Depression.

The central section of this mountaintop road was opened to the public before the Park officially existed. Roosevelt also ordered up to 1,200 young men of his new Civilian Conservation Corps (CCC) to create camp and picnic grounds and make other recreational improvements. Roosevelt came in person several times to inspect the progress. He praised the Skyline Drive and commented once that it was a "relief project" and "it was by Herbert Hoover." The northern section of Skyline Drive opened in October 1936 and the southern section in 1939. Costs, which were covered from one or another emergency fund, averaged $47,000 a mile. All told, the 105.4-mile Skyline Drive from Front Royal to Rockfish Gap cost well over $5 million to complete.

Skyline Drive construction caused relocation of most of the Appalachian Trail originally routed in the late 1920s and early 1930s along the Blue Ridge skyline by the Potomac Appalachian Trail Club. The CCC, working under National Park supervision, built much of the present-day trail between 1933 and 1937.

In 1976, Congress included 79,579 acres of the Park (about 123 square miles of the Park's present 306 square miles) in the National Wilderness Preservation System. This action was hailed as confirming Shenandoah in the status Congress had in mind when authorizing the Park in 1926 to protect and preserve the resources in the Appalachian Range.

Today, Shenandoah National Park is one of the most heavily visited parks in the National Park system—15th overall. In 2011, over 1.1 million visitors came to Shenandoah to behold the beauty of the gentle blue hills, which in the past 70 years have regenerated into an almost continuous mountain woodland.

For those interested in learning more about the history of Shenandoah National Park, the most comprehensive historical overview by far is contained in *The Undying Past of Shenandoah National Park*, written by Darwin Lambert, the first employee of SNP. For additional history about the Park, the following books may be sold by the Shenandoah National Park Association at Shenandoah National Park visitor centers. Some are also available from PATC Headquarters. Books published by PATC include *Shenandoah Heritage*, *Shenandoah Vestiges* and *Shenandoah Secrets*, all by Carolyn and Jack Reeder; *Lost Trails and Forgotten People,* by Tom Floyd; *The Dean Mountain Story,* by Gloria Dean; and *Memories of a Lewis Mountain Man,* by John Stoneberger.

Other books of interest are *Everything Was Wonderful* (on the CCC in the Park), *In the Light of the Mountain Moon* (on Skyland), and *The Greatest Single Feature… A*

Sky-line Drive, all by Reed L. Engle; and *In the Shadow of Ragged Mountain,* by Audrey Horning.

The Shenandoah National Park Association publishes many other books and trail guides, available from the Association's web site: *www.snpbooks.org*.

A Recycled Park

Despite the disturbances resulting from the previous century of users, the forest community was still intact at the time of SNP's establishment. With each cutting of a forest, the succession of the forest towards a "climax forest" was set back, but not changed in nature. More of the same species of plants and trees would replace them, and the forest community would continue. This is much unlike today, when an opening of the canopy would likely bring about an uncontrolled explosion of exotic plant growth and elimination of native plant populations by uncontrolled deer.

The first SNP forest-mapping inventory of 1937 showed that only 14.5% of the Park acreage was open, either as cultivated or pastureland and that only 25.7% of the Park land showed evidence of burning. Furthermore, although much of the Park had been logged in the past, eleven watersheds, or parts of watersheds, were identified that retained significant forest communities with no evidence of previous logging activity. Only four watersheds were identified as having serious erosion

The Civilian Conservation Corps (CCC), created in FDR's first year of office in 1933, was given the task of making the "unnatural" Park "natural" again. From 1933 to 1942 an estimated 10,000 men planted hundreds of thousands of trees, shrubs, and vines in SNP, including Fraser fir, red spruce, Canadian yew, table mountain pine, Virginia creeper, trumpet creeper, and others. Many of these were grown in three CCC plant nurseries from seeds collected within the Park.

Many of the displays of mountain laurels that today

line the Skyline Drive were, in fact, planted by the CCC. After the November 2000 fires, remnants of the contoured planting beds paralleling the Drive between Thornton Gap and Skyland were once again revealed.

Most of the blue-blazed trails within the Park take the hiker along former wagon roads that took the mountain residents from one side of the mountain to the other. The astute hiker might notice that every former roadbed in the Park has a nice flat, or horizontal, surface. These improvements were the result of extensive efforts expended by the CCC, who leveled every mountain road, rut and trail in the Park, adding most of the rock retaining walls as they proceeded, in order to make the roads suitable for car and truck traffic.

A hike in the Park, especially in winter, can reveal some of the plethora of mountain resident artifacts still visible throughout the Park. Rusty galvanized buckets, mason jars, auto bodies and carriage parts, even broken 78 rpm records and bits of shoe leather may be found among the stone walls and hundreds of rock piles that are the result of generations farming and living on the land.

Other artifacts from these former residents can also be observed. Tulip poplars, all of the same diameter and height, and all lacking branches on the lower third of their boles, now repopulate acres of land. This represents former cropped or grazed open lands, and the tulip poplars represent the growth that has occurred since these fields went fallow at the time of the Park's establishment in the 1930s.

The SNP has been called a recycled park. Unlike the untouched virgin forests of the western national parks of its time, the forest community of the initial SNP showed the results of generations of natural resources extraction and subsistence farming when it was formally established on Dec. 26, 1935. This is not the same place it was 200 years ago, or even 20 years ago.

Seventy-five years of forest growth has enabled today's

Park to recycle its resources, nurtured by the deposition of two tons of leaf and twig litter per acre every year, producing our current mature forest community. However, throughout this period of regrowth, many factors have influenced the natural systems within the parkland, creating a new community unlike any that has occurred in the past.

As the introduction of exotic plants, animals and fungi and natural catastrophic events continue to affect the forest community, we can be assured that SNP will not remain the same. We must appreciate what we have now and make decisions that will protect our natural environment for future generations to appreciate.

Geology of Shenandoah National Park

Approximately 800 million years ago (Pre-Cambrian time), the area that is now Shenandoah National Park had hills about 1,000 feet above the valleys. The underlying rock was deeply eroded granite and other igneous rocks that had shallow soil on the hilltops and slopes but a thicker soil and accumulations of eroded material in the valleys. A major period of volcanic activity then violently disturbed this region with fire fountains, explosive eruptions and earthquakes. The earth rifted apart, and lava welled up through fissures and fed immense fire fountains, like those sometimes seen on Kilauea Volcano, Hawaii. Lava flowed from these fissures, first filling the valleys and finally drowning even the roughly 1,000-foot hills.

There was not just a single flow but a series of at least seven major ones, for a total thickness of about 2,000 ft., of which about 1,800 ft. remain. Volcanic ash deposits, soil development, volcanic mudflows, and eroded material accumulated between the flows and today help mark flow contacts. Finally, the volcanic action ceased, and normal weathering and erosion led to soil development and the accumulation of sand and gravel. At this time, the land was barren, for land plants had yet to evolve.

Geologists today believe that major mountain building has almost always been caused by collisions of earth's brittle plates, also termed the lithosphere. Beneath these plates is the asthenosphere, a slowly moving but solid layer that carries the plates apart, together, or along one another. There is evidence that the Atlantic Ocean has opened and closed at least two times in the past 1.2 billion years. For reference, the earth is about 4.6 billion years old.

One important era of mountain building occurred about 420 million years ago during a slow collision between North America, the first Atlantic Ocean lithosphere and finally Europe. Although the mountains formed by this collision have been eroded away, traces still exist. This collision destroyed the eastern part of the first Atlantic Ocean, termed the Iapetus Sea, and largely affected the region north of our central Appalachians. This episode of collision is termed the Taconic Orogeny, named for the Taconic Mountains of New York state, where the evidence of the event is well exposed.

These first collisions created land areas on what had been the oceanic margin of the Iapetus Sea. This land closed the eastern margin of the Iapetus Sea, forming a great inland sea, termed the Appalachian Basin. To the east, streams and rivers eroded these eastern highlands, carrying a tremendous amount of sediment (sand, silt and clay) into the shallow inland sea. These sediments deeply buried the older volcanic soil, lava beds and granitic rocks that formed the basement of the Appalachian Basin. Marine invertebrate animals flourished in the seas, leaving behind many fossil-rich rocks. Compaction and higher temperature turned the sediment into rock.

About 250 million years ago, near the end of the Permian period, Africa and Euro-America slowly converged, closing the ancestral Atlantic Ocean. On the Euro-American side, the continent was crumpled and uplifted, forming mountains. In some places the African plate was thrust over the North American plate. The tremendous pressure, coming from the southeast in the mid-Atlantic coastal area, caused the earth's crust to compress and fold like a rug into long subparallel ridges.

The mountain chain so formed extended from Poland and Germany (Harz Mountains) west through Belgium, France and southern England, then on to Newfoundland and thence southwest to Birmingham, Alabama. As the pressure continued the folds became higher and steeper and rocks that had been laid down in horizontal beds were tilted vertically in places.

The deeply buried basaltic lava and ash and the granitic rocks were shoved westward over upturned layers of sandstone, shale and even limestone of the now folded rocks of the Appalachian Basin. The Blue Ridge Thrust Fault zone marks the surface trace of this great deformed zone and can be traced from Alabama to Roanoke, Virginia, and north into Pennsylvania. The present Blue Ridge Mountains were then the western edge of a huge anticlinorium, an anticline of regional extent composed of smaller synclines and anticlines folds. Some researchers believe this great fold and others in the Piedmont Province closer to the center of the convergence zone formed a mountain range as high as the Himalayas are today, possibly five miles high. Other researchers believe that erosion may have kept pace with the lifting of the land, in which case this early mountain range was never so high.

The high pressures and temperatures associated with continental collision caused much of the rock, both igneous and sedimentary, to be altered (metamorphosed)— the basalt into greenstone, the sandstone into quartzite, and the shale into phyllite.

The supercontinent, made up of Euro-America and Africa and many other continents, was named *Pangaea* by Alfred Wegener. Pangaea broke up around 190 million years ago, when the Atlantic reopened between North America and Africa, leaving remnants of the African continent along a southeastern strip of North America. Separation of North America from Europe was not completed for another 100 million years.

By the beginning of Cretaceous time, 130 million years ago, the last period in the age of the dinosaurs, the period of mountain building was over and erosion had leveled much of the land, leaving low hills here and there. River drainage was now to the east, into the Atlantic Ocean. Sometime in Early Cretaceous time the land was gently tilted, with the Appalachian region lifted as the coastal areas were lowered. This gave the formerly lazily flowing rivers renewed vigor, and they were now able to cut through the hard rocks of the Blue Ridge.

As time went on, the headwaters of many of the rivers and streams west of the present Blue Ridge were captured by the biggest rivers—the Potomac, the James and the Roanoke. The gaps cut by the beheaded rivers ceased to deepen and rose as the land rose. They make today's wind gaps. Thornton Gap may have originally been cut by the Thornton River. Manassas Gap, just north of the Park, is one of the deepest of the wind gaps.

Looking at the mountains in the SNP of today, we can see reminders of their vast history. Most of the Blue Ridge crest in Shenandoah is capped by the hard, erosion-resistant greenstone. Although changed from the original basalt, this rock still retains many of its original volcanic characteristics. One can find amygdules—spherical gas bubbles in the basalt, later filled with crystalline minerals—in many greenstone outcrops.

In many places columnar jointing, polygonal-shaped cracks formed when lava cools, shrinks and hardens, is still quite evident. It can be seen very strikingly at the southeastern viewpoint on Compton Mtn., just off the *AT* in the North District. One must get down below the rocks to see this display. It can also be seen on cliffs above the *AT* about 0.15 mi. north of Hawksbill Gap, and again about 200 ft. south of Little Stony Man Parking Area. Evidence of the multiple layers of lava originally laid down can be seen along the *AT* below Franklin Cliffs and Crescent Rocks. In both places the *AT* follows a shelf "between layers," as shown by the vertical cliffs above and below the Trail. One of the ancient granite hills that was drowned by the lava flows can be seen along the walls of Whiteoak Canyon. The stepwise series of waterfalls in this canyon also indicates the multiple lava flows.

In some places along the Blue Ridge crest in the Park, the greenstone has been completely eroded away and it is the "base rock" that crops out. In such places, it is also possible that the lavas never covered the granite. One such place is Marys Rock, where the outcrop is the igneous rock granodiorite. Radiometric age measurements, such as the uranium lead method, give an approximate age of 1,200,000,000 years to the intrusion of the granites. Some of the peaks on the eastern side of the main ridge consist primarily of light-colored, coarse-grained granite. The popular Old Rag Mountain is one of these. Numerous greenstone dikes are present on Old Rag. Here the greenstone is eroding faster than the surrounding granite, leaving narrow passageways with vertical sides and surprisingly regular "steps" made by erosion of the columnar-structured dike material.

To the west of the main crest are the remnants of two lower paralleling ridges, both of sandstone-quartzite. These ridges took shape as the limestone west of them, the shale between them, and the conglomerate between the sandstone and greenstone of the main crest eroded much faster than they did. The remnants of these sandstone ridges show today as peaks on the side ridges that run from the Blue Ridge crest westward. On these side ridges the peak farthest from the main crest is composed of a type of sandstone-quartzite known as the Antietam formation. This sandstone is easily recognized, as it is characterized by fine straight parallel tubes that cross the bedding at right angles. These tubes are presumed to be fossil burrows of sea worms—skolithos—filled with sand. Because of its appearance, this rock has been called pipe-rock. Estimated age of the wormhole-like fossils is about 500,000,000 years, the lower Cambrian. Fossils like these are termed trace fossils for they are only markings, or traces, in rocks. The exact nature of the organisms that created skolithos is unknown.

Peaks underlain by the old Antietam sandstone include Rockytop (the highest and westernmost peak, 2,556 ft., of the Rockytop ridge), Lewis Peak, Austin Mtn., Turk Mtn. and Brown Mtn. in the South District of the Park. The Antietam sandstone in the Central and North districts is not as obvious to the hiker. In some places the greenstone and base rock was thrust west overtop of the sandstone and shale deposits and even some of the limestone. This is true at the very northern end of the Park and explains the location of Skyline Caverns, a limestone cave, located under the western slopes of the Blue Ridge.

Natural History

Over the past two million years, more than 15 glacial advances have resulted in the ebb and flow of forest migration through SNP. These migrations have created new forest communities every time, each like the former, but each unique.

Change occurs not only in the time frame of millennia, but also in the moment. Catastrophic weather events and fires routinely, if infrequently, reshape the land and recycle the nutrients to form a new forest community. For example, the June 27, 1995 storm that dropped 30.5 in. of rain during a 16-hour period in Madison County, VA was a once-in-a-few-thousand-years event. However, such an event happens in SNP, on average, every 80 years.

Despite such changes, the southern Appalachians constitute one of the oldest plant communities on Earth. The resilience of SNP forests can be reflected in the number of its inhabitants whose ancestors evolved from these same mountains. The heath family (including the rhododendron, azaleas, mountain laurel, and blueberries, among others), ferns (specifically the spleenworts), the lungless salamanders and, to some extent, the wood warblers, all reach their peak of development in the mountains of the Appalachians. Other organisms that are representative of the Appalachians include orchids, brook trout, white-tailed deer and black bear.

Forest Communities

The forest communities of SNP are representative of much of the deciduous forest formation of the central and southern Appalachian Mountain chain, which stretches from Alabama in the south to the Gaspé Peninsula in Canada. Within this formation, three associations exist in SNP.

Oak-Chestnut Association

The majority of SNP lies within the Oak-Chestnut association of the eastern North American deciduous forest formation. It is dominated by white oak and, formerly, the American chestnut. Additional dominants include red oak, chestnut oak, hickories and tulip poplar.

With the loss of the American chestnut from the eastern forest communities, oaks, hickories, and tulip poplar have replaced them. Red oaks preferred the lower and more moist habitats, while chestnut oak prevailed in higher elevations. Tulip poplar, yellow birch, and sugar maple replaced American chestnut in coves with superior soils.

Some of the moister areas in valleys at the base of the ridge contain beech, hemlock, tulip poplar and an occasional white pine. In the moist coves of higher elevations (over

3,000 ft.), sugar maple, basswood, and red oak are the usual dominants, while black birch and white ash are also common.

On rocky or windswept slopes, chestnut oak dominates, with table mountain pine often present. On more protected rockslide communities, black birch will dominate. Along ridge tops with poor soils, which have been subjected to lumbering and fires, scrub (bear) oak becomes the dominant species.

Hemlock-White Pine-Northern Hardwoods Association

At the higher elevations within the Park, the Hemlock-White Pine-Northern Hardwoods association reaches down from the north. Only here, along the summits of Stony Man, Hawksbill, and Crescent Rock, can the visitor view the relic populations of red spruce and balsam fir. Balsam fir, red spruce, speckled alder, gray dogwood, round-leaved dogwood, quaking aspen, fly honeysuckle, and gray birch are found only in the stretch of the Park from Skyland to Big Meadows. About six small stands of native white (or paper) birch exist in the Park. Other typically northern trees that are natives here include the American mountain ash, black ash, and mountain and striped maple, and the three-toothed cinquefoil, which may be found along a few very high rock outcrops, such as Hawksbill's. Bunchberry or dwarf cornel grows in the South District of the Park—the only place in Virginia where it is found.

Oak-Pine Association

At the lower elevations in the Park, the southern Oak-Pine association creeps up from the south. This region is characterized by the dominance of oak and hickory, in which white oak is the most abundant species. However, the widespread occurrence of pines throughout the region has resulted in the term "oak-pine." Here, we find a few plants that are near the northernmost limit of their range, including the shortleaf pine, umbrella magnolia and Carolina willow. The Catawba rhododendron, responsible for the colorful balds found farther to the south, is found only in the southern third of the Park.

The Oak-Chestnut Forest

For more than 6,000 years, oaks and chestnuts have been the major components of the eastern forests. Their fruits provide the most significant wildlife food in the deciduous forests. They are the fuel that runs the eastern US forests, being eaten by literally hundreds of forest wildlife. With the loss of the American chestnut tree, oaks have largely taken their place.

Since European settlement, the preponderance of oak species in eastern forests has increased. With few exceptions, oak species are shade intolerant, meaning they cannot regenerate in a closed canopy forest habitat. Thus, their contribution is directly related to openings provided in the forest canopy. Logging and subsequent burnings that have occurred throughout most of the eastern US for timber and the charcoal-fueled iron industry have enabled a regeneration of oak species. In fact, current forest acreage in eastern North American is approaching about two-thirds of the forest areas estimated to have existed at the time of the arrival of Europeans.

However, this trend of oak recruitment throughout most of the eastern forest biome and SNP has declined dramatically in the last 50 years. This decline can be attributed to a number of factors, including fire suppression, deer browsing, insects and diseases, and exotic plant competition. How the oak species can respond to these pressures will ultimately determine the future viability of our eastern forest communities.

Fire

Fire in our eastern forests is a natural part of the

ecosystem. Fires set back the successional stage of development. Low temperature non-catastrophic ground fires historically occurred in this region at a 5- to 25-year interval. This regime tended to eliminate thin-barked trees, such as red maple, sugar maple, beech, birch, black cherry and black gum. With the absence of such fires, these faster growing species out-compete the oaks, thus becoming a more dominant member of the forest understory. Additionally, with the increase in understory vegetation, oak reproduction is restricted, yielding to more shade-tolerant species, such as maples. Formerly, catastrophic fires, intense enough to induce stand replacement, occurred on a 200- to 500-year basis, providing widespread new habitat for the recruitment of a new population of oak species.

Deer Browse

Deer herbivory has been a major concern in most national parks of the northeastern U for over two decades. Intensive browsing has removed oak seedlings, enabling a conversion of forests from oak to species such as tulip poplar, maple, and birch. Recent studies within SNP and adjacent forest communities provide evidence that deer browse is negatively impacting oak recruitment.

Exotic Plants

Exotic plants have been an issue in SNP since its inception. One of the many activities of the CCC was the removal of the ailanthus tree, or tree of heaven, and the removal of currants and gooseberries, alternate hosts to the introduced fungus that causes white pine blister rust.

Invasive exotic plants can reduce oak recruitment. Introduction of exotics is associated with openings in the forest canopy. Such openings are often the result of man-made disturbances, such as roads, recreational services, power lines, or tree mortality due to introduced diseases or insect infestations.

Extensive surveys have been conducted by SNP staff to address exotics within the Park. The most frequently encountered herbaceous species was garlic mustard, followed by Japanese stiltgrass and Oriental ladysthumb.

Non-native shrubs and vines of significance found in the Park include multiflora rose, wineberry, and the woody vines Japanese honeysuckle and Oriental bittersweet

While tree of heaven was, by far, the most common species of exotic tree species found, Norway maple and princess tree were also notable exotics.

Other identified exotic invasives with the potential for significant impact within the Park are wavyleaf basketgrass, the annual mile-a-minute, and perennials Japanese knotweed and kudzu.

Gypsy Moth

Gypsy moths have been responsible for the loss of a significant portion of the oak species from the Appalachians throughout the last century.

The introduced gypsy moth was first detected in the SNP in 1981. Serious defoliation first occurred in 1986 in the North District. During the next decade, as the gypsy moth population migrated south, oak mortality continued throughout the Park, with some parts of the Park losing more than 50% of the forest canopy.

A fungus was introduced to the gypsy moth population as a biological control from its native Asian habitat as far back as 1910. Within SNP, the fungus has kept the gypsy moth population at low levels, with the exception of localized outbreaks in 2002 and a larger outbreak in 2007, defoliating more than 7,300 acres in the Park. It is believed that the fairly reliable presence of the fungus will continue to act as an effective regulator of gypsy moth populations in the Park.

Sudden Oak Death

Sudden Oak Death (SOD), first identified in California in 1995, is a fungus that has been imported to the east coast. SOD causes a bleeding canker on the stem of numerous oak species, ultimately resulting in mortality. Unfortunately, many nursery crops are carriers of SOD. Chestnut oaks and white oaks appear the most susceptible to the fungus, followed by northern red oak and pin oak.

The US Forest Service has stated, "Based on past history, it is not a matter of 'if' but 'when' SOD will gain a foothold in eastern oak forests. Due to a lack of basic epidemiological research on eastern species, the range of outcomes is extremely uncertain—from innocuous to a potential chestnut blight scenario." Under the worst-case scenario, this disease may ultimately result in an ecological disaster greater than the loss of the American chestnut.

Vertebrates of the Oak-Chestnut Forest

Approximately 70 species of mammals can be found in this Appalachian region, from Pennsylvania south to North Carolina. Like plants, some of the species will only be found in boreal habitats, while others require more southern oak-pine forests.

A joint ATC/PATC and Smithsonian Institution project is utilizing 50 infrared, motion-detection cameras along the Appalachian Trail (from the VA/NC border to the MD/PA border) to identify warm-blooded animals (birds and mammals). Using a scent to lure animals to the camera from as far away as 150 ft., photos were taken for a month at each site before the cameras were moved to another location along the *AT*. The results of the first two years (2007, 2008) showed that white-tailed deer were seen at the most number of monitored sites (82%), followed by black bear (35%), raccoons (28%), gray squirrels (27%), opossum (9%), coyotes (7%), domestic dogs (6%) and bobcats (5%).

Black Bear

At the time of the Park's establishment, the only two known bears in the Park belonged to the Panorama resort management, who used the two cubs for entertainment purposes. Black bear repopulated the Park on their own, migrating from the western mountains

Today's estimate of black bear in SNP is roughly between 400 and 800 or more. A 1985 study found a density of 2.6 bear/mi^2 in the Central District of the SNP, the highest density of black bear of any national park. It is quite possible that the bear population in SNP has doubled since 1985. Overall, SNP estimates Park-wide bear densities are probably closer to one to two bears per square mile.

Bears in SNP average 200 pounds for females and 400 for males. The availability of oak trees and oak mast is critical to black bear health. In the fall, black bear are totally focused on eating acorns and other seasonal foods (apples, hickory nuts, corn). They will feed up to 20 hours a day, consuming 20,000 calories and adding two to four pounds of fat daily. During good mast years, bears may more than double their body weights between August and December. The need to feed becomes so important in the life cycle of the black bear, that even sex is put on hold, literally. With an actual gestation of only six to eight weeks, it would be natural to presume that the mating season would be in late fall. However, it is imperative that black bear focus their attention on feeding.

In order to accommodate both needs, black bear have evolved the ability to temporarily suspend the growth of the fertilized egg by withholding implantation of the egg in the uterus. This "delayed-implantation" enables the black bear to mate in June, maintain an arrested state of development for five or six months, implant the egg in late November, and give birth in late January. Delayed implantation also occurs with most members of the weasel family.

Black bear will continue foraging until the hard mast is

depleted. As a result, a fall season of good hard mast pro-
duction, or a "mast year," will keep the bear active later in
the season than a poor mast year.

Oak trees also provide ideal denning environments. A
SNP study found 84% of pregnant females denned in trees.
These trees had an average diameter of three feet.

It is interesting to note that in the Southern Appalachians, the second most important food for bear is squawroot, a parasitic plant that grows on the roots of oak trees.
Squawroot is believed to be an important source of protein
for lactating females emerging from dens. Thus, the top two
foods of black bear are associated with the oak tree.

White-tailed deer

Prior to European settlement, white-tailed deer populations in SNP probably averaged about 10-20 deer/mi^2.
Prior to the time of the Park's establishment, white-tails
had been extirpated from the area. In 1934, 13 deer were
released along Big Run in the South District. With the pro-
hibition of hunting, lack of predators, and vast areas of
ideal habitat, the deer population in the Park soared.

Oak mast is a preferred food of deer. Studies report that
deer densities above 25 deer/mi^2 prevent the natural recruitment of oaks to the forest community. By 1988, the deer population within and around the SNP had exceeded these levels, and was above the biological carrying capacity. Within
SNP, the highest densities are found in the more open grassy
areas associated with campgrounds, visitor centers, and
Skyline Drive. From 1999-2007, documented densities in the
Big Meadows area averaged 182 deer/mi^2, with one single
night count as high as 451 deer/mi^2.

The impact of white-tails on the plant communities has
been viewed as a "catastrophic event" comparable to wind
throw, fire, or insect outbreak. Regeneration failure,
reduced species richness and biomass, and loss of struc-
tural diversity are long-term ecosystem impacts from such

excessive white-tailed deer populations.

The future of white-tailed deer in the eastern US, as well as SNP, may be determined by the spread of chronic wasting disease (CWD). This neurological brain and nervous system disease of deer and elk was identified in West Virginia in 2005, and in 2007 a CWD-positive deer was identified in Yellow Spring, WV.

Canids

The canids are represented in SNP by the coyote, the red and the gray fox, as well as the feral domesticated dog.

Until the early 1900s, the range of coyotes extended only as far east as northern Wisconsin and central Texas. Removal of the gray wolf in the east made room for the gradual move into the east by the coyote. Coyotes are now known to exist in every county in Virginia. The eastern U.S. population is about ten pounds bigger than the western subspecies, due to interbreeding with Canadian wolves (20-25 lbs. vs 35-40 lbs.).

The red fox of the mid-Atlantic states is believed to be a descendant of the English fox, with interbreeding from the northern native American red fox. Gray fox have a black-tipped tail, while a red fox has a white-tipped tail. Gray fox are the only canid that can climb trees.

Felids

Bobcats exist in abundant numbers within SNP. Shrieks in the winter night, sounding like the wailing of wild women, is likely to be the mating, or caterwauling, of these 25-pound cats.

Mustelids

Of the seven species in the weasel family found in the Appalachian region, only the long-tailed weasel is a common member of the SNP community, with mink occupying lower stream habitats. The long-tailed weasels of SNP do not don a winter white coat with their fall molt. Instead, a lighter shade of brown pelage appears.

Skunks

SNP has two skunk species as residents; the striped and spotted. The spotted skunk is a southern species, with the Mathews Arm area being near its northern-most location. The unusual defense of the spotted skunk starts with the skunk stomping the ground rapidly with its front feet. The next stage includes doing a series of handstands with the rear end and tail held straight up in the air. If the intruder hasn't caught on by now, the spotted skunk will either drop to all fours, or remain in its handstand position, and let go with the spray. The potent musk glands secrete the spray 12 to 15 ft. in distance.

Skunks are preyed upon by great-horned owls, which, although having terrific hearing and sight senses, suffer a bit in the olfactory sense.

Insectivores

Of the nine species of shrew and three of moles found in the Appalachian region, four species of shrews and one mole species are found in SNP. Shrews, the smallest mammals in North America, are extremely common. Look for their characteristic 1-inch diameter holes and tunnels under logs and rocks.

These primitive mammals essentially do everything extremely fast. With a life spans of a year or less, a whole "lifetime" must be condensed basically one into season. For example, shrews have extremely high energy/metabolic rates. Under stress, their heart rates have been recorded as high as 1,200 beats per minute.

Opossum

At the time of European arrival in North America, opossum were limited to south of the Potomac River to

Harpers Ferry, and on a line to Wheeling, then northwest including most of Ohio, Indiana and Illinois. With the removal of natural predators, they have moved north since that time and now reach Canada.

Opossums, like the more primitive monotremes (echidna and duck-billed platypus), and some shrew, have only a single opening, or cloaca, closed by a sphincter muscle into which all of the fecal, urinal and genital products are discharged. This characteristic is shared with reptiles and birds.

Strangely enough, they can also prey upon rattlesnakes, copperheads and water moccasins due to their apparent immunity to pit viper venom.

Rodents

Rodents are the largest order of mammals in the Appalachian region (as well as the world), both in species and actual numbers. In fact, 40% of the world's mammalian species are rodents. They include squirrels, beaver, mice, rats, lemmings, voles, groundhog, porcupine and jumping mice. Of the 24 native species found in the Appalachian region, approximately 14 can be found in SNP. By far, the white-footed mouse and the deer mouse are the most common in the SNP.

More information on Appalachian mammals can be found at *www.bobpickett.org*.

Birds

Over 200 species of birds have been documented in SNP, with nearly half of these known to breed in the Park. Depending on the source, approximately 70 species are year-round residents, with 75 being summer residents only, and 20 only found in the Park during the winter season.

SNP maintains a long-standing peregrine falcon restoration program in cooperation with the Virginia Department of Game and Inland Fisheries and the Center for Conservation Biology at the College of William and Mary. Between 1978 and 1993, 37 falcons were successfully released from the Park. Nesting peregrines were documented on Stony Man Mountain from 1994-1998 and another pair from 2004-2007. During 2000-2008, the Park hacked, released, and successfully fledged 69 young peregrine falcons at sites within the Park. In general, the hacked/released falcons have not returned to the SNP in subsequent years. Only one chick has been naturally produced by a breeding pair during this period of time (2005). The same pair reared two additional foster chicks in 2006 after their own eggs were flooded out.

Turkeys were reintroduced into the Park in the 1930s. They are now quite prolific throughout SNP. While the eastern turkey's diet is quite omnivorous, acorns can be the primary food consumed during fall, winter and spring. Turkeys are one of the few animals that can eat walnuts and hickories whole; the nuts pass through the gizzard, are crushed and absorbed.

A small but healthy population of ravens nests in the Park. The raven, larger than the common crow, can be identified by its hoarse/guttural call and wedge-shaped tail, rather than the fan-like tail of the crow.

Amphibians

SNP is home to ten species of toads and frogs and fourteen species of salamanders or newts.

The cool, moist habitat of the Appalachians provides ideal habitat for amphibians. The red-backed salamander is the most common amphibian in the Park, as well as the Appalachian chain in general. Research has found that the biomass of red-backed salamanders exceeds that of all birds and mammals combined in the Appalachians.

The Shenandoah salamander is a federally listed endangered species, found only on dry rocky talus slopes of the Pinnacles, Hawksbill Mountain, and Stony Man

Mountain. The limited range of the Shenandoah salamander is due in part to competition with the red-backed salamander. These salamanders have adapted to drier habitat conditions than red-backed salamanders, maintaining a stronghold on these isolated island habitats.

Reptiles

There are 28 species of reptiles found in the SNP, including 18 snakes, five turtles, three skinks, and two lizards. The cool, moist weather that makes the Appalachians such a haven for amphibians has the opposite effect on reptiles.

The most common snake in the Park is the northern ring-necked snake, followed by the northern garter snake, northern copperhead, eastern black rat snake, and timber rattlesnake. Northern water snakes are commonly found in or around mountain streams.

The two venomous snakes, timber rattlesnake and northern copperhead, are commonly found at rocky, high-elevation talus areas in late April and September as they enter or exit their wintering dens. Both species produce new fangs almost once a month, with the old passing through the snake's digestive system. The venom of rattlesnakes is approximately two to six times more toxic than copperheads'.

Fish

By the time SNP was established in 1936, brook trout populations within most streams had been severely depleted due to local harvesting pressure.

Today, the most common fish in SNP streams is the eastern brook trout. Over 50 of the Park's 70 perennial streams support brook trout. It is the only trout native to the Park. Although stocking of "brookies," brown, and rainbow trout has occurred in many streams since the early days of the Park, nearly half of current stream populations still support the original native brook stock, making SNP the repository of one of the largest strongholds of native brook trout in the northeastern US.

The SNP allows catch and release fishing in all Park streams (aka "fish for fun"). Harvesting of trout is allowed from 22 streams, subject to size and creel limitations.

Within the SNP, trout populations are affected during summer droughts, when streams become isolated pools, and brook trout become "swimming ducks" for northern water snakes, which will remove all fish from one pool before traveling to the next.

Insects and Diseases of the Forest Community

The eastern forests are being invaded by a large number of alien species, which are causing serious damage to the natural balance of life. It has been estimated that 23% of the vegetation in the SNP is exotic plants. The forests of our eastern deciduous forests have probably suffered the most severe damage in the country.

In addition to gypsy moths and Sudden Oak Death, mentioned earlier, below is a summary of the most (or potentially most) damaging introduced species.

Emerald ash borer

The emerald ash borer (EAB) has recently been discovered again in northern Virginia. The 2008 populations are at least two to three years old, meaning the beetle has already spread beyond a controllable limit. With the EAB already established in West Virginia, Pennsylvania and Maryland, SNP has recently implemented a Firewood Movement Restriction Program. At this time (2011), visitors who live more than 50 miles from the Park are not permitted to bring in outside firewood. Firewood can be purchased locally or "dead and down" firewood can be collected within the Park.

Throughout the eastern US, the EAB has the ability to

kill millions of ash trees, just as the hemlock woolly adelgid has killed millions of hemlock trees.

Hemlock woolly adelgid

The hemlock woolly adelgid is a tiny aphid-like insect that is associated with the decline of thousands of Eastern and Carolina hemlocks in eastern North America, from southwestern North Carolina to Massachusetts and west to Pennsylvania and West Virginia. Introduced from Japan in 1924 and first identified in a large municipal park in Richmond, Virginia in 1952, the adelgid damages the tree by sucking sap from twig tissues; the tree loses vigor and prematurely drops needles, to the point of defoliation, which, stressing the tree, enables the hemlock woolly adelgid to ultimately kill the tree in four to six years. As of 2011, 95% of the Park-wide hemlock population had succumbed to the adelgid.

Current treatment relies on the use of a systemic pesticide, using a portable soil injection method. Soil injections provide for three years of treatment longevity and are much more effective (and cheaper) at preserving hemlock health versus twice-yearly insecticidal soap treatments. At this time, existing treated trees are holding their own.

Even though eastern hemlocks comprised only 0.5% of the Park's forest before the adelgid, the loss of the hemlock community will have a likely significant impact on Blackburnian and black-throated green warblers, who nest in coniferous forests.

Dogwood Anthracnose

Dogwood anthracnose is an introduced fungal disease, first reported in 1978, decimating widespread areas of flowering dogwoods. Since that time, SNP has seen a 90% decline in dogwood due to the anthracnose. Currently, there is no known way of preventing this blight from continuing its destruction of our native dogwood populations.

Beech Bark Disease

Beech bark disease refers to a disease relationship between a non-native sap-feeding scale insect and at least two species of Nectria fungus (one fungus is native, and one is nonnative).

The disease was first identified in the upper Whiteoak Canyon of SNP in 2007.

While it is projected that 90% of the native beech trees in the mid-Atlantic region may be destroyed, there are some beech trees that have shown a natural resistance to the scale insects.

Chronic Wasting Disease

Chronic Wasting Disease (CWD) is a disease that affects the brain and nervous system of elk, deer and moose, ultimately causing death. The disease is related to mad cow disease in humans and scrapie in sheep. CWD was first identified in 1967 in Colorado and is spreading eastward. It has recently been confirmed (2005) in Hampshire County, West Virginia, only 25 miles from the SNP. It is reasonable to presume CWD will be found in SNP in the next five to 20 years.

Dark Hollow Falls, Central District   *Photo by Lee Sheaffer*

HEIGHTS OF THE HIGHEST WATERFALLS IN SHENANDOAH NATIONAL PARK

(Reproduced, with permission, from the Shenandoah National Park's PARK GUIDE, copyrighted 1968.)

Waterfall	Ht Ft.	District	Stream
Overall Run Falls	93	North	Overall Run
Whiteoak #1	86	Central	Whiteoak Run
South River Falls	83	Central	South River
Lewis Falls	81	Central	Hawksbill Cr.
Dark Hollow Falls	70	Central	Hogcamp Br.
Rose River Falls, Upper	67	Central	Rose River
Big Falls, Doyles River	63	South	Doyles River
Whiteoak #2	62	Central	Whiteoak Run
Whiteoak #6	60	Central	Whiteoak Run
Whiteoak #5	49	Central	Whiteoak Run
Jones Run Falls	42	South	Jones Run
Whiteoak #4	41	Central	Whiteoak Run
Whiteoak #3	35	Central	Whiteoak Run
Twin Falls	29	North	Overall Run
Little Falls, Doyles Riv.	28	South	Doyles River
Rose River Falls, Low.	22	Central	Rose River

(NOTE: The waterfalls on Whiteoak Run are numbered from top to bottom.)

Measurements were made by Robert Momich and Gary Miller (Volunteers in the Parks) using a Wallace and Tiernan Altimeter accurate within 2 ft. One might consider an unrestricted drop of water a waterfall and a steeply slanting, downhill rush of water a cascade. Shenandoah Park falls of water are usually a combination; in particular, the tops and bottoms of the Park waterfalls are often indefinite and so the establishment of recording stations for the above measurements was necessarily arbitrary.

North District - Appalachian Trail

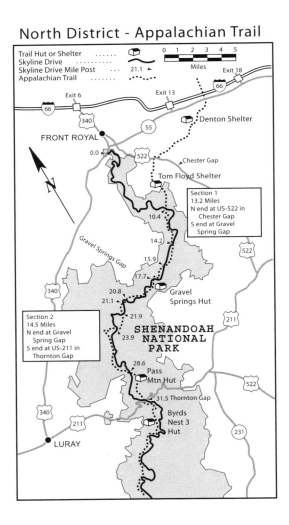

Trail Hut or Shelter	. . . . . .
Skyline Drive	. . . .
Skyline Drive Mile Post	21.1 ►
Appalachian Trail	. . . .

0 1 2 3 4 5
Miles

Exit 18

66

Exit 6

Exit 13

66

Denton Shelter

340

55

FRONT ROYAL

0.0

522

Chester Gap

Tom Floyd Shelter

Section 1
13.2 Miles
N end at US-522 in
Chester Gap
S end at Gravel
Spring Gap

10.4

14.2

522

15.9

17.7

20.8

21.1

Gravel
Springs Hut

340

211

21.9

Section 2
14.5 Miles
N end at Gravel
Spring Gap
S end at US-211 in
Thornton Gap

23.9

**SHENANDOAH
NATIONAL
PARK**

28.6

Pass
Mtn Hut

522

31.5 Thornton Gap

340

Byrds
Nest 3
Hut

211

231

LURAY

APPALACHIAN TRAIL
NORTH DISTRICT
Shenandoah National Park

The Appalachian Trail in the North District of Shenandoah National Park has its northern terminus on US 522 near Front Royal, its southern terminus in Thornton Gap where US 211 crosses Skyline Drive. It includes a total of 27.7 miles of trail, and Section 1 and Section 2 in this guidebook.

> *NOTE: The Skyline Drive in the North District may be gated and locked from dusk to 8 a.m. during November and December. Check with the Park information line before you hike (540-999-3500). In the event that you are locked in the Park, call the emergency number (800-732-0911) for assistance.*

In the North District of the Park, open areas that were once fields, orchards and farmlands are long gone, so that good viewpoints are limited to occasional rock outcroppings. Through most of this area the Trail and Skyline Drive parallel each other closely, with many intersections, making the Trail readily accessible. However, the deep woods through which it passes make the hiker feel remote.

For the first 3.5 miles the Trail is along easements, passing property of the National Zoological Park Conservation Center, the Northern Virginia 4-H Educational Center and private property in Harmony Hollow. From here the Trail enters SNP and soon reaches the crest of the Blue Ridge.

Numerous side trails and fire roads can be used in conjunction with the *AT* for a variety of walking trips, including some circuit hikes. For more information, see section titled "Side Trails," as well as the PATC publication *Circuit Hikes in Shenandoah National Park*.

Maps:

PATC Map #9, Appalachian Trail and Other Trails in SNP North District, (Edition 18, 2009) is recommended for use with this Guide. The following USGS 1:24,000 scale sheets cover the *AT*: Front Royal, Bentonville, Chester Gap, Luray, Thornton Gap. Additional USGS sheets complete the coverage of the North District: Luray and Washington, VA.

Large-flowered trillium　　　　*Photo by Lee Sheaffer*

SECTION 1
US 522 to Gravel Springs Gap

13.2 miles — PATC Map #9

General Description: From US 522, just below Lake Front Royal (940 ft.), the *AT* leads south along the edge of National Zoological Park Conservation Center property. It crosses SR 602 and reaches an elevation of 1,475 ft. at SR 601. From here it climbs steadily via graded trail, crossing into Shenandoah National Park a short distance before reaching the crest of the Blue Ridge, where it comes into the old road from Chester Gap to Compton Gap (former route of the *AT*). The Trail follows the Compton Gap Rd. south to Skyline Drive at Compton Gap (2,415 ft.), then climbs over Compton Mtn. and North and South Marshall mountains before reaching Gravel Springs Gap. The *AT* either crosses Skyline Drive or comes quite close to it in several places, so that all parts of it are easily accessible. Spring water is available in several locations near the Trail.

Trail Approaches: The northern end of this section begins at US 522, just west of Lake Front Royal and 3.2 miles east of its junction with VA 55 in Front Royal.

The southern end is on Skyline Drive, SDMP 17.7, at its intersection with old Browntown-Harris Hollow Road in Gravel Springs Gap. Paved parking for 12 cars here.

Side Trails: The Dickey Ridge Trail, Bluff Trail, Lands Run Gap Road, Hickerson Hollow Trail, Mt. Marshall Trail, Jordan River Trail, and Browntown Trail offer good hiking. For details see "Side Trails." Also refer to PATC publication: *Circuit Hikes in Shenandoah National Park.*

Accommodations: There are many motels and restaurants in Front Royal and a number of private campgrounds

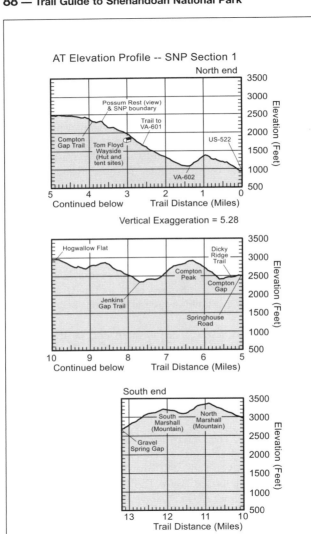

AT Elevation Profile -- SNP Section 1

North end

Compton Gap Trail
Possum Rest (view) & SNP boundary
Trail to VA-601
Tom Floyd Wayside (Hut and tent sites)
US-522
VA-602

Continued below

Trail Distance (Miles)

Vertical Exaggeration = 5.28

Hogwallow Flat
Dicky Ridge Trail
Compton Peak
Compton Gap
Jenkins Gap Trail
Springhouse Road

Continued below

Trail Distance (Miles)

South end

South Marshall (Mountain)
North Marshall (Mountain)
Gravel Spring Gap

Trail Distance (Miles)

in the Front Royal area.

The Tom Floyd Wayside is located along the *AT*, 3.1 mi. south of US 522. This is a primitive camping area with a few tent sites and a three-sided shelter, to be used by overnight hikers.

Trail Description, North to South

0.0 US 522. Descend and cross footbridge over polluted Sloan Creek. The Trail ahead follows a National Park Service easement over land belonging to the Research and Conservation Center. (The Center is a 4,000-acre wildlife preserve belonging to the National Zoological Park, an agency of the Smithsonian Institution. The land was formerly a USDA livestock research station and, before that, a US Cavalry remount post.) *Camping and hunting are prohibited.*

0.1 Cross footbridge over polluted marsh. Ascend, steeply at times, with fenced meadow and good view on right. (A World War II prisoner-of-war camp was on top of the ridge above the former cavalry post.) Ticks are common in this area. Frequent inspections for ticks are recommended.

0.5 Enter woods dominated by yellow poplars (tulip trees).

0.8 Just before crossing ditch, evening orchids may be seen beside large yellow poplar.

0.9 Cross crest of spur ridge. Descend steeply.

1.4 Cross VA 602. Trail undulates ahead through forest where beech trees predominate. In 50 yd., cross Moore Run. Do not take water from here, nor at the stream ahead, for there are houses upstream.

1.5 Cross intermittent stream and ascend.

1.7 Go straight at cross-trail in a densely overgrown meadow. Good view of Harmony Hollow from bench just ahead.

1.8 Enter woods again.

1.9 Giant beech on right. Oak, hickory, sassafras forest.

2.0 Bench on left. Descend, sometimes steeply. Blue-blazed trail leads right to Northern Virginia 4-H Center.

2.6 Bear left. Sign here points to Harmony Hollow Trailhead Parking.

2.8 Blue-blazed trail leads right 0.7 mi. to Harmony Hollow Trailhead Parking. This trail also leads to another side trail in 0.2 mi which leads to *Ginger Springs* and Tom Floyd Wayside Tent Camp #1. Oakland hickory predominate ahead.

2.9 Path on right leads to Tom Floyd Wayside Shelter and Tent Camp #2.

3.3 Ridge crest. Level, descend ahead.

3.4 Cross old road and ascend.

3.5 Ascend steeply up cliff face via switchbacks and rock steps.

3.6 Possums Rest. 180-degree view west from top of cliff and the boundary of SNP. (A self-registration back-country permit booth is located 100 yds. further north on the *AT*. Backpackers intending to camp in the Park must stop here and follow instructions for completing their backcountry camping permit.)

3.8 Horse trail, former Compton Gap Road. Follow it right, blazed both white and yellow. (To left, horse trail leads 0.5 mi. down to SR 610 at the Park boundary. Via 610 it is 1.8 mi. farther to US 522 at Chester Gap. Until 1974 this was route of *AT*.)

5.0 Springhouse Road, yellow-blazed on right.

5.3 Reach trail junction marked by concrete post. (To right, Dickey Ridge Trail leads 9.2 mi. north to Front Royal town limits and entrance to Skyline Drive, SDMP 0.0. Interesting Fort Windham Rocks are 0.2 mi. from *AT* on this trail. To left of *AT*, a Park service road leads 0.4 mi. to PATC Indian Run Maintenance Bldg, not available for camping. *Spring* is 250 ft. from service road, on left, about

0.1 mi. before reaching building.

5.6 Cross to right (south) of Skyline Drive, SDMP 10.4, in Compton Gap (2,415 ft.). (Paved parking area for 14 cars here.) Ascend Compton Mtn. by switch-backs, passing several large outcrops of basalt. (A patch of white clintonia, speckled wood lily, along Trail here and a small clump of yellow lady's slippers. The latter bloom in mid-May, the former in early June.)

6.4 Signpost marks short blue-blazed trails leading right and left to viewpoints. Both are ungraded and offer only rough footing but are worthwhile. (Trail on left leads 0.2 mi. to a spectacular outcrop of columnar basalt. To see columnar structure it is necessary to climb down below the rocks via rough trail to left of outcrop. Trail to right of *AT* leads over top of Compton Mtn. [2,909 ft.] and down 0.2 mi. to rocky ledge offering excellent views to west and north.)

6.8 Pass *Compton Springs*. (Original springhead, unmarked, is approximately 25 yd. to left of trail. A second intermittent seep is 100 ft. downhill and to right.) About 150 ft. beyond springs, *AT* crosses small stream fed by them. *AT* descends fairly steeply for about 0.5 mi. then levels off. (Much mountain laurel, blooming in early June, and pink azalea, blooming in mid-May, between here and Jenkins Gap.)

7.7 Cross yellow-blazed Jenkins Gap Trail in Jenkins Gap (2,398 ft). (Paved parking area to left for 14 cars just off Skyline Drive at Jenkins Gap. Mt. Marshall Trail can be reached by walking south along Skyline Drive about 0.3 mi.)

7.8 Cross abandoned road diagonally. Trail climbs unnamed mountain, then passes through an old orchard of apple trees that still persist but are now mostly overgrown.

9.1 Trail passes along foundations of an old building. This building was an old comfort station facility during the early days of the Park. A close inspection of the foundation will show an entrance leading toward nearby Skyline Drive.

9.4 Cross to left of Skyline Drive at Hogwallow Gap, SDMP 14.2 (2,739 ft.). (Some parking available.) Trail ascends gently through Hogwallow Flat area.

9.9 Pass short trail 30 ft. left to *Hogwallow Spring*, unmarked and easy to miss. (Most springs in Park along *AT* are marked with concrete post.)

10.9 Reach summit of North Marshall (3,368 ft.). (The name of this mountain grows out of fact that these lands were formerly part of Blue Ridge holdings of John Marshall, noted Chief Justice of the United States from 1801 to 1835.) Along crest of mountain, cliffs to right of Trail offer some good views to west. As Trail descends, just where it jogs sharply to left, there is one outstanding viewpoint.

11.6 Cross to right (west) of Skyline Drive, SDMP 15.9 (3,087 ft.). (Paved parking area for 12 cars just before Drive.)

12.1 Summit of South Marshall (3,212 ft.). Trail descends gradually, with ledges on right affording splendid views to west.

13.2 Gravel Springs Gap at intersection of old Browntown-Harris Hollow Rd. with Skyline Drive, SDMP 17.7 (2,666 ft.). To right, Browntown Trail, yellow-blazed, leads northwest down mountain. To left and across Skyline Drive, Harris Hollow Trail, also yellow-blazed, descends hollow. *AT* continues from end of parking lot.

Trail Description, South to North

0.0 West of Skyline Drive at its intersection with Browntown Trail (yellow-blazed), SDMP 17.7 (2,666 ft.). Browntown Trail follows route of old Browntown-Harris Hollow Rd. northward down mountain. East of Drive first 0.3 mi. of old road serves as Harris Hollow Trail as well as an access road to Gravel Springs Hut. *AT* follows Browntown Trail for few feet, then turns right and ascends gradually. Ledges on left, near top of mountain, afford splendid views to west.

1.1 Summit of South Marshall (3,212 ft.).

1.6 Cross to right (east) of Skyline Drive, SDMP 15.9 (3,087 ft.). (Paved parking area for 12 cars here.) Ascend North Marshall by switchbacks. Near top is an excellent view of Browntown Valley to the west.

2.1 Crest of ridge. Cliffs to left of Trail offer some good views to west.

2.3 Summit of North Marshall (3,368 ft.). (These lands were formerly a part of Blue Ridge holdings of John Marshall, noted Chief Justice of the United States from 1801-1835.) Trail now descends gradually.

3.2 Pass short trail leading right 30 ft. to *Hogwallow Spring*. (Piped spring and easy to miss.) Continue to descend, very gently, through Hogwallow Flat.

3.8 Cross to left of Skyline Drive at Hogwallow Gap, SDMP 14.2 (2,739 ft.). (Some parking available here.) For 0.5 mi. *AT* proceeds across relatively level terrain.

4.0 Foundation of old building on right. This building was an old comfort station facility during early days of Park. A close inspection of foundation will show an entrance leading toward nearby Skyline Drive. Trail climbs unnamed mountain, passing through old orchard with many old apple trees persisting, although now topped by black locust trees.

5.4 Cross abandoned road diagonally. (Old road leads left 0.1 mi. to an old quarry.)

5.5 Cross yellow-blazed Jenkins Gap Trail in Jenkins Gap (2,398 ft.). (Parking space for 14 cars in Jenkins Gap just off Drive. To left, Jenkins Gap Trail descends mountain; to right it leads 150 ft. to Skyline Drive and Mt. Marshall Trail.) Trail now passes through a level area containing extensive growth of mountain laurel (blooms early

June) and pink azalea (blooms late May). Beyond, Trail ascends fairly steeply.

6.4 *Compton Springs.* Original springhead, unmarked, is approximately 25 yd. to right of trail. A second intermittent seep is 100 ft. to left.

6.8 Signpost at top of climb marks short blue-blazed trails leading left and right to viewpoints. Though ungraded and offering only rough footing, both trails are worthwhile. (Trail on right leads down 0.2 mi. to spectacular outcrop of columnar basalt. To see columnar structure it is necessary to climb down below rocks via rough trail to left of viewpoint. Top of outcrop affords good view east. Trail on left leads over crest of Compton Mtn. [2,909 ft.] and down 0.2 mi. to a rocky ledge offering excellent views to west and north.) *AT* continues along ridge of Compton Mtn. for about 0.2 mi. then descends, passing several large boulder-like outcrops of basalt. (At least one clump of yellow lady's slipper, blooms mid-May, and some white clintonia, bloom early June, along this stretch of Trail.)

7.6 In Compton Gap cross to right side of Skyline Drive, SDMP 10.4 (2,415 ft.). (Parking for 14 cars here.) *AT* follows old Compton Gap-Chester Gap Road, both white and yellow blazes, continuing along Blue Ridge crest.

7.9 Intersection with blue-blazed Dickey Ridge Trail (left) and service road (right) to PATC Indian Run Maintenance Bldg. (Dickey Ridge Trail begins here and leads northwest 9.2 mi. to entrance to Skyline Drive at Front Royal town limits. Fort Windham Rocks are 0.2 mi. from *AT* along this trail. Service road leads 0.4 mi. to PATC Indian Run Maintenance Bldg., not available for camping. *Spring* 250 ft. to left of service road about 0.1 mi. before reaching building.)

8.2 Springhouse Road, yellow-blazed on left.

9.4 Turn left from Compton Gap Trail onto narrower footpath (white-blazed only). (Compton Gap Trail, yellow-blazed, continues down mountain. This was route of *AT* until 1974.)

9.6 SNP boundary. Reach Possums Rest in 50 ft., 180-degree view west from top of cliff. Turn right and descend cliff steeply via switchbacks and rock steps. Trail ahead is on Harmony Hollow scenic easement, first such easement established in Virginia.

9.7 Bottom of cliff. Descend ahead through oak and hickory forest.

9.8 Cross old road and ascend.

10.3 Path on left leads to Tom Floyd Wayside Shelter and Tent Camp # 1 & 2. Pass through extensive growth of white ash and yellow poplar (tulip tree) ahead.

10.4 Blue-blazed trail leads 0.7 mi. to Harmony Hollow trailhead parking (an additional trail 0.2 mi down this trail leads to *Ginger Springs* and Tom Floyd Tent Camp #1). Ahead, a strong aroma of sassafras may be detectable in places.

10.6 Bear right. Sign here pointing to Harmony Hollow trailhead parking, which may be reached by blue-blazed trail 0.2 mi. back in opposite direction.

11.3 Bear right at fork. Blue-blazed trail leads to Northern Virginia 4-H Center. Giant beech on left.

11.4 Densely overgrown meadow. Good view of Harmony Hollow from bench just ahead.

11.5 Go straight at cross-trail and re-enter woods just ahead.

11.7 Cross intermittent stream. Do not take water from here, or at stream ahead, for there are houses upstream. Trail undulates ahead through forest where beech trees predominate.

11.8 Cross Moore Run. In 50 yds., cross VA 602. Enter land belonging to Research and Conservation Center. (Center is a 4,000-acre wildlife preserve belonging to National Zoological Park, an agency of the Smithsonian Institution. Land was formerly a USDA livestock research station and, before that, a U.S. Cavalry remount post.) *Camping and hunting are prohibited.* Ascend steeply ahead.

12.3 Cross crest of spur ridge. Descend through forest dominated by yellow poplar.

12.5 Just after crossing ditch, evening orchids may be seen beside large yellow poplar.

12.7 Leave woods and descend, sometimes steeply, with fenced meadow and good view on left. (A World War II prisoner-of-war camp was on top of ridge above former cavalry post.) Ticks are common in this area. Frequent inspections for ticks are recommended.

13.1 Cross footbridge over polluted marsh, then cross footbridge over polluted Sloan Creek.

13.2 US 522. To continue on Trail, cross US 522 and ascend embankment.

Hikers on SNP ridge line   *Photo by Lee Sheaffer*

SECTION 2
Gravel Springs to Thornton Gap

14.5 miles — PATC Map #9

General Description: From Gravel Springs (2,666 ft.)
the *AT* climbs to Little Hogback and just below Hogback
Mtn. It descends over 1,000 ft. to Elkwallow Gap, then
ascends several lesser high points and the summit of Pass
Mtn. before descending to Thornton Gap (2,307 ft.). Near
Range View Cabin and also on Pass Mountain the Trail
passes through areas that were once quite open. Large old
oak trees with widespreading low branches are being
crowded by slender young forest trees. The old oaks
remind the hiker that these areas were open fields in the
pre-Park days, during which these oaks grew to maturity.

Side Trails: At 3.8 mi. the Tuscarora Trail connects
with the *AT*. This trail offers a 220-mile route west of the
AT, rejoining it northeast of Carlisle, Pa. For more infor-
mation see "Side Trails," as well as the PATC publication
Guide to the Tuscarora Trail. The Gravel Springs-
Thornton Gap area is rich with side trails, too many to enu-
merate here. See "Side Trails" and the PATC publication
Circuit Hikes in Shenandoah National Park.

Trail Approaches: The northern end of this section is on
Skyline Drive, SDMP 17.7, at intersection with old
Browntown-Harris Hollow Rd. Paved parking area for 12
cars.
   The southern end is in Thornton Gap, SDMP 31.5,
where US 211 crosses Skyline Drive. Trail is 0.2 mile west
of Skyline Drive.

Accommodations: Two three-sided huts are available
for overnight hikers. Gravel Springs Hut is 0.2 mi. south of

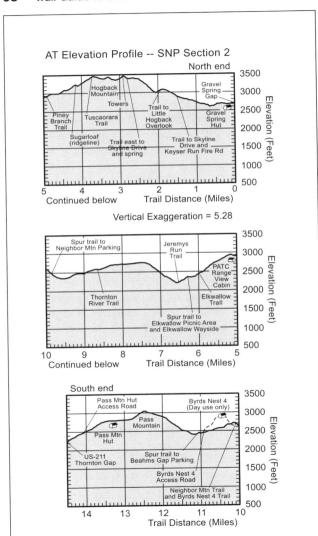

AT Elevation Profile -- SNP Section 2

North end

Gravel Spring Gap

Hogback Mountain

Towers

Trail to Little Hogback Overlook

Piney Branch Trail

Tuscaorara Trail

Gravel Spring Hut

Sugarloaf (ridgeline)

Trail east to Skyline Drive and spring

Trail to Skyline Drive and Keyser Run Fire Rd

Vertical Exaggeration = 5.28

Spur trail to Neighbor Mtn Parking

Jeremys Run Trail

PATC Range View Cabin

Thornton River Trail

Elkwallow Trail

Spur trail to Elkwallow Picnic Area and Elkwallow Wayside

Continued below

South end

Pass Mtn Hut Access Road

Byrds Nest 4 (Day use only)

Pass Mountain

Pass Mtn Hut

US-211 Thornton Gap

Spur trail to Beahms Gap Parking

Byrds Nest 4 Access Road

Neighbor Mtn Trail and Byrds Nest 4 Trail

Gravel Springs Gap and another 0.2 mi. down the Bluff Trail. Pass Mtn. Hut is 1.2 mi. north of Thornton Gap and 0.2 mi. down a spur trail. Range View Cabin, a locked PATC cabin requiring advance reservations, is located 5.1 mi. south of Gravel Springs Gap (see "Shelters, Huts and Cabins").

Mathews Arm Campground, SDMP 22.2, near Trail 4.4 mi. south of Gravel Springs Gap, offers extensive camping facilities, no reservations accepted. (Campground is open during summer season.) Restrooms and water available at Thornton Gap. Short-order food can be purchased at Elkwallow Wayside, SDMP 24.0. None of these facilities is open during the cold months.

Trail Description, North to South

0.0 Intersection of old Browntown-Harris Hollow Rd. with Skyline Drive, SDMP 17.7 (2,666 ft.). (Paved parking area for 12 cars here.) *AT* crosses to left (east) side of Drive and parallels old Harris Hollow Rd. for several hundred feet. (This road, on left of *AT*, is utilized as access road to Gravel Springs Hut, 0.3 mi. Harris Hollow Trail, yellow-blazed, goes down the east side.

0.2 *AT* turns right at concrete post where Bluff Trail comes in on left. (Bluff Trail starts here, descends by switchbacks to Gravel Springs and hut in 0.2 mi.) *AT* passes through extended level area.

1.3 Cross to right side of Skyline Drive, SDMP 18.9.

1.5 Spur trail to left leads 100 ft. to Skyline Drive, SDMP 19.4, at junction of Keyser Run Fire Rd. on east side of Drive. Paved parking area. Keyser Run Fire Rd. leads south along east slopes of Blue Ridge.

1.8 *AT* reaches top of Little Hogback. Fine outlook from ledge 30 ft. to right of Trail.

1.9 Spur trail, at signpost, leads straight ahead 50 ft. to Little Hogback Parking Overlook on Skyline Drive,

SDMP 19.7. *AT* veers right and descends, passing below overlook. Trail then ascends steeply, by switchbacks, up east face of first peak of Hogback.

2.5 Ridge crest; continue along ridge.

2.6 Pass few feet to left of first peak of Hogback (3,420 ft.).

2.7 Hogback Spur Trail leads left, downhill, 0.2 mi. to walled-in *spring* which is within sight of Skyline Drive. *AT* ascends.

2.8 Trail veers left immediately after hang-glider site.

3.1 *AT* comes into tower road just before it reaches the Drive. Road leads to summit of second peak of Hogback (3,474 ft.). Cross to left of Skyline Drive, SDMP 20.8. (Junction with Sugarloaf Trail, leading left, is 50 ft. beyond the Drive.) Ascend toward third peak of Hogback (3,440 ft.). Near top a side trail leads right 15 ft. to a spot offering splendid view north over Browntown Valley and Dickey Ridge. Skyline Drive is directly below; enormous rocks here.

3.4 Cross to right of Skyline Drive, SDMP 21.1, at paved parking area. Continue along crest of Hogback Mtn.

3.7 Side trail leads left 30 ft. to summit of fourth peak (3,440 ft.), with view south, now mostly overgrown. From fourth peak, *AT* descends.

3.8 Junction with Tuscarora-Overall Run Trail. (Tuscarora forms a 220-mile loop, rejoining *AT* near Carlisle, Pa.)

4.2 Spur trail on right leads 50 ft. to summit of Sugarloaf. *AT* continues to descend.

4.4 Cross to left of Skyline Drive, SDMP 21.9. (Entrance road to Mathews Arm Campground is 0.2 mi. to right along Drive. Rattlesnake Point Overlook [3,105 ft.] is 50 yd. left of *AT* on Drive. Views east over Piney Branch.) Pass Rattlesnake Point, a large rock formation, to right of Trail.

4.6 Junction with Piney Branch Trail, which crosses *AT*. Immediately beyond, *AT* comes to Range View Cabin service road and follows it left a few feet before turning left away from it.

5.0 Pass under power line.

5.1 Post marks second side trail leading 0.1 mi. to Range View Cabin. *Spring* is below cabin. (Cabin is a locked structure. Advance reservations required. See "Shelters, Huts and Cabins.") In 200 ft. *AT* crosses access road to cabin. (A few feet down road Piney Ridge Trail takes off from right of road, just as road bends left toward cabin.) *AT* descends gently toward Elkwallow Gap.

5.9 Cross to right of Skyline Drive, SDMP 23.9 (2,480 ft.). (Elkwallow Wayside is 200 yd. south on Drive. Short-order food available spring, summer, fall. Elkwallow Picnic Area is beyond wayside. No overnight accommodations. Restroom, pay phone, *water* available.) *AT* swings right, then circles wayside and picnic area. Cross Elkwallow Trail 250 ft. beyond Drive. (To left, trail leads 0.1 mi. to wayside; to right, it is 1.9 mi. to Mathews Arm Campground.)

6.1 *Spring*, marked with concrete post to left.

6.3 Trail leads left 200 ft. to Elkwallow Picnic Area. *AT* turns sharply right here and descends.

6.4 *Spring* marked with concrete post is to left of Trail.

6.5 Junction with Jeremys Run Trail, which is straight ahead. *AT* turns sharply left at this junction, crosses creek in 100 ft. and ascends.

7.5 Reach crest of narrow ridge and follow it.

8.7 Junction with blue-blazed Thornton River Trail. (Thornton River Trail crosses Skyline Drive in 0.3 mi. then descends along a branch of Thornton River to eastern Park boundary.)

9.8 Trail leads left 0.1 mi. to Neighbor Mtn. (Parking area on Skyline Drive, SDMP 26.8.)

10.1 Intersection with yellow-blazed Neighbor Mountain Trail. (To left, horse trail continues to Skyline Drive, SDMP 28.1, in 1 mi. passing near Byrds Nest #4.

No camping here.) *AT* now tops rise, then descends following main ridge.

10.3 *AT* leaves ridge crest and slabs southwest side of ridge.

11.0 *Spring*, marked with concrete post, is to right of Trail, 100 ft. farther along *AT*.

11.1 Spur trail on left leads 0.1 mi. to Beahms Gap Parking Overlook on Skyline Drive, SDMP 28.5.

11.4 Cross to left of Skyline Drive, SDMP 28.6. *AT* ascends gently from here. Intersection with yellow-blazed Rocky Branch Trail.

12.1 Rocky area on right affords wintertime views to The Neighbor and Knob Mtn.

12.5 Reach summit of Pass Mtn. (3,052 ft.).

13.3 Pass Mountain Trail leads left. (Pass Mountain Hut is 0.2 mi. down trail. Hut for use of overnight hikers. *Spring* is few feet behind hut.)

14.1 *AT* comes to service road and follows it to right for 150 ft., then turns off road to right.

14.4 Trail descends bank to service road within sight of Drive. Follow road to Drive and cross it.

14.5 Cross US 211 at a point 0.2 mi. west of Skyline Drive in Thornton Gap, SDMP 31.5 (2,307 ft.).

Trail Description, South to North

0.0 Intersection with US 211 at a point 0.2 mi. west of Skyline Drive in Thornton Gap, SDMP 31.5 (2,307 ft.). Trail leads uphill through woods.

0.1 Cross to right side of Skyline Drive and follow service road for few feet; then turn left, up bank, into woods.

0.4 *AT* turns left onto service road, follows it about 150 ft., then turns left, away from road. Trail ascends gradually.

1.2 Pass Mountain Trail leads right 3 mi. to its lower terminus on US 211. (Pass Mtn. Hut is 0.2 mi. from *AT* down this trail. *Spring* is few feet behind hut. Hut for use of overnight hikers.)

2.0 Wooded summit of Pass Mtn. (3,052 ft.).

2.4 *AT*, descending, passes through rocky area with winter views west of Kemp Hollow, Neighbor Mtn. and Knob Mtn.

3.1 Intersection with yellow-blazed Rocky Branch Trail crosses to left (west) of Skyline Drive, SDMP 28.6, in Beahms Gap

3.4 Spur trail leads right 0.1 mi. to Beahms Gap Parking Overlook on Skyline Drive, SDMP 28.5.

3.5 Cross well-defined old road trace. Just beyond, trail on left leads 100 ft. to *spring* (concrete signpost). Trail now slabs southwest side of ridge.

4.1 Reach ridge crest and follow it.

4.2 Top of rise. In 200 ft. reach junction with yellow-blazed Neighbor Mountain Trail. (To left leads to peak of The Neighbor, then continues down to Jeremys Run.)

4.7 Spur trail leads right 0.1 mi. to parking area on Skyline Drive, SDMP 26.8. Beyond this junction *AT* continues along crest of long narrow ridge for over 2 mi., then descends.

5.8 Junction with blue-blazed Thornton River Trail. (Right leads 0.3 mi. to Skyline Drive, then follows branch of Thornton River to Park boundary.)

8.0 Cross creek. In 100 ft., where *AT* turns sharply right, is intersection with Jeremys Run Trail.

8.1 On right of *AT* a short trail, marked with concrete signpost, leads to *spring*.

8.2 Trail straight ahead leads 200 ft. to Elkwallow Picnic Area. *AT* turns sharply to left here to swing around developed area of Elkwallow Picnic Area and Wayside.

8.4 *Spring* marked with concrete post to right.

8.5 Intersect Elkwallow Trail. (To left this trail leads 1.9 mi. to Mathews Arm Campground; to right it leads 0.1 mi. to Elkwallow Wayside. Short-order food available spring, summer, fall. Restrooms, *water*, pay phone available.)

8.6 *AT* crosses to right of Skyline Drive, SDMP 23.9, and ascends gently.

9.4 Cross service road to Range View Cabin, a locked structure requiring advance reservations from PATC Headquarters. To right, road leads down 0.1 mi. to cabin. *Spring* is below cabin. (To left, road leads 0.6 mi. to Skyline Drive, SDMP 22.1.) In 200 ft. spur trail leads right 0.1 mi. to Range View Cabin.

9.5 Pass under power line.

9.8 Turn right onto access road and follow it a few feet before leaving it again as road bends to left. Immediately ahead is junction with Piney Branch Trail, which leads right from *AT*.

10.1 Cross to left side of Skyline Drive, SDMP 21.9. Rattlesnake Point is to left of Trail as you reach Drive. (Rattlesnake Point Overlook [3,105 ft.] is on Drive, 50 yd. right of *AT*, with views east over Piney Branch. To left of *AT*, 0.2 mi. along Drive, is entrance road to Mathews Arm Campground.) *AT* now ascends.

10.3 Spur trail on left leads 50 ft. to summit of Sugarloaf.

10.7 Junction with Tuscarora-Overall Run Trail. (Tuscarora Trail provides a 220-mi. loop, rejoining *AT* near Carlisle, Pa.)

10.8 Side trail leads right 30 ft. to summit of fourth peak of Hogback (3,440 ft.), with overgrown view south. Continue along ridge, descending slightly.

11.1 Cross to right of Skyline Drive, SDMP 21.1. (Paved parking area.) Ascend third peak of Hogback (3,440 ft.). Just beyond top, side trail leads 15 ft. to spot offering splendid view north over Browntown Valley and Dickey Ridge. (Skyline Drive is directly below; enormous rocks here.)

11.4 Junction with new Sugarloaf Trail, which leads right. In 50 ft. cross Skyline Drive, SDMP 20.8. Follow tower access road few feet, then bear right off road. Road continues to second peak of Hogback (3,475 ft.).

11.7 *AT* veers right past old hang-glider site on left.

11.8 Graded trail to right leads 0.2 mi. downhill to walled-in *spring* which is within sight of Skyline Drive. *AT* now ascends.

11.9 Pass few feet to right of first peak of Hogback (3,420 ft.). Continue along ridge crest, then descend steeply by switchbacks down east face of mountain.

12.6 Spur trail, at signpost, leads right 50 ft. to Little Hogback Overlook on Skyline Drive, SDMP 19.7. *AT* veers left here, and climbs.

12.7 Top of Little Hogback; fine outlook from ledge 30 ft. to left of Trail. *AT* now descends gradually.

13.0 Spur trail to right leads 100 ft. to Skyline Drive, SDMP 19.4, at junction of Keyser Run Fire Road on east side of Drive. Paved parking area is available.

13.2 Cross to right side of Skyline Drive, SDMP 18.9. Trail passes along an almost level area.

14.3 Junction with Bluff Trail. *AT* bears left, paralleling old Browntown-Harris Hollow Rd. from here to Drive. (Bluff Trail starts here and descends by switchbacks to *Gravel Springs* in 0.2 mi. and Gravel Springs Hut 50 ft. beyond.)

14.5 Cross to left side of Skyline Drive, SDMP 17.7 (2,665 ft.), at its intersection with old Browntown-Harris Hollow Rd. (Paved parking area for 12 cars here. Harris Hollow Rd., right of Drive and *AT*, is utilized as service road to Gravel Springs Hut for 0.3 mi. Harris Hollow Trail, yellow-blazed, follows route of old road down mountain.)

SUMMARY OF DISTANCES ALONG THE *AT*
North District

	Miles	
	N-S	**S-N**
US 522	0.0	27.7
Indian Run Maintenance Bldg.	5.3 +0.4	22.4 +0.4
Compton Gap	5.6	22.1
Jenkins Gap	7.7	20.0
North Marshall summit	10.9	16.8
Gravel Springs Gap	13.2	14.5
Gravel Springs Hut	13.4 +0.2	14.3 +0.2
Hogback, 2nd peak (tower)	16.1	11.6
Tuscarora Trail	17.0	10.7
Piney Branch Trail	17.8	9.9
Range View Cabin	18.3 +0.1	9.4 +0.1
Piney Ridge Trail	18.3	9.4
Elkwallow Gap, Skyline Drive crossing	19.2	8.5
Jeremys Run Trail	19.7	8.0
Thornton River Trail	21.9	5.8
Neighbor Mtn. Trail	23.3	4.4
Byrds Nest #4	24.2 +0.5	3.5 +0.5
Beahms Gap, Skyline Drive crossing	24.4	3.4
Pass Mtn.	25.7	2.0
Pass Mtn. Hut	26.5 +0.2	1.2 +0.2
US 211, Thornton Gap	27.7	0.0

SUMMARY OF DISTANCES BY SKYLINE DRIVE
TO POINT ON *AT*
North District

SDMP N to S		Miles S to N
0.0	Park Entrance; US 340 east of Front Royal	31.5
10.4	Compton Gap; *AT* crossing	21.1
12.3	Jenkins Gap; *AT* is 0.1 mi. to west	19.2
14.2	Hogwallow Gap; *AT* crossing	17.3
15.9	*AT* crossing just south of North Marshall Mtn.	15.6
17.7	Gravel Springs Gap; *AT* crossing	13.8
18.9	*AT* crossing	12.6
19.4	Keyser Run Fire Rd; *AT* is 100 ft. via spur trail	12.1
19.7	Little Hogback Parking Overlook; *AT* is 50 ft. north via spur trail	11.8
20.8	*AT* crossing, sag between second and third peaks of Hogback	10.7
21.1	*AT* crossing, between third and fourth peaks of Hogback	10.4
21.9	Rattlesnake Point; *AT* crossing 0.3 mi. north of Mathews Arm Campground	9.6
23.9	Elkwallow Gap; *AT* crossing 200 yds. north of wayside	7.6
24.2	Elkwallow Picnic Area; *AT* is 200 ft. from second parking area via spur trail	7.3
26.8	Neighbor Mtn. Trail parking area; *AT* is 0.1 mi. west via spur trail	4.7
28.5	Beahms Gap Overlook; *AT* is 0.1 mi. west of Drive via spur trail	3.0
28.6	Beahms Gap; *AT* crossing	2.9
31.5	Thornton Gap; *AT* crosses US 211 0.2 mi. west of Drive	0.0

Central District - Appalachian Trail

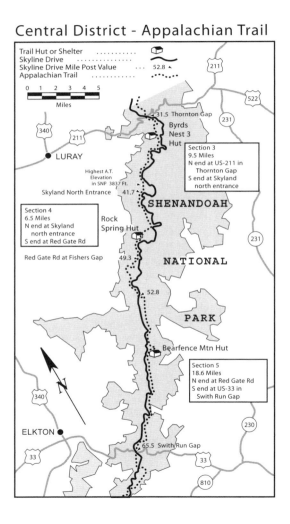

Trail Hut or Shelter ....
Skyline Drive ....
Skyline Drive Mile Post Value ... 52.8 ▲
Appalachian Trail ....

0 1 2 3 4 5
Miles

211

522

231

31.5 Thornton Gap

Byrds
Nest 3
Hut

340

211

LURAY

Section 3
9.5 Miles
N end at US-211 in
Thornton Gap
S end at Skyland
north entrance

Highest A.T.
Elevation
in SNP 3837 Ft.

Skyland North Entrance   41.7

SHENANDOAH

Section 4
6.5 Miles
N end at Skyland
north entrance
S end at Red Gate Rd

Rock
Spring Hut

231

Red Gate Rd at Fishers Gap   49.3

NATIONAL

52.8

PARK

Bearfence Mtn Hut

N

Section 5
18.6 Miles
N end at Red Gate Rd
S end at US-33 in
Swith Run Gap

340

ELKTON

230

33

65.5 Swith Run Gap

33

810

APPALACHIAN TRAIL
CENTRAL DISTRICT
Shenandoah National Park

This district begins where US 211 crosses the Blue Ridge and intersects Skyline Drive in Thornton Gap, SDMP 31.5, at a point 9 miles east of Luray, 7 miles west of Sperryville, and 83 miles from Washington, D.C. The southern end is at Swift Run Gap, SDMP 65.7, where US 33 crosses the Blue Ridge. From Swift Run Gap it is 7 miles west to Elkton, 8 miles east to Stanardsville, and 110 miles to Washington, D.C. The Central District includes Section 3, Section 4, and Section 5 for a total of 34.4 miles of the *AT*.

The Blue Ridge crest is higher in this part of the Park than in the northern and southern parts. The highest peak in the Park, Hawksbill, just south of Skyland, has an elevation of 4,050 feet. The *AT* reaches its highest point in the Park, 3,837 ft., on Stony Man Mtn. Skyline Drive reaches its highest altitude, 3,680 ft., at the northern entrance to Skyland.

The Central District of Shenandoah National Park is the part most widely used by the motoring public, by campers, and by hikers. The *AT* is heavily used, as are the chief side trails. Favorite short hikes include the Stony Man and Story of the Forest trails, the Bearfence and *AT* loop, the Passamaquoddy and *AT* loop, the Dark Hollow Falls Trail, the trails up Hawksbill, and the Limberlost Trail. Longer favorites are the Whiteoak Canyon Trail, the trails up Old Rag Mountain, and the stretch of *AT* from Thornton Gap (Panorama) to Marys Rock. There are also special trails for horseback riding, with a stable at Skyland.

There are two campgrounds in this district, the largest at Big Meadows and another at Lewis Mountain. Skyland, Big Meadows, and Lewis Mountain have lodging facilities available, in season, for tourists.

The Skyland resort antedates the Park, having been developed by George F. Pollock in the early 1900s. Rapidan Camp (formally Camp Hoover), on the eastern slope of the Blue Ridge near Big Meadows, was a summer retreat for President Herbert Hoover (1929-32). It is now managed by the Park Service. For more information about the history of this area, read "Skyland Before 1900" by Jean Stephenson in the July 1935 PATC *Bulletin* and the books, *In the Light of the Mountain Moon* by Reed L. Engle (Shenandoah National Park Association, 2003), *Skyland*, by George Freeman Pollock (Washington, Judd and Detwiler, 1960), *Herbert Hoover's Hideaway* by Darwin Lambert (Shenandoah National Park Assoc. Inc., Luray, Va. 1971), and *The Undying Past of Shenandoah National Park* by Darwin Lambert (Roberts Rinehart, Inc. 1989).

Maps: PATC Map #10, SNP Central District, Edition 21 (2008) is recommended for use with this Guide. The following USGS 1:24,000 scale sheets cover the *AT*: Thornton Gap, Old Rag, Big Meadows, Fletcher, Elkton East, and Swift Run Gap. The following additional USGS sheets complete the coverage of the Central District: Luray, Stanley, Madison, and Stanardsville.

SECTION 3
Thornton Gap to Skyland

9.5 miles — PATC #10

General Description: From US 211 in Thornton Gap (2,307 ft.), the Trail climbs to the ridge crest just beyond Marys Rock (3,514 ft.). Here a side trail leads to one of the most outstanding panoramic views in the entire Park. The Trail then follows the ridge crest, climbs over The Pinnacle (3,730 ft.), passes below the Jewell Hollow Overlook and continues on to the Pinnacles Picnic Area. Until Hughes River Gap, the Trail stays a little below the ridge crest on

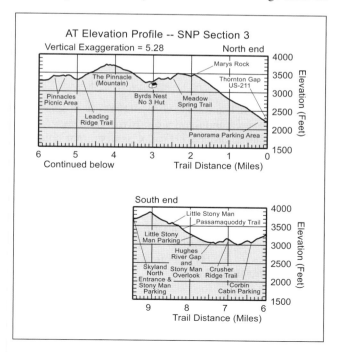

the western side. As the western slopes are generally quite steep in this area there are many good views westward.

From Hughes River Gap, the *AT* climbs to the cliff tops of Little Stony Man then continues ascending to within 0.4 mi. of the summit of Stony Man, formed by the erosion of layer upon layer of ancient lava flows. From here the Trail descends gently to the Stony Man Trail Parking Area at the end of the section.

There are no dependable sources of water on the *AT* along this stretch of trail except the piped water, available "in season," at Panorama and Pinnacles Picnic Area. The springs at Meadow Spring and Shaver Hollow (difficult to find) are each 0.3 mile downhill from the *AT*. The spring at Byrds Nest #3 Hut is 0.2 mile downhill from *AT*.

Trail Approaches: The northern end is on US 211 in Thornton Gap, 0.1 mile west of Skyline Drive, SDMP 31.5. The southern end is at Stony Man Trail Parking Area, SDMP 41.7.

Side Trails: The Park is wide on the eastern side of the Drive in this area and there are many trails. One group of trails is centered around "Hazel Country," that area near the Hazel River and Hazel Mountain. These interconnect with trails in the Nicholson (Free State) Hollow and Corbin Cabin area. (Archaeological studies by Audrey Horning suggest that Aaron Nicholson and clan not only owned their own land but were seen in Sperryville often for medical attention and other necessities.) Skyland area also includes a wide variety of trails. See "Side Trails." Also refer to PATC publication *Circuit Hikes in Shenandoah National Park*.

Accommodations: Skyland has an excellent restaurant, a lodge, and cottages. A stable is maintained here, and there is a network of horse trails as well as hiking trails in this area. Reservations may be made by calling 800-999-4714. The nearest public campground is at Big Meadows, SDMP 51.2, about 9 mi. south of Skyland.

The only hut available for camping in this section is Byrds Nest #3 Hut, available for overnight use. Corbin Cabin, a locked structure reached via the Corbin Cabin Cutoff Trail, is 1.4 mi. east of Skyline Drive, SDMP 37.9. For its use, reservations must be obtained in advance from PATC Headquarters. See "Shelters, Huts and Cabins."

Trail Description, North to South

0.0 This section of *AT* begins at Trail's intersection with US 211, about 0.1 mi. west of Skyline Drive, SDMP 31.5 (2,307 ft.).

0.2 Proceed through woods, passing west of Panorama parking. (Spur trail here leads left to parking area at Panorama. *Water* and restrooms available.) *AT* ascends steadily along northern and then eastern slopes of mountain.

1.9 Spur trail leads right 0.1 mi. to northern tip of Marys Rock. Views from this point are unsurpassed anywhere in Park. (Highest point [3,514 ft.] is reached by climbing to top of huge rock outcrop; dangerous in wet or windy weather. The rock is granodiorite, and geologists have determined its age to be over one billion years!) Beyond junction, *AT* follows ridge crest south, with occasional views westward, then descends gradually.

2.5 In a sag, Meadow Spring Trail intersects *AT*. (Meadow Spring Trail leads left, downhill, passing *Meadow Spring* on left in 0.3 mi.) *AT* continues along ridge crest, which is narrow here. There is an excellent view to west from a rock outcrop 0.1 mi. farther along Trail.

2.9 Reach another good viewpoint. Trail switches back to left, then descends toward sag at base of The Pinnacle.

3.2 *AT* comes into service road and follows it right 180 ft. to Byrds Nest #3 Hut. (To left, service road leads 0.3 mi. to Skyline Drive, SDMP 33.9.) Spring *water* available 0.2 mi. down service road. Beyond hut *AT* ascends gradually.

4.0 Obscure spur trail, right, leads 100 ft. to fine view north.

4.1 50 ft. to right of *AT* are jagged rocks forming north peak of The Pinnacle. Beyond, *AT* leads along level ridge crest for a short distance, affording splendid views of sheer western slopes of this ridge.

4.2 Pass to left of highest point of The Pinnacle (3,730 ft.). Descend through heavy growth of mountain laurel (blossoming in early June).

4.9 Cross blue-blazed Leading Ridge Trail. (To left, trail leads 0.1 mi. to the Drive.) *AT* now passes through some tall white pine, descending gently.

5.0 *AT* passes below Jewel Hollow Overlook.

5.2 Side trail, left, leads back 75 ft. to Jewell Hollow Overlook, SDMP 36.4 (3,335 ft.). *AT* ascends gradually along crest of a narrow ridge. There are fine views westward across Jewell Hollow.

5.3 *AT* comes up to, then parallels to right, entrance road to Pinnacles Picnic Area, SDMP 36.7. At fork in path *AT* follows unpaved right fork, which leads around picnic area. Follow white blazes! Trail route is through tall laurel.

5.4 Trail passes toilets and drinking fountain. (*Water* available here "in season.") Enter woods, ascend slightly, then descend.

5.8 An impressive old white pine grows to left of *AT* here. In 0.1 mi. *AT* passes under power lines. Trail then ascends knob at head of Nicholson Hollow.

6.3 Where *AT* switchbacks sharply to right, descending, there is an excellent viewpoint. *AT* here is close to, but above, Skyline Drive and presents an unobstructed view of Nicholson Hollow and Old Rag Mountain beyond.

6.4 Abandoned trail leads 0.3 mi. downhill to right to *spring* near location of razed Shaver Hollow Shelter. From this intersection, *AT* continues with several gentle dips and climbs.

7.0 Cross Crusher Ridge Trail, blue-blazed, which here follows an old woods road known as Sours Lane.

7.1 Junction with blue-blazed Nicholson Hollow Trail. (It is 0.1 mi. to Drive.)

7.5 A side trail, left, leads 200 ft. to south end of Stony Man Mountain Overlook in Hughes River Gap, SDMP 38.6 (3,097 ft.). Continuing around head of Nicholson Hollow, *AT* parallels Drive and ascends.

7.9 Spur trail, left, leads 150 ft. to Little Stony Man Parking Area on Skyline Drive, SDMP 39.1. Ascend Stony Man Mountain gradually, by long switchbacks, first left, then right.

8.2 At trail junction, take left fork. (Right fork is Passamaquoddy Trail leading 1.4 mi. to Skyland Lodge; Passamaquoddy is a Maine Indian word translating as "abounding in pollock"—as in George Freeman Pollock, founder of Skyland. This is former *AT* route.)

8.4 Reach cliff tops of Little Stony Man. (Climbers frequently "top rope" here.) Continue ascent, climbing more gradually.

9.1 Trail junction and highest elevation of *AT* in Shenandoah National Park (3,837 ft.). (Here hiker may ascend summit of Stony Man via a 0.4 mi. loop, or continue south on *AT*.) *AT* turns left here and descends gradually.

9.5 Reach Stony Man Trail Parking Area and end of this section. (To right it is 0.3 mi. on paved road to Skyland and Dining Hall; to left 0.1 mi. to Skyline Drive, SDMP 41.7.)

Trail Description, South to North

0.0 This section of *AT* starts at Stony Man Trail Parking Area, near northern entrance to Skyland, SDMP 41.7. Ascend gently.

0.4 Trail junction and highest elevation of *AT* in Shenandoah National Park at 3,837 ft. Turn right here and continue on *AT* toward Little Stony Man. (Straight ahead is 0.4 mi. loop around summit of Stony Man Mountain. To left, a spur trail connects with Skyland-Stony Man Mountain Horse Trail.)

1.1 Reach cliffs of Little Stony Man. From here Trail descends steeply by switchbacks.

1.3 Base of Little Stony Man cliffs. (Skyland is 1.4 mi. left (south), on Passamaquoddy Trail, former *AT*, which passes under sheer cliffs of Stony Man.)

1.6 Spur trail, right, leads 150 ft. to Little Stony Man Parking Area on Skyline Drive, SDMP 39.1. *AT* drops well below Drive, then parallels it, clinging to steep western slopes of main ridge.

2.0 Spur trail, right, leads 200 ft. to southern end of Stony Man Mountain Parking Overlook in Hughes River Gap, SDMP 38.6 (3,097 ft.). *AT* now descends.

2.4 Trail junction. (To right, blue-blazed Nicholson Hollow Trail leads 0.1 mi. to Skyline Drive, SDMP 38.4, then continues into Nicholson Hollow.)

2.5 Intersection with blue-blazed Crusher Ridge Trail. (This trail utilizes an old road known as Sours Lane.) *AT* descends, passes over a slight rise, then descends again.

3.1 To left a trail leads downhill 0.3 mi. to *spring* near location of former Shaver Hollow Shelter. From this intersection *AT* ascends.

3.2 Where *AT* switchbacks sharply to left there is an excellent viewpoint. *AT* is immediately above Skyline Drive here and offers an unobstructed view of Nicholson Hollow and Old Rag Mountain beyond.

3.5 Pass under power lines. About 0.1 mi. farther, notice impressive old white pine growing to right of *AT*. From here Trail ascends over knob, then descends to reach Pinnacles Picnic Area.

3.9 Come onto paved path in picnic area and bear left, following *AT* blazes. In 200 ft. turn left at drinking fountain (*water* in season). Pass toilets and follow path through tunnels of mountain laurel. Trail now follows picnic area path, paralleling entrance road to the Pinnacles Area for about 0.1 mi.

4.2 Bear left, away from road. Descend gradually along narrow ridge crest. Fine views westward over Jewell Hollow.

4.3 Spur trail, right, leads 75 ft. to Jewell Hollow Parking Overlook, SDMP 36.4. *AT* passes below overlook.

4.5 Pass second spur trail leading back to overlook. Trail now ascends gently through some tall white pines.

4.6 Cross Leading Ridge Trail, blue-blazed, which leads right 0.1 mi. to Skyline Drive and left over Leading Ridge. *AT* now ascends, passing through thick growth of mountain laurel.

5.3 Pass to right of highest point of The Pinnacle (3,730 ft.). For a short distance Trail follows level ridge crest with excellent views. Pass, on left, jagged rocks forming north peak of The Pinnacle. From here Trail descends to a sag at base of The Pinnacle.

5.5 Pass obscure trail, left, leading 100 ft. to fine view north. *AT* descends by switchbacks along a rocky, picturesque ridge.

6.3 Reach Byrds Nest #3 Hut, which is available for overnight camping. Spring *water* available 0.2 mi. down forest road. Beyond shelter, *AT* follows access road for 180 ft. then turns left, away from road. (Road leads 0.3 mi. to Skyline Drive, SDMP 33.9.) From road, *AT* ascends slightly by switchbacks on east slope of ridge, passing viewpoint at 6.7 mi., then bearing right along ridge. Descend into

Byrds Nest #3 Hut *Photo by John Hedrick*

slight sag.

7.0 Junction with Meadow Spring Trail which leads right, downhill, passing *Meadow Spring* on left in 0.3 mi. and ending at US 211. From trail junction *AT* follows ridge crest. At large rock outcrop, southern tip of Marys Rock, *AT* swings to right of ridge and starts to descend.

7.6 Spur trail leads left 0.1 mi. to exposed northern tip of Marys Rock. (Views from this point are unsurpassed anywhere in Park. Here there are splendid views of Central and North districts of the Park, Massanutten Mtn., Great North Mtn. and the Alleghenies to west, and rolling hills of Virginia Piedmont to east. Highest point [3,514 ft.] is reached by climbing to top of rock outcrop of granodiorite. It can be dangerous in icy, wet, or windy weather. Geologists believe rock of Marys Rock is over one billion years old!) From trail junction *AT* descends steadily to Thornton Gap, at first through laurel and scrub oak. Here there are splendid views of Hazel Mtn. to southeast, Oventop Mtn. with its many peaks to northeast, and the Blue Ridge as far north as Mt. Marshall.

9.3 Spur trail, right, leads into Panorama Upper Parking Area. *AT* passes to left and below Panorama Parking. (Restrooms and *water* available.)

9.5 Junction with US 211, about 0.1 mi. west of Skyline Drive in Thornton Gap, SDMP 31.5 (2,307 ft.).

SECTION 4
Skyland to Fishers Gap

6.5 miles — PATC Map #10

General Description: Most of the Blue Ridge in this area was at one time covered by a series of lava flows. Today this lava, in its present form of greenstone, is the rock seen in the various rock outcrops along Skyline Drive and along the Appalachian Trail in this section. On the western side of the ridge, where the slope is very steep, the old layers of lava show as a series of vertical cliffs, one above another. The route of the *AT* below Crescent Rocks, along Hawksbill and Franklin Cliffs, follows these cliff shelves from one level to another, thus affording a very rugged and photogenic section of trail.

Hawksbill Mountain is the highest in the Park. The *AT* slabs its northwestern slope; side trails lead to the summit, (4,050 ft.). Native red spruce and balsam fir can be found in disjunct colonies at high elevations from Hawksbill to Stony Man Mountain, and from The Pinnacles to Marys Rock. They do not grow along the *AT* north of this area until one reaches Vermont, or south of this area until one

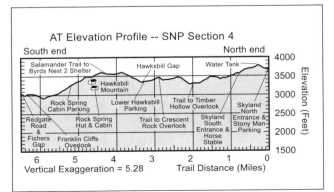

reaches Mt. Rogers (5,729 ft.), and nearby Whitetop in southwest Virginia.

Trail Approaches: The northern end is at Stony Man Trail Parking Area on Skyline Drive, SDMP 41.7.

The southern end is in Fishers Gap, SDMP 49.3, at intersection with Red Gate Fire Road just north of Fishers Gap Overlook.

Side Trails: As in Section 3, the Park is wide here, especially to the east of Skyline Drive. The lovely White-oak Canyon-Cedar Run circuit hike is in this area. The scenic rock-sculptured top of Old Rag Mountain beckons the hiker. Several routes lead to the top of Hawksbill Mountain. For details see "Side Trails." Also refer to PATC publication *Circuit Hikes in Shenandoah National Park.*

Accommodations: Public accommodations are open at Skyland from mid-April through November. Skyland has 179 guestrooms. There is a stable here with a network of horse trails in the area. For information and lodging reservations call 800-999-4714, FAX 540-743-7883 or write to: ARAMARK Shenandoah National Park Lodging, Box 727, Luray, VA 22835.

Rock Spring Hut, 1.9 mi. north of Fishers Gap, is available for overnight hikers. One locked cabin, Rock Spring, also 1.9 mi. north of Fishers Gap, may be reserved in advance from PATC Headquarters. See "Shelters, Huts and Cabins." Byrds Nest #2, an open-faced shelter for day use only (no fires), is atop Hawksbill Mtn. It can be reached from the *AT* in 0.9 mi. via the Hawksbill Trail from Hawksbill Gap.

Trail Description, North to South

0.0 This section of *AT* begins at Stony Man Trail Parking Area near Skyline Drive, SDMP 41.7. From parking lot, cross paved road (watch for posts and blazes) and enter woods. Ascend gradually.

0.2 Intersection with dirt service road leading right 0.2 mi. to Skyland Dining Hall and left to water tank. At top of climb, reach open field with large green water tank. (Do NOT camp here!) *AT* now begins a gradual descent.

0.8 Cross paved Skyland Road, which leads left to Skyline Drive and right to Skyland accommodations. Pass stables to right. Horse trail leads left to Skyline Drive and beyond to Whiteoak Canyon and Big Meadows.

1.1 Trail leads along cliffs on western edge of ridge under Pollock Knob, 3,560 ft. (named for George Pollock, founder of Skyland). There are occasional views to right from Trail.

1.5 Where *AT* begins descent by switchbacks, there is a spectacular view of Hawksbill Mtn. and Ida Valley. Beyond, *AT* parallels Drive, passing through a thicket of laurel.

2.0 Reach open area. Spur trail, left, leads uphill 300 ft. to Timber Hollow Parking Overlook on Skyline Drive, SDMP 43.3.

2.2 Trail climbs over small ridge, then descends gently, slabbing steep western slopes of Blue Ridge. Here Trail passes some picturesque contorted trees. A big oak on right extends a "sitting limb."

2.9 Concrete post marks spur trail on left leading uphill 0.1 mi. to junction a few feet north from Crescent Rock Parking Overlook, SDMP 44.4. *AT* next passes under cliffs of Crescent Rock. Excellent views of Nakedtop and Hawksbill Mtn. from Trail along here.

3.3 Reach Hawksbill Gap. (Trail to right leads downhill 450 ft. to *spring*. To left, uphill, it is 300 ft. to Hawksbill Gap Parking Area on Drive, SDMP 45.6 (3,361 ft.). On east side of Drive here is start of Cedar Run Trail. From Hawksbill Gap Parking Area, Hawksbill Trail leads steeply up for 0.8 mi. to Byrds Nest #2 and summit of Hawksbill just beyond. During summers of 2007 and 2008 summit of Hawksbill (4,050 ft.), was site of a peregrine falcon release program reintroducing falcon to Park. Wonderful view of mountains from summit. From summit, Hawksbill Trail descends southward to Upper Hawksbill Parking Area on Drive, SDMP 46.7.) From Hawksbill Gap, *AT* ascends then slabs steep north face of Hawksbill Mtn., passing under cliffs in a wild, rugged setting. (This is home of the endangered Shenandoah salamander. Splendid views, looking backward, of Crescent Rocks and Stony Man.)

4.3 Reach sag between Hawksbill and Nakedtop. Salamander Trail to left leads 0.9 mi. to summit of Hawksbill.

4.6 *AT* comes out of deep woods into old orchard now rapidly being overgrown with black locust, sumac, and pines. Road entering from left is used as service road to Rock Spring Cabin. It appears as a grassy meadow. Do NOT camp here! To left it is 0.2 mi. to Skyline Drive, SDMP 47.8. 20 ft. farther along *AT* signpost marks graded spur trail leading right 0.2 mi. downhill to Rock Spring Cabin, a locked structure, and to Rock Spring Hut, available for overnight hikers. A *spring* is 50 yds. north of cabin.

5.1 Spur trail, left, marked by post, leads 300 ft. uphill to Skyline Drive at Spitler Knoll Parking, SDMP 47.9. (This small parking area for four cars is used mainly for Rock Spring Cabin parking.) Beyond overlook *AT* continues, again slabbing western slopes of main Blue Ridge.

6.5 Intersect Red Gate Fire Road in Fishers Gap. (This road was known as Gordonsville Turnpike in days before SNP. To right it leads down mountain to SR 611. To left it is 350 ft. to northern end of Fishers Gap Parking Overlook, SDMP 49.3 [3,061 ft.]. East of Drive is Rose River Fire Road, leading to Dark Hollow Falls Trail.)

Trail Description, South to North

0.0 Intersection of *AT* and Red Gate Fire Road in Fishers Gap. (To right [east] it is 350 ft. to Skyline Drive just north of Fishers Gap Parking Overlook, SDMP 49.3 [3,061 ft.]. To east of Drive is Rose River Fire Road leading to Dark Hollow Falls Trail.)

0.2 From here *AT* passes below Franklin Cliffs, then along ledge above more cliffs. Birdfoot violets bloom here in May. (Cliffs, composed of altered basaltic rock, are result of erosion of ancient lava beds laid down in layers 100 ft. to 250 ft. thick for total thickness of 2,000-3,000 ft. and later tilted about 90 degrees.)

0.5. *AT* continues to slab west side of ridge.

1.4 Spur trail, right, marked by post, leads 300 ft. uphill to Skyline Drive at Spitler Knoll Parking, SDMP 47.9. (This small parking area for four cars is used mainly for Rock Spring Cabin parking.) *AT* now ascends gradually, passing old road at 1.5 mi. Trail soon levels off, then descends gently.

1.9 *AT* comes into slightly open area. Post marks spur trail which leads left 0.2 mi. downhill to Rock Spring Hut, for use by overnight hikers, and Rock Spring Cabin, a locked PATC cabin requiring advance reservations. *Spring* is 150 ft. north of cabin. 20 ft. farther along *AT* an old road, which serves as Park access road to cabin, leads 0.2 mi. to Drive, SDMP 47.8. This road appears to be a grassy meadow. Do NOT camp here! *AT* passes old orchard rapidly being overgrown with pine, sumac, and locust.

2.2 Reach sag between Hawksbill and Nakedtop. Salamander Trail to right leads 0.9 mi. to summit of Hawksbill. From sag *AT* slabs north face of Hawksbill, passing below steep cliffs, home of the endangered Shenandoah salamander. Good views to north of Ida Valley and Luray, views ahead of Crescent Rock and Stony Man.

3.2 Reach Hawksbill Gap and trail intersection. (To left trail leads downhill 0.1 mi. to *spring*. To right it is 300 ft.

uphill to Hawksbill Gap Parking Area on Drive, SDMP 45.6 [3,361 ft.]. From parking area, Hawksbill Trail leads steeply to summit of Hawksbill (4,050 ft.), highest point in SNP. In summers of 2007 and 2008 summit of Hawksbill was site of peregrine release program, reintroducing falcon to Park. Wonderful views of the mountains from here.) Byrds Nest #2, an open-faced shelter for day use only (no fires), is just below summit.)

3.5 *AT* passes under cliffs of Crescent Rock. These, like Franklin Cliffs, are eroded remnants of ancient lava beds.

3.6 Side trail, marked by concrete post, leads right, uphill 0.1 mi., to northern end of Crescent Rock Parking Overlook, SDMP 44.4.

4.5 In open area, spur trail, right, leads uphill 300 ft. to Timber Hollow Parking Overlook on Drive, SDMP 43.3. From junction *AT* parallels Drive, passing through thicket of mountain laurel, blooming in early June. Trail then ascends by switchbacks to Pollock Knob (3,560 ft.). Good views of Hawksbill Mtn. and Ida Valley.

5.0 Reach top of ridge with splendid views of Hawksbill Mtn. and Ida Valley. Trail now follows cliffs along west side of Pollock Knob, with fine views west. Trail ascends slightly, then follows corral fence to Skyland stables.

5.7 Horse trail leads right to Skyline Drive and beyond to Whiteoak Canyon and Big Meadows. *AT* continues ahead, crossing blacktop trail at stables, then crossing paved Skyland Road before entering woods. *AT* now ascends gently. At top of hill, reach open area and large green water tank. (Do NOT camp here!) Begin gradual descent.

6.3 Intersection with dirt service road leading left 0.2mi. to Skyland Dining Hall and Lodge. *AT* continues gradual descent.

6.5 Reach paved Skyland Road near northern entrance to Skyland, SDMP 41.7. (To left it is 0.3 mi. on paved road to Skyland Dining Hall.) Follow concrete posts, crossing road to Stony Man Trail Parking Area.

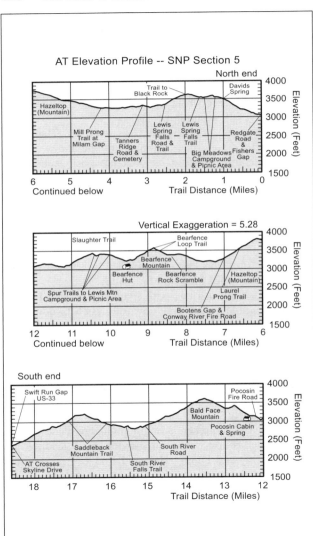

AT Elevation Profile -- SNP Section 5

North end

Hazeltop
(Mountain)

Mill Prong
Trail at
Milam Gap

Tanners
Ridge
Road &
Cemetery

Trail to
Black Rock

Lewis
Spring
Falls
Road &
Trail

Lewis
Spring
Falls
Trail

Big Meadows
Campground
& Picnic Area

Davids
Spring

Redgate
Road &
Fishers Gap

Vertical Exaggeration = 5.28

Slaughter Trail

Spur Trails to Lewis Mtn
Campground & Picnic Area

Bearfence
Hut

Bearfence
Mountain

Bearfence
Loop Trail

Bearfence
Rock Scramble

Bootens Gap &
Conway River Fire Road

Laurel
Prong Trail

Hazeltop
(Mountain)

Continued below

South end

Swift Run Gap
US-33

AT Crosses
Skyline Drive

Saddleback
Mountain Trail

South River
Falls Trail

South River
Road

Bald Face
Mountain

Pocosin
Fire Road

Pocosin Cabin
& Spring

SECTION 5
Fishers Gap to Swift Run Gap

18.6 miles — PATC Map #10

General Description: From Fishers Gap (3,061 ft.), the *AT* skirts the Big Meadows developed area, then continues on to Milam Gap where it crosses Skyline Drive. It climbs to the summit of Hazeltop Mountain (3,816 ft.). It descends to Bootens Gap before climbing two low mountains, Bush and Bearfence; the latter is very scenic. The *AT* skirts the Lewis Mountain developed area, climbs over Baldface Mtn., drops down to skirt the South River Picnic Area, then follows an old road over a spur of Saddleback Mtn., finally descending to Swift Run Gap (2,367 ft.).

Trail Approaches: The northern end of this section is on Skyline Drive just north of Fishers Gap Overlook, SDMP 49.3, at intersection with Red Gate Fire Road, 350 ft. west of Drive. The southern end is at Swift Run Gap, SDMP 65.5, where entrance road from US 33 joins Drive. It is 7 mi. east of Elkton and 8 mi. west of Stanardsville via US 33.

Side Trails: In the Big Meadows area there are many trails and a number of circuit hikes that are popular. The Dark Hollow-Rose River Loop circuit is a favorite one. The Rapidan Fire Road and several trails lead eastward from Skyline Drive and the *AT* to Rapidan Camp (formerly Camp Hoover), located within the Park on the Rapidan River. On Laurel Prong near Rapidan Camp one can find rosebay rhododendron. The Lewis Spring Falls Trail, combined with the Lewis Spring service road and the *AT,* makes a spectacular circuit.

Farther south is the short, but very scenic, South River Falls Trail. An excellent circuit hike can be made from

Pocosin Cabin by using the Pocosin Fire Road, the Pocosin Trail, the South River Fire Road, the South River Falls Trail, and the *AT*. See "Side Trails"; also see PATC publication *Circuit Hikes in Shenandoah National Park*.

Many blue-blazed trails, fire roads and old roads beckon the hiker. Some are well-marked and easy to follow, but others may be poorly marked or badly overgrown and should be attempted only by the experienced woodsman.

Accommodations: The Big Meadows developed area, SDMP 51.2, just south of Fishers Gap, includes a lodge and cottages offering meals and lodging for 350 persons. It also contains a wayside (meals and supplies available in season) gas station and automated teller machine. The Byrd Visitor Center is a great place to visit. Big Meadows campground has standard facilities for campers—ice, laundry, showers (handicapped accessible), etc.—and is open from spring to late fall. During the summer and fall, campground reservations may be made by calling 877-444-6777 or online at *www.recreation.gov*. The lodge is open mid-May through October and the Byrd Visitor Center is open April through November. Lewis Mountain has a campground, open summer only, cabins mid-May through October, and a camp store. For information and lodging reservations at Big Meadows and Lewis Mtn., call 800-999-4714, FAX 540-743-7883 or write to: ARA-MARK Shenandoah National Park Lodging, Box 727, Luray, VA 22835.

The open-faced Bearfence Mountain Hut, 9.1 mi. north of Swift Run Gap, is available for overnight hikers with backcountry permits. One locked structure, Pocosin Cabin, is near the trail here but must be reserved in advance. A second cabin, Jones Mountain Cabin, is located too far to the east for easy accessibility from the *AT*. See "Shelters, Huts and Cabins."

Trail Description, North to South

0.0 Intersection with Red Gate Fire Road 350 ft. west of Skyline Drive, SDMP 49.3 (3,061 ft.). (To right, fire road leads down mountain to SR 611. East of Drive is Rose River Fire Road and Dark Hollow Falls.)

0.1 Pass below Fishers Gap Overlook. (Look for blooms of hepatica in spring and clematis in summer.) Pass post marking spur trail, left, which leads 100 ft. to Fishers Gap Parking Overlook.

0.2 Pass to right of split rock. Ascend gradually. Pass through once beautiful hemlock grove. Continue to ascend, crossing small stream twice.

1.0 *David Spring* is 50 ft. to right of *AT*. (See Big Meadows inset on back of PATC Map #10.) *AT* skirts north edge of Big Meadows Campground. (Several short unmarked trails lead left to campground.) Openings along *AT* give fine views north and west—Hawksbill Mtn. is in foreground, Stony Man Mtn. is farther away, and, in the distance, Knob Mtn. and Neighbor Mtn. Across Page Valley, Signal Knob can be seen at northern end of Massanutten range.

1.3 Cross a small rocky knob, the Monkey Head. Views here also. Beyond, *AT* skirts western edge of ridge.

1.6 Concrete post marks trail intersection. *AT* is straight ahead. Trail to right, downhill, leads 1.2 mi. to Lewis Falls. Trail to left leads to Amphitheater Parking Area, picnic ground and campground.

1.9 Pass under sheer cliffs of Blackrock. Rocks to right of *AT* provide a grandstand view west of Shenandoah Valley, Massanutten Mtn., Great North Mtn., and distant Alleghenies.

2.0 Trail to left of *AT* leads 0.1 mi. to Blackrock view-point and another 0.2 mi. to Big Meadows Lodge. *AT* continues along western slope of ridge, descending, with occasional views to west from rocks to right of Trail.

2.5 Cross service road. To left it is 0.3 mi. to Skyline Drive, SDMP 51.4, at a point 0.1 mi. south of Big Meadows Wayside. Meals and supplies are available at Wayside in season. Harry F. Byrd Sr. Visitor Center located here, also. (To right of *AT*, service road leads downhill about 150 ft. to small pumphouse to right of road. Turn left off road onto footpath that leads 0.5 mi. downhill to Lewis Falls.) Beyond service road intersection *AT* passes outlet of housed-in *Lewis Spring*. Trail continues through woods, descending gradually.

3.1 Reach Tanners Ridge Cemetery on right. Cross Tanners Ridge Road. (Road, gated at Drive and Park boundary, leads right 1.4 mi. to Park boundary where it becomes SR 682. To left it leads 0.1 mi. to Drive, SDMP 51.6.) From here to Milam Gap *AT* is a level path.

3.3 Pass *spring* 50 ft. to left of *AT*. Beyond, pass through stands of pioneering locust.

4.2 Cross Skyline Drive, SDMP 52.8, just south of Milam Gap (3,257 ft.). (Parking space for 20 vehicles on west side of Milam Gap.) *AT* bears east through a field. Concrete post marks Mill Prong Trail, which leads left from *AT* and continues 1.8 mi. to Rapidan Camp. Beyond junction, *AT* ascends north ridge of Hazeltop.

4.6 Bear right along ridge crest. From rock to left of Trail is wintertime view of Doubletop and Fork mtns. (Former President Herbert and First Lady Lou Henry Hoover's Rapidan Camp is in Rapidan Valley between these peaks.) *AT* ascends very gradually along ridge crest. Here may be found a fine stand of stiff gentians among white and purple asters in autumn.

5.7 Reach north end of Hazeltop.

6.1 Cross wooded summit of Hazeltop (3,812 ft.). A few red spruce and balsam can be found here.

6.6 Junction with blue-blazed Laurel Prong Trail, leading left 2.8 mi. to Rapidan Camp. (This is one of few trails in Park that passes through areas with rosebay rhododendron, or great laurel, which blooms in late June or early July. Other wild flowers found here include false lily-of-the-valley, trillium, and wild iris.)

7.0 In Bootens Gap (3,243 ft.) cross gated Conway River Fire Road. (Skyline Drive, SDMP 55.1, is 50 ft. to right with parking space for five cars. To left, road leads down mountain to VA 230.) *AT* descends gradually for 0.2 mi. then continues with little change in elevation, paralleling Skyline Drive.

7.7 Ascend gradually, following western slope of Bush Mtn.

7.9 *AT* approaches within 150 ft. of Drive. Ascent continues for about 0.2 mi., then Trail is level for about 0.2 mi. before again ascending along ridge of Bearfence Mtn.

8.4 Trail intersection. (To right, blue-blazed trail leads 0.1 mi. to Bearfence Mountain Parking Area on Skyline Drive, SDMP 56.4. To left, a blazed trail leads to spectacular jagged rocks of Bearfence Mtn. Views from rocks are excellent. This is a rough trail requiring use of hands in some places. In 0.3 mi. it connects with graded loop trail over Bearfence Mtn. The two trails, with *AT*, make a rough figure eight.)

8.6 Bearfence Mtn. Loop Trail (graded) leaves *AT* on left. (Views along this trail are rewarding. Loop trail is only 150 ft. longer than stretch of *AT* between junctions.)

8.8 Bearfence Loop Trail comes in from left. *AT* now descends by switchbacks. From a rock ledge near top there is a splendid view to east.

9.4 In gap, cross yellow-blazed Slaughter Trail. (Slaughter Trail leads 0.1 mi. to access road to Bearfence Hut, then down to Park boundary. Bearfence Mountain Hut is used by overnight hikers. *Spring* is 50 ft. south of hut, frequently dry in summer. To right it is a few feet to Skyline Drive, SDMP 56.8. Across Drive it continues as Meadow School Trail.)

9.6 *AT* now ascends gradually north slope of Lewis

Mtn. As Trail levels off (about 3,400 ft.), several paths lead right, first to Lewis Mtn. Picnic Area (*water* available "in season") and then to Lewis Mtn. Campground. Camp store on campground road is open May through October.

10.3 Post marks trail, right, leading 300 ft. to campground.

10.4 Pass trail intersection. (To right, trail leads to campground; to left, obscure Lewis Mtn. East Trail, blue-blazed, ends in less than one mile.)

11.1 Old road descends left toward Pocosin Hollow; to right, Skyline Drive is only a few feet away. *AT* soon bears away from Drive.

12.0 Pass *spring* to right of Trail. (In early May vast fields of trillium, chickweed, cutleaf toothwort, plus yellow and purple violets can be found here.)

12.2 Cross Pocosin Fire Road. (To right, fire road leads 0.1 mi. to Skyline Drive, SDMP 59.5; to left it is 0.1 mi. downhill to Pocosin Cabin.) Beyond fire road intersection, *AT* ascends gradually.

12.3 Graded spur trail leads left, 250 ft. downhill, to Pocosin Cabin and *spring* just south of cabin. (This is a locked cabin and reservations must be made in advance from PATC Headquarters. From cabin there is a fine view east over Conway River Valley. Three mountains can be seen across valley. Local mountaineers called them, from right to left: Panther, Bear Stand, and Sawney Macks. These names are not recognized on current maps. "Pocosin" is said to be of Indian derivation meaning "dismal" or swamp.)

12.4 Pass *spring* to right of trail.

12.5 *AT* ascends steeply by switchbacks for 0.1 mi. (At top is view north of Lewis Mtn., Hazeltop, Jones Mtn., and Fork Mtn. crowned with a radio transmitter tower.) *AT* next passes through a relatively flat area known as Kites Deadening, now completely wooded. (A deadening was an area where early settlers, instead of felling trees to clear land for a field, saved time and effort by ringing them—removing the lower bark—thus killing trees without task of cutting them down. They would then plant their crops amid "deadened" trees.)

13.6 Reach crest of Baldface Mtn. (3,600 ft.).

13.8 Rocks to right of Trail offer views to west. *AT* begins gentle descent of Baldface Mtn.

14.2 Cross old road, which leads left past an old quarry. (To right, road leads 0.1 mi. past site of former CCC camp, then to Skyline Drive, SDMP 61.8.)

15.1 Cross South River Fire Road, yellow-blazed. (To left, road leads 0.8 mi. to blue-blazed trail which goes right to South River. Follow a footpath for 0.1 mi. up river to base of South River Falls. To right, fire road leads to Skyline Drive, SDMP 62.7 [2,960 ft.] in 0.3 mi.)

15.6 Cross graded South River Falls Trail. (To left, trail leads 1.5 mi. downhill to South River Falls. To right, it is 0.1 mi. to eastern edge of South River Picnic Area. *Water* and restroom are available here "in season.")

l5.9 In pine thicket, old road comes in on right from Drive, SDMP 63.1. *AT* turns left onto this road and follows it.

16.1 *AT* takes right fork of road. (Left fork is blue-blazed Saddleback Trail which leads 0.3 mi. to PATC South River Maintenance Bldg. where there is a *spring* 200 ft. west of building. Trail continues to south and west to rejoin *AT* in 1.4 mi.)

16.5 At bend in Trail an old road comes in from left. *AT* ascends.

16.7 Still following old road, reach top of rise, just west of westernmost peak of Saddleback Mtn. (3,296 ft.). There is much trillium along Trail here in early May.

17.1 Junction with Saddleback Mtn. Trail, which comes in from left.

17.9 *AT* turns left off old road.

18.3 Trail passes under power line.

18.4 Pass side trail on left, which leads 100 yds. to a cemetery.

18.6 Reach Skyline Drive, where US 33 crosses Drive in Swift Run Gap, SDMP 65.5 (2,367 ft.).

Trail Description, South to North

0.0 This section begins on eastern side of Skyline Drive in Swift Run Gap, SDMP 65.5 (2,367 ft.), where entrance road from US 33 joins Drive. Trail ascends through woods.

0.2 Pass a side trail, right, which leads 100 yds. east to a cemetery.

0.3 *AT* passes under power line.

0.7 Trail turns right onto old road, which it follows over Saddleback Mtn., passing west of summit. Follow old road for about 2 mi.

1.5 Saddleback Mtn. Trail, blue-blazed, leads right from *AT* for 1.1 mi. to PATC South River Maintenance Bldg. where there is a *spring* 200 ft. west of building.

1.9 Still following old road, *AT* reaches top of rise just west of westernmost peak of Saddleback Mtn. (3,296 ft.). (One may find a profusion of trillium blooming here in early May.) Trail now descends.

2.1 At sharp left bend in *AT* an old road comes in from right.

2.5 At junction of old roads, *AT* follows left fork. (Right fork is Saddleback Trail, which leads 0.3 mi. to PATC South River Maintenance Bldg.)

2.7 *AT* turns right off old road and passes through a pine woods. (Road bears left and leads 0.1 mi. to Skyline Drive, SDMP 63.1.) *AT* skirts eastern side of South River Picnic Area.

3.0 Cross graded South River Falls Trail. (To left, trail leads 0.1 mi. to picnic area. *Water* and restrooms available here "in season." To right, trail leads steeply downhill for 1.5 mi. to lovely South River Falls.)

3.5 Cross South River Fire Road, yellow-blazed. (To left goes to Skyline Drive, SDMP 62.7 [2,960 ft.] in 0.2 mi.) *AT* begins long gentle ascent of Baldface Mtn.

4.4 Cross old road which leads, right, past an old quarry. (To left, road leads past site of former CCC camp 0.1 mi. to Skyline Drive, SDMP 61.8.)

4.8 Rocks to left of Trail offer views to west.

5.0 Reach summit of Baldface Mtn. (3,600 ft.), then descend gently.

5.9 *AT* passes through a relatively flat area known as Kites Deadening, now completely wooded. (Instead of felling trees for a field, early settlers saved time and effort by ringing trees and removing lower bark, thus killing them without task of removing them. They would plant their crops amid "deadened" trees.)

6.0 View north of Lewis Mtn., Hazeltop, Jones Mtn. and Fork Mtn. with radio transmitter tower. Trail descends steeply by switchbacks for 0.1 mi.

6.2 Pass *spring* to left of trail.

6.3 Spur trail leads 250 ft. right, downhill, to Pocosin Cabin (3,120 ft.) and *spring* south of cabin. (Pocosin is a locked cabin which may be reserved in advance at PATC Headquarters. From cabin there is a fine view east over Conway River Valley. Three mountains can be seen across valley. Local mountaineers called these, from right to left: Panther, Bear Stand and Sawney Macks; these names are not shown on today's maps. The word "Pocosin" is said to be of Indian derivation meaning a "dismal" or swamp.) Beyond spur trail *AT* descends gently.

6.4 Cross Pocosin Fire Road. (To left, fire road leads 0.1 mi. to Skyline Drive, SDMP 59.5. To right, it leads back to Pocosin Cabin.)

7.5 Where *AT* is close (30 ft.) to Drive, an old road leads right and descends toward Pocosin Hollow. *AT* soon ascends.

8.2 Pass trail intersection. (To left, trail leads to Lewis

Mountain Campground. To right, blue-blazed Lewis Mtn. East Trail leads along ridge crest of Lewis Mtn., then disappears.)

8.3 A post marks trail, left, which leads 300 ft. to Lewis Mtn. Campground. (*Water* fountain "in season" directly across camp road. Camp store is located on road.) *AT* now descends gently. Several paths, unmarked, lead left to camping area and then picnic area of Lewis Mtn. *Water* available "in season."

9.2 Cross yellow-blazed Slaughter Trail. (To right it joins access road to Bearfence Mtn. Hut. *Spring* 50 ft. to right of hut is frequently dry by late summer. Hut is for use of overnight hikers. To left it leads to Skyline Drive, SDMP 56.8.)

9.8 Junction with Bearfence Loop Trail, which leads right. (Views on this short trail are very rewarding. Loop Trail is only 150 ft. longer than *AT* between junctions.)

10.0 Loop Trail re-enters *AT* from right.

10.2 Cross blue-blazed trail. (To left, trail leads 0.1 mi. to Bearfence Mtn. Parking Area on Skyline Drive, SDMP 56.4. Hikes led by SNP interpreter or ranger start here during summer months. To right, trail leads to spectacular jagged rocks of Bearfence Mtn.; they offer excellent views. This rough trail requires use of hands in some places. It connects with loop trail over Bearfence Mtn., making a rough figure-eight with *AT*.) Beyond intersection *AT* remains rather level for 0.3 mi. then descends gradually along western slope of Bush Mtn.

11.6 In Bootens Gap (3,243 ft.), cross Conway River Fire Road. (Skyline Drive, SDMP 55.1, is 150 ft. to left, with parking space for five cars; to right, leads down mountain to VA 230.) *AT* now starts ascent of Hazeltop Mtn.

12.0 Pass blue-blazed Laurel Prong Trail on right. (It leads 2.8 mi. down to Rapidan Camp, passing through one of few areas in Park where rosebay rhododendron grows.)

AT continues to ascend.

12.5 Cross wooded summit of Hazeltop (3,812 ft.). (A few red spruce and balsam here.) *AT* now descends gently.

12.9 Along a level area there is a fine stand of stiff gentians mixed with purple and white asters, blooming in autumn. Beyond this area Trail again descends.

14.0 Trail bears left, due west. From a rock to right of *AT* at this turn is a good wintertime view of Doubletop and Fork mtns. (Former President Hoover's Camp is in Rapidan Valley between these peaks.)

14.4 Come into overgrown field. Concrete post marks Mill Prong Trail leading right from *AT*. (This trail leads 1.8 mi. to Rapidan Camp. See "Side Trails.") A few feet farther, just south of Milam Gap, *AT* crosses Skyline Drive, SDMP 52.8. (This is only crossing of Drive in Central District of Park. On west side of Milam Gap is parking for 20 cars.) Cross a field and enter woods.

15.3 Pass *spring* 50 ft. to right of *AT*.

15.5 Cross Tanners Ridge Road with cemetery on left. (To right it is 0.1 mi. to Drive, SDMP 51.6; to left leads out of Park.)

16.1 Pass outlet of housed-in *Lewis Spring*. Immediately beyond, cross Park service road. (To right, road leads 0.3 mi. to Skyline Drive, SDMP 51.4, at a point 0.1 mi. south of Big Meadows Wayside. Meals and supplies available at Wayside in season. Harry F. Byrd Sr. Visitor Center located here also. To left, road leads to Lewis Falls in 0.6 mi. Follow road down about 150 ft. to small pumphouse on right of road. Turn left off road onto footpath that continues downhill 0.5 mi. to Lewis Falls.) *AT* ascends steadily along western slope of ridge with occasional views from rocks to left of Trail.

16.6 Trail to right of *AT* leads 0.1 mi. to Blackrock Viewpoint and 0.2 mi. farther to Big Meadows Lodge. (About 50 yds. north of Blackrock Trail is incredible view west encompassing length of Massanutten Mtn. and beyond to Great North Mtn. and the Alleghenies.) Continuing on *AT*, pass under sheer cliffs of Blackrock in 0.2 mi.

17.0 Trail intersection marked by concrete post. (Trail to left leads back 1.2 mi. to Lewis Falls; to right leads up to amphitheater, picnic area and campground.) *AT* now passes below Big Meadows Amphitheater.

17.3 Cross small rocky knob, the Monkey Head, where there are views. Beyond, *AT* skirts north edge of Big Meadows Campground. Several small unmarked trails lead right to camping area. Openings along *AT* give fine views north and west. (Hawksbill Mtn. is in foreground, Stony Man Mtn. farther away and, in distance, Knob Mtn., The Neighbor, and, across Page Valley, Signal Knob is at northern end of Massanutten range.

17.6 Reach northern end of campground. *David Spring* is 50 ft. to left of *AT*. *AT* now descends. (A large, disjunct colony of gray birch, southernmost stand of this northern tree, is found here.) Begin gradual descent to Fishers Gap. Cross small stream twice. Pass once-beautiful hemlock grove.

18.4 Pass to left of split rock.

18.5 Spur trail leads right 100 ft. to Fishers Gap Parking Overlook on Skyline Drive. Pass below overlook. (Look for blooms of hepatica in spring and clematis in summer.)

18.6 Intersection with Red Gate Fire Road, 350 ft. west of Skyline Drive, just north of Fishers Gap Parking Overlook, SDMP 49.3 (3,061 ft.). (Across Drive, Rose River Fire Rd. leads down mountain, crossing Hogcamp Branch in 1 mi. Dark Hollow Falls is a few hundred feet above crossing.)

Dark Hollow Falls   *Photo by Robert Kuhns*

SUMMARY OF DISTANCES ALONG THE *AT*
Central District

	Miles	
	N-S	**S-N**
Thornton Gap and US 211	0.0	34.6
Marys Rock summit	1.9+0.1	32.7+0.1
Meadow Spring Trail	2.5	31.1
Byrds Nest #3 Hut	3.2	31.4
Pinnacles Picnic Area	5.5	29.1
Nicholson Hollow Trail	7.1	27.5
Stony Man Parking Overlook	7.5	27.1
Little Stony Man Parking Area	7.9	26.7
Stony Man Trail Parking	9.5	25.1
Whiteoak Canyon Trail at entrance road to Skyland Lodge	10.3+0.1	24.3+0.1
Hawksbill Gap	12.8	21.8
Byrds Nest #2 and summit of Hawksbill	12.-8+0.8 from north	20.8+0.9 from south
Rock Spring Cabin	14.1+0.2	20.5+0.2
Rock Spring Hut	14.1+0.1	20.5+0.1
Fishers Gap	16.0	18.6
Big Meadows—Amphitheater	17.2	17.4
Lewis Spring Service Road	17.6	17.0
Skyline Drive crossing, Milam Gap	20.2	14.4
Hazeltop Mtn. summit	22.2	12.4
Bearfence Mtn. Loop Trail (north end)	24.6	10.0
Bearfence Mtn. Hut	25.6+0.1	9.0+0.1
Lewis Mtn. Campground (north end)	26.3	8.3
Pocosin Cabin	28.3+0.1	6.3+0.1
South River Falls Trail	31.6	3.0
Swift Run Gap and US 33	34.6	0.0

SUMMARY OF DISTANCES BY SKYLINE DRIVE TO POINTS ON THE *AT*
Central District

SDMP N-S		Miles S-N
31.5	US 211 at Thornton Gap	34.0
33.5	Buck Hollow Trail, 0.7 mi. from *AT*	32.0
33.9	Service Road to Byrds Nest #3 Hut; 0.3 mi. to *AT*	31.6
36.4	Jewell Hollow Overlook	29.1
36.7	Pinnacles Picnic Area	28.8
37.9	Shaver Hollow Parking Area	27.6
38.4	Nicholson Hollow Trail; 0.1 mi. to *AT*	27.1
38.6	Stony Man Mtn. Overlook	26.9
39.1	Little Stony Man Parking Area	26.4
41.7	Skyland, North Entrance; 0.3 mi. to *AT*	23.8
42.5	Skyland, South Entrance, 0.1 mi. to *AT*	23.0
43.3	Timber Hollow Overlook	21.2
44.4	Crescent Rock Overlook	21.1
45.6	Hawksbill Gap	19.9
48.1	Spitler Knoll Parking Overlook	17.4
49.0	Franklin Cliffs Overlook	16.5
49.3	Fishers Gap	16.2
51.2	Big Meadows dev. area; 0.1 mi. to *AT*	14.3
51.6	Tanners Ridge Fire Road; 0.1 mi. to *AT*	13.9
52.8	Milam Gap; *AT* crossing	12.7
55.1	Bootens Gap	10.4
56.4	Bearfence Mtn. Parking; 0.1 mi. to *AT*	9.1
56.8	Slaughter Trail	8.7
57.5	Lewis Mtn. Campground; 0.1 mi. to *AT*	8.0
59.5	Pocosin Fire Road; 0.1 mi. to *AT*	6.0
62.7	South River Fire Road; 0.2 mi. to *AT*	2.8
62.8	South River Picnic Area; 0.3 mi. to *AT*	2.7
63.1	Service Road to PATC South River Maintenance Bldg; 0.1 mi. to *AT*	2.4
65.5	Swift Run Gap	0.0

South District - Appalachian Trail

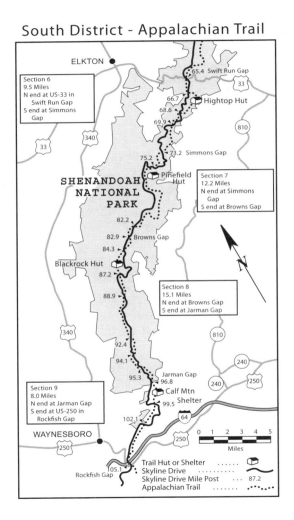

ELKTON

65.4 Swift Run Gap

Section 6
9.5 Miles
N end at US-33 in
Swift Run Gap
S end at Simmons
Gap

66.7
Hightop Hut
68.6
69.9

SHENANDOAH
NATIONAL
PARK

73.2 Simmons Gap

75.2

Pinefield
Hut

Section 7
12.2 Miles
N end at Simmons
Gap
S end at Browns Gap

82.2
82.9 Browns Gap
84.3

Blackrock Hut

87.2

Section 8
15.1 Miles
N end at Browns Gap
S end at Jarman Gap

88.9

92.4
94.1
95.3

Jarman Gap
96.8
Calf Mtn
Shelter
99.5

Section 9
8.0 Miles
N end at Jarman Gap
S end at US-250 in
Rockfish Gap

102.1

WAYNESBORO

0 1 2 3 4 5
Miles

Trail Hut or Shelter . . . . . .
Skyline Drive . . . .
Skyline Drive Mile Post . . . 87.2
Appalachian Trail . . . .

105.1
Rockfish Gap

APPALACHIAN TRAIL
SOUTH DISTRICT
Shenandoah National Park

In the northern end of this district, the Appalachian Trail commences where US 33 (Spotswood Trail) crosses the Blue Ridge at Swift Run Gap, SDMP 65.5 (2,367 ft.). The southern end is in Rockfish Gap, where US 250 and I-64 cross Skyline Drive. The South District of the Park includes Section 6, Section 7, Section 8, and Section 9 in this guidebook, for a total of 44.9 miles.

NOTE: The Skyline Drive in the South District may be gated and locked from dusk to 8 a.m. during November and December. Check with Park personnel before hiking.

The South District is the wildest and least developed area of the Park. Much of it has wilderness status. The *AT* follows the main crest of the Blue Ridge, is rarely far from Skyline Drive and crosses it often.

There are many side trails and fire roads that can be used in conjunction with the *AT* for interesting hiking trips. Some points of particular interest are the Doyles River-Jones Run Loop Trail, Big Run Loop Trail, Riprap Ravine and Blackrock. Traveling south, the *AT* leaves the Park at Jarman Gap and, except for a short stretch on Calf Mountain, passes through a corridor of land acquired by the National Park Service for the Trail. See "Side Trails"; also the PATC publication *Circuit Hikes in Shenandoah National Park*.

There is one large campground in this district, Loft Mountain Campground, and one campground for groups only, Dundo Picnic Area.

Maps: PATC Map #11, SNP South District, Edition 16 (2009) is recommended for use with this Guide. The following USGS 1:24,000 scale sheets cover the *AT*: Swift Run Gap, McGaheysville, Browns Cove, Crimora and

Waynesboro East. The following additional USGS sheets complete the coverage of the South District: Grottoes, Elkton East and Crozet.

Ridge line panorama   *Photo by Lee Sheaffer*

SECTION 6
Swift Run Gap to Simmons Gap

9.5 miles — PATC Map #11

General Description: The highest elevation of the *AT* in the South District of the Park is reached near the summit of Hightop Mtn. (3,587 ft.). This means a climb of over 1,200 ft. traveling in either direction. Open ledges to the west of the summit afford excellent views south and west.

Trail Approaches: Access to the northern end of this section is at the junction of US 33 and Skyline Drive, SDMP 65.5, on east side of Drive, about 300 ft. north of

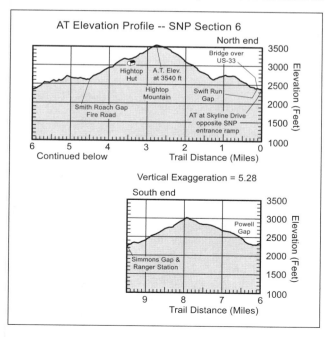

bridge and directly opposite place where entrance road from US 33 reaches Drive in Swift Run Gap; marked by concrete post.

The southern end is in Simmons Gap, SDMP 73.2, at intersection of Simmons Gap Fire Road and Skyline Drive, 7.7 miles south of the Swift Run Gap/US 33 entrance to Skyline Drive.

Side Trails: Because SNP is very narrow through most of this section there are few side trails and those that do exist lead out of the Park.

Accommodations: There are no public accommodations along this section. Closest public lodgings, open only during warmer months, are at Lewis Mtn., SDMP 57.5, in the Central District of the Park. There are neither gasoline nor food available at Swift Run Gap.

Hightop Hut, 3.4 mi. south of Swift Run Gap, is available for use by overnight hikers. See "Shelters, Huts and Cabins."

Trail Description, North to South

0.0 From concrete post on east side of Skyline Drive, SDMP 65.5, *AT* follows pedestrian footway along edge of bridge. Beyond bridge, cross to right side of Skyline Drive and climb bank. Trail shortly comes into old road, which it follows for few feet.

0.1 Trail turns sharply left from old road and climbs. It soon levels off and follows an old farm road through what remains of an apple orchard, then descends gently.

1.3 In grassy sag, Trail crosses to left (east) of Skyline Drive, SDMP 66.7 (2,637 ft.). From sag, Trail ascends steeply, by switchbacks, northern slope of Hightop Mtn.

2.8 As *AT* nears summit there are two excellent viewpoints from ledges to right of Trail, one about 100 ft. farther along Trail than the other. In another 100 ft. spur trail, left, leads 350 ft. to site of former Park Service lookout tower at summit of Hightop Mtn. (3,587 ft.). No view from summit. *AT* now descends.

2.9 Protected *spring* at foot of large boulder just to left of *AT*. Trail continues to descend.

3.4 Spur trail leads right 0.1 mi. to Hightop Hut, for use by overnight hikers. *Spring* is 400 ft. downhill from hut on graded trail.

3.5 Cross dirt road. (Service road leads right to Hightop Hut and left to Smith Roach Gap Fire Road.) *AT* descends steadily.

4.5 Trail crosses Smith Roach Gap Fire Road, then turns right and parallels it to Skyline Drive.

4.6 Cross to right (west) of Skyline Drive at Smith Roach Gap, SDMP 68.6 (2,622 ft.). Trail continues with little change in elevation around east and south sides of Roundtop Mtn., affording wintertime views of Powell Gap and Flattop Mtn. Continue along ridge crest.

5.8 Summit of Little Roundtop Mtn. is 50 yds. to right. View of Powell Gap just as Trail starts steep descent of western slope of mountain.

6.2 Powell Gap, SDMP 69.9 (2,294 ft.). Cross to left of Drive. *AT* now ascends shoulder of Flattop Mtn.

6.5 Turn sharply left where old road, which *AT* has been following, continues straight ahead. Continue to ascend.

6.8 Excellent views of Roach River Valley (Powell Gap and Bacon Hollow) from rock ledges to left of Trail. Continue to ascend very gently.

8.0 Summit of shoulder of Flattop Mtn. Start gradual descent.

8.1 Views, especially of Flattop Mtn. (3,325 ft.), from open field 50 ft. to left of Trail. Trail continues to descend.

8.9 Trail bends right to parallel old road on left, and descends steeply.

9.0 Trail comes into old road and follows it right for

about 0.1 mi.

9.2 Trail bends right, uphill, and ascends three rock steps.

9.4 Descend under power lines.

9.5 Simmons Gap, SDMP 73.2 (2,253 ft.) at intersection of Simmons Gap Fire Road and Skyline Drive. (A short distance south on road is ranger's office and beyond it are Park Service maintenance facilities. *Water* available here.) *AT* crosses to right (west) of Skyline Drive.

Trail Description, South to North

0.0 Begin at intersection of Simmons Gap Fire Road and Skyline Drive, SDMP 73.2 (2,253 ft.). *AT* follows Simmons Gap Road east of Drive for about 40 ft., then turns left onto path. (A short distance south on road is ranger's office and Park Service maintenance facilities. *Water* available here.)

0.1 Ascend under power lines.

0.3 Descend and bend left.

0.9 *AT* turns sharply left while old road continues ahead. Trail continues to ascend.

1.4 Near top of rise, open field about 50 ft. to right of Trail affords views of Flattop Mtn. (3,325 ft.).

1.5 Summit of shoulder of Flattop Mtn. *AT* continues along northern ridge crest.

2.7 Excellent views of Roach River Valley (Bacon Hollow and Powell Gap) from rock ledges to right of Trail. *AT* descends gradually.

3.0 Turn sharply right onto well-worn trail, former road, leaving old roadbed (now overgrown) in 0.1 mi. Continue descent.

3.3 Powell Gap, SDMP 69.9 (2,294 ft.). Cross to left (west) of Drive. Trail crosses grass, angles along edge of woods, then ascends western slope of Little Roundtop Mtn.

3.8 Summit of Little Roundtop Mtn. is 50 yd. to left of

AT. Trail continues along ridge crest, then swings around south and east sides of Roundtop Mtn., affording wintertime views of Powell Gap and Flattop Mtn. *AT* continues with little change in elevation.

4.9 Cross to right (east) of Skyline Drive in open Smith Roach Gap, SDMP 68.6 (2,622 ft.). From Drive, *AT* parallels Smith Roach Gap Fire Road a few feet to right of road for about 300 ft., then crosses road and ascends steadily through woods.

6.0 Cross Hightop Hut service road. (Hut is to left.)

6.1 Spur trail leads left 0.1 mi. to Hightop Hut, to be used by overnight hikers. *Spring* is 400 ft. downhill from hut on graded trail.

6.7 Piped, covered *spring* at foot of large boulder to right of *AT*. Trail continues to ascend. Side trail leads right 350 ft. to site of former Park Service lookout tower at summit of Hightop Mtn. (3,587 ft.). No view from summit. About 100 ft. farther along Trail is excellent view from ledges to left of Trail. A little farther yet is second good viewpoint. Beyond, Trail descends sharply, veering east then switchbacking down northern slope of mountain.

8.2 Trail crosses to left (west) of Skyline Drive in grassy sag, SDMP 66.7 (2,637 ft.). *AT* continues along former farm road, ascending slightly, passing through remains of old apple orchard, then descending.

9.4 Trail turns sharply right on old road which comes in from left. It follows road a few feet only, then climbs to its right. Just beyond, Trail drops steeply down to highway bridge which carries Skyline Drive over US 33. *AT* follows pedestrian footway along edge of bridge.

9.5 Concrete post marking *AT* on east side of Drive in Swift Run Gap, SDMP 65.5 (2,376 ft.).

SECTION 7
Simmons Gap to Browns Gap

12.2 miles — PATC Map #11

General Description: The Shenandoah Park is much wider in this section than in Section 6. Most of the Park west of the *AT* is designated as a wilderness area. A roughly triangular area between the ridges of Rockytop, Brown Mtn. and Loft Mtn., and drained by the tributaries of Big Run, comprises the largest watershed in the Park, 11 square miles.

Elevations in this section range from 2,253 ft. at Simmons Gap to over 3,300 ft. in the area of Big Flat Mtn.

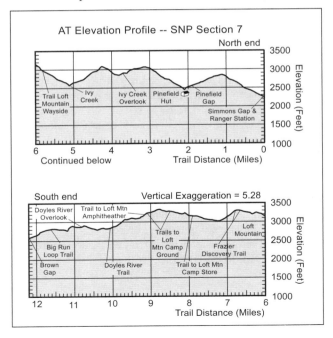

(where Loft Mountain Campground is located) and back to 2,599 ft. at Browns Gap. Traveling from the north there are two 600-ft. climbs and one 800-ft. one from Ivy Creek to the summit of Loft Mtn., but little other climbing.

Trail Approaches: The northern end of this section begins on the west side of Skyline Drive, at its junction with Simmons Gap Fire Rd, SDMP 73.2. This is 7.7 miles south of Swift Run Gap and US 33.

The southern end starts at its junction with Madison Run Road about 100 ft. west of Skyline Drive, SDMP 82.9, in Browns Gap.

Side Trails: The greater width of the Park here gives space for a wide variety of trails. The Big Run Loop Trail and the Doyles River-Jones Run trails are both loop trails, connected at each of their ends with either the *AT* or Skyline Drive. There are, in addition, other blue-blazed trails, a number of horse trails, and three gated Park fire roads—Simmons Gap Rd., Browns Gap Rd., and Madison Run Fire Rd. For details see "Side Trails." Also refer to PATC publication *Circuit Hikes in Shenandoah National Park*.

Accommodations: The Loft Mtn. developed area includes a wayside, camp store, campground with shower and laundry facilities (handicapped accessible), one discovery trail and the Loft Mountain Information Center (open weekends during season). Open dates vary between May and October.

One open-faced hut, Pinefield Hut, 2.1 mi. south of Simmons Gap, is available for overnight hikers.

One locked cabin, the Doyles River Cabin, 2.2 mi. north of Browns Gap, may be reserved in advance from PATC Headquarters. See "Shelters, Huts and Cabins."

Trail Description, North to South

0.0 West side of Skyline Drive, at junction with Simmons Gap Fire Rd., SDMP 73.2 (2,253 ft.). (A short distance to south on fire road is ranger's office and beyond it Park Service maintenance facilities. *Water* available here.) Trail ascends northwestern face of Weaver Mtn.

1.1 Top of Weaver Mtn. Descend gently through sparse, scraggly woods, primarily black locust.

1.9 Cross to left (east) of Skyline Drive at Pinefield Gap, SDMP 75.2. Continue through level area.

2.1 Cross access road to Pinefield Hut, for use by overnight hikers. (*Spring* is located along this road, 20 yds. left of *AT,* but is dry much of year. Hut is 150 yds. farther. A second *spring* is 250 ft. behind hut.) Trail now ascends.

2.3 *AT* comes within 100 ft. of Skyline Drive.

2.7 At spot where *AT* turns sharply left, Skyline Drive is approximately 200 ft. to right. (Twomile Run Parking Overlook is 0.1 mi. north, SDMP 76.2.) *AT* continues to ascend.

3.1 Reach unnamed summit (3,050 ft.), then descend gently.

3.7 North end of Ivy Creek Overlook, SDMP 77.5. *AT* passes along overlook, then parallels Drive a few feet farther.

3.9 Ascend unnamed peak (3,080 ft.), then descend.

4.5 Trail reaches excellent viewpoint with Skyline Drive immediately below Trail. (View covers area from Trayfoot Mtn. on left to Rockytop on right.) *AT* continues to descend.

5.1 Cross Ivy Creek in lovely miniature canyon (2,550 ft.). Trail starts ascent of Loft Mtn., longest climb in this portion of *AT,* climbing along east bank of Ivy Creek for 0.2 mi., then bearing left away from it.

5.8 Spur trail leads right 0.1 mi. to PATC Ivy Creek Maintenance Bldg. (no camping permitted) and a *spring.*

(This trail leads to an old road and in 0.3 mi. to Skyline Drive. Left is 0.1 mi to Wayside.)

6.1 *AT* passes to right of peak of Loft Mtn. (about 3,320 ft.) and follows ridge crest. For next mile or so, as far as Big Flat Mtn., *AT* passes through Patterson Field, an area that was once a 240-acre pasture. (Grass has been replaced by blackberry vines and other shrubby growth. Black locust now covers much of land, but in midst of young woods stand several old oak trees with very large low-spreading branches, showing that these oaks gained their maturity while the land was still open pasture.)

6.7 Panoramic (270 degree) view from Trail. A short distance farther Frazier Discovery Trail (see Loft Mtn. inset, back of PATC Map #11), a Park Service trail, enters from right and follows *AT*. (This interpretive trail starts from Skyline Drive at entrance to Loft Mtn. Campground, SDMP 79.5, climbs to *AT*, follows it south about 0.1 mi., then descends to starting point.)

6.8 Frazier Discovery Trail leaves *AT*. *AT* begins descent toward sag between Loft Mtn. and Big Flat Mtn.

7.5 *AT* crosses old road in sag. (Right leads to paved Loft Mtn. Campground road. Left is a dead-end.)

7.9 Spur trail leads right, uphill, to Loft Mtn. camp store, which is open "in season," generally mid-May through October. (Store carries complete line of groceries. Adjoining laundry is equipped with coin-operated washers, dryers, and showers.) Trail climbs gently toward Big Flat Mtn. (3,387 ft.).

8.1 *AT* circles clockwise around Loft Mtn. Campground. Excellent views east, then south, and finally to west, as *AT* swings around camping area on summit of Big Flat Mtn. *AT* is almost level here. Concrete posts at 8.5 mi. and 9.0 mi. mark side trails leading to campground.

9.2 Concrete post marks trail leading right 0.3 mi. to Loft Mtn. Amphitheater.

9.7 Excellent panoramic view, from left to right: Rockytop, Brown Mtn., Rocky Mtn., Rocky Mount, and to right (east) of Drive, Loft Mtn. *AT* continues to descend.

10.0 *AT* intersects Doyles River Trail. (Skyline Drive, SDMP 81.1, is 200 ft. to right. Big Run Parking Overlook is 250 ft. south on Drive. To left leads below Doyles River Cabin and *spring* in 0.3 mi. Cabin must be reserved in advance at PATC Headquarters.) From Doyles River Trail intersection *AT* closely parallels Skyline Drive and is relatively level.

10.9 Trail passes through Doyles River Parking Overlook, SDMP 81.9.

11.1 Trail follows ledges with wintertime views south.

11.3 *AT* crosses to right (west) of Skyline Drive, SDMP 82.2, with fine view from Drive of Cedar Mtn. and Trayfoot Mtn.

11.6 Junction with Big Run Loop Trail. (Big Run Loop Trail, 4.2 mi. long, runs from here to Big Run Parking Overlook, SDMP 81.1, near Doyles River Trail.) Beyond junction, *AT* gradually descends.

12.2 Concrete post marks junction with Madison Run Fire Road 100 ft. right of Skyline Drive, SDMP 82.9 (2,599 ft.) in Browns Gap. (Browns Gap was used several times by Gen. Stonewall Jackson during Civil War's Valley Campaign.)

Trail Description, South to North

0.0 Browns Gap. (Gen. Stonewall Jackson used this gap several times during Valley Campaign of Civil War.) Start of this section is at junction with Madison Run Rd. (western portion of old Browns Gap Rd.) about 100 ft. to left (west) of Skyline Drive, SDMP 82.9, in Browns Gap (2,599 ft.), and is marked by concrete post. Trail ascends, gaining 250 ft. in elevation, then levels off.

0.5 Big Run Loop Trail, blue-blazed, leads left 4.2 mi. to its northern trailhead at Big Run Parking Overlook, SDMP 81.1.

0.9 *AT* crosses to right of Skyline Drive, SDMP 82.2, with fine view of Cedar Mtn. and Trayfoot Mtn.

1.1 Trail follows ledges affording wintertime views south.

1.3 Trail passes through Doyles River Parking Overlook, SDMP 81.9.

2.1 *AT* intersects Doyles River Trail. (Skyline Drive is 200 ft. to left, SDMP 81.1, just north of Big Run Parking Overlook. Doyles River Trail leads right, passing below Doyles River Cabin and *spring* in 0.3 mi. Cabin must be reserved in advance at PATC Headquarters.) *AT* now ascends Big Flat Mtn. (3,389 ft.).

2.5 Excellent panoramic view, from left to right, of: Rockytop, Brown Mtn., Rocky Mtn., Rocky Mount, and, to the right (east) of the Drive, Loft Mtn.

3.0 Concrete post marks side trail leading left 0.3 mi. to Loft Mountain Amphitheater. *AT* now skirts southern and eastern edges of Loft Mtn. Campground for about 1 mi., with good views west, then south, and finally due east. Concrete posts at 3.2 mi. and 3.7 mi. mark side trails leading left to campground.

4.3 Trail leads left, 0.1 mi. uphill, to Loft Mtn. camp store, usually open mid-May through October. (Store carries complete line of groceries. Laundry with coin-operated washers, dryers, and showers, adjoins store.) For next mile or so, to summit of Loft Mtn., Trail passes through Patterson Field, once a 240-acre pasture. (Now grass has been replaced by berry vines, other shrubby growth and black locust trees. In the midst of young woods stand several old oak trees with very large, low-spreading branches, indicating that these oaks gained their maturity while land was still pasture.)

4.7 Trail crosses old road. (To left, road leads to paved road to Loft Mtn. Campground. To right is dead-end.)

5.4 Ridge crest of Loft Mtn. Frazier Discovery Trail enters *AT* from left. (Discovery Trail starts on Skyline

Drive at entrance to Loft Mtn. Campground, SDMP 79.5, joins *AT*, follows it north 0.1 mi., then descends to starting point. See inset, back of PATC Map #11.) Excellent 270 degree panoramic view about 150 ft. farther along *AT*.

6.1 Trail passes slightly to left of peak of Loft Mtn. (3,320 ft.), then starts descending toward Ivy Creek.

6.4 Trail leads left 200 yd. to PATC Ivy Creek Maintenance Bldg. and *spring* (no camping here). *AT* continues to descend, following right bank of Ivy Creek.

7.1 Trail crosses Ivy Creek, very picturesque (about 2,550 ft.), then ascends.

7.8 Excellent viewpoint showing area from Trayfoot Mtn. on left to Rockytop on right. Skyline Drive is immediately below Trail. *AT* continues to ascend for 0.2 mi., then descends.

8.5 South end of Ivy Creek Overlook, SDMP 77.5. Trail passes along overlook, then ascends gently for 0.5 mi.

9.1 Unnamed summit (3,080 ft.). Trail descends through patches of white pine, interspersed with areas of locust and young oak.

9.5 At spot where *AT* turns sharply right, spur trail leads left approximately 200 ft. to Skyline Drive, 0.1 mi. south of Twomile Run Parking Overlook.

9.9 *AT*, still descending, again comes within 100 ft. of Drive.

10.1 *AT* crosses access road to Pinefield Hut. (Hut available for use by overnight hikers. *Spring* 20 yds. to right along this road is often dry. Hut is 0.1 mi. farther with another *spring* behind it.)

10.3 *AT* crosses to left (west) of Skyline Drive at Pinefield Gap, SDMP 75.2. Trail now ascends, winding through sparse, scraggly woods, primarily black locust.

11.1 Top of Weaver Mtn. Trail descends along northwestern side of ridge.

12.2 *AT* reaches Simmons Gap at junction of Simmons

Gap Fire Road and Skyline Drive, SDMP 73.2 (2,253 ft.). (A short distance to south on fire road is ranger's office and beyond it Park Service facilities. *Water* available here.)

Falls of North Fork Moormans River

Photo by Lee Sheaffer

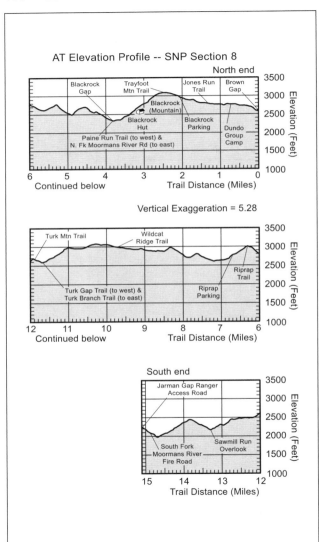

AT Elevation Profile -- SNP Section 8

North end

Blackrock Gap
Trayfoot Mtn Trail
Jones Run Trail
Brown Gap
Blackrock (Mountain)
Blackrock Hut
Blackrock Parking
Paine Run Trail (to west) &
N. Fk Moormans River Rd (to east)
Dundo Group Camp

Elevation (Feet)
3500
3000
2500
2000
1500
1000

6   5   4   3   2   1   0
Continued below   Trail Distance (Miles)

Vertical Exaggeration = 5.28

Turk Mtn Trail
Wildcat Ridge Trail
Turk Gap Trail (to west) &
Turk Branch Trail (to east)
Riprap Trail
Riprap Parking

Elevation (Feet)
3500
3000
2500
2000
1500
1000

12   11   10   9   8   7   6
Continued below   Trail Distance (Miles)

South end

Jarman Gap Ranger Access Road
South Fork Moormans River Fire Road
Sawmill Run Overlook

Elevation (Feet)
3500
3000
2500
2000
1500
1000

15   14   13   12
Trail Distance (Miles)

SECTION 8
Browns Gap to Jarman Gap

15.1 miles — PATC Map #11

General Description: The highlight of this section is Blackrock, a tumbled mass of large, lichen-covered blocks of stone, interesting of itself but also a spot for splendid views. As in Section 7, this part of the Park is quite wild and most of it is designated a wilderness area. Rhododendron, which is quite scarce in the Park, is found along the Riprap Trail and along the *AT* in the same general area. Mountain laurel is very plentiful in this area, especially along the Moormans River Fire Road east of the Drive from Blackrock Gap.

From Browns Gap the Trail climbs to Blackrock, drops 750 ft. to Blackrock Gap, then, after a succession of short climbs and dips, gradually ascends to over 3,000 ft. The final 5 mi. to Jarman Gap (2,173 ft.) is primarily downhill.

Trail Approaches: The northern end of this section begins in Browns Gap, SDMP 82.9. This is 17.4 mi. south of the Swift Run Gap entrance to Skyline Drive from US 33 or 22.5 mi. north of the Rockfish Gap entrance from US 250. A concrete post marks junction of *AT* and Madison Fire Road 100 ft. west of Skyline Drive. *AT* crosses the Drive here, then continues on east side.

The southern end begins in Jarman Gap, SDMP 96.9, 8.5 mi. north of the Rockfish Gap entrance to Skyline Drive from US 250/I-64. The *AT* is at junction with Bucks Elbow Mtn. Fire Road, 0.1 mile. east of Skyline Drive.

Side Trails: There are many worthwhile side trails in this section. Some lead to places of special interest, such as Riprap Ravine, Calvary Rocks, Trayfoot Mtn., and the falls on both Jones Run and Doyles River. The old Moormans River Road, former route of the *AT*, leads from Jarman Gap down the South Fork of Moormans River and up the North Fork to Blackrock Gap. See "Side Trails." Also refer to PATC publication *Circuit Hikes in Shenandoah National Park.*

Accommodations: One open-faced hut, Blackrock Hut, 3 mi. south of Browns Gap, is available for overnight hikers. See "Shelters, Huts and Cabins."

Trail Description, North to South

0.0 Concrete post marks junction of *AT* and Madison Run Fire Road, 100 ft. west of Skyline Drive, SDMP 82.9 (2,599 ft.). *AT* crosses diagonally to left side of Drive, then ascends gently.

0.4 Trail skirts eastern side of Dundo Picnic Area, SDMP 83.7, for next 0.2 mi. Several unmarked paths lead up to Dundo. *Water* may be obtained there May through October.

0.7 *AT* turns sharply left. A trail to right leads to Dundo.

1.3 Intersection with Jones Run Trail. (Jones Run Parking Area is 100 ft. to right. Left leads down Jones Run then ascends Doyles River Trail to return to *AT*.) *AT* now passes through remnants of old apple orchard.

1.5 Cross to west side of Skyline Drive, SDMP 84.3, and ascend very gently.

2.1 *AT* and Trayfoot Mtn. Trail come within few feet of each other and run parallel but do not cross. After 0.1 mi., *AT* bears right away from road and circles north, west, and south sides of Blackrock (3,092 ft.). (This area is reminiscent of New Hampshire's White Mountain terrain above tree-line. View from rocks is excellent.)

2.5 Blue-blazed Blackrock Spur Trail leads right from *AT* at its highest elevation at Blackrock and follows ridge leading to Trayfoot Mtn.

2.6 *AT* crosses Trayfoot Mtn. Trail, then descends steadily toward Blackrock Gap, following east side of narrow ridge. (An old road parallels Trail on western side of ridge, just out of sight.)

3.1 Spur trail, left, leads steeply down 0.2 mi. to Blackrock Hut. (Hut located in deep ravine. *Spring* 10 yds. in front of it. Hut for use of overnight hikers.) In 100 ft., *AT* crosses to west of old road, parallels it for 0.2 mi., then joins it and follows it down to intersection with Skyline Drive.

3.6 Cross to left of Skyline Drive, SDMP 87.2, and continue along east side for quarter mile.

3.8 Cross Moormans River Fire Road, yellow-blazed, in Blackrock Gap, SDMP 87.4 (2,321 ft.). (Moormans River Fire Road follows north fork of river down to Charlottesville Reservoir, then climbs along south fork of river to Skyline Drive at Jarman Gap; hiking distance 9.4 mi. This is former route of *AT*.)

4.9 From road intersection *AT* climbs over small knob, then descends to sag, with Skyline Drive 50 ft. to right. Trail now climbs over second small knob.

5.6 Trail crosses to right (west) of Skyline Drive, SDMP 88.9, in sag, then climbs.

6.3 Junction with blue-blazed Riprap Trail, at summit of knob (2,988 ft.). (Riprap Trail, Wildcat Ridge Trail and *AT* make excellent circuit of 9.3 mi.) *AT* descends steeply.

6.7 Graded trail, left, leads to Riprap Parking Area on Skyline Drive, SDMP 90.0. Trail continues to descend steeply another 0.1 mi., then more gradually. For next 2 mi. Trail alternately climbs and dips gently. Occasional rhododendron.

9.4 Intersection with Wildcat Ridge Trail. (Wildcat Ridge Parking Area, SDMP 92.1, is to left.) *AT* ascends gently.

9.7 *AT* crosses to left (east) of Skyline Drive, SDMP 92.4, and continues to ascend, reaching summit (3,080 ft.) in 0.5 mi. (Beyond summit are wintertime views of peaks in George Washington National Forest, Pedlar District, south of Rockfish Gap.) Trail descends to slight sag, reclimbs to about same elevation, then descends fairly steeply toward Turk Gap.

11.7 *AT* passes concrete post marking start of Turk Branch Trail, then crosses to right side of Skyline Drive at Turk Gap, SDMP 94.1 (2,610 ft.).

11.9 Turk Mtn. Trail leaves *AT*, right, and follows side ridge which shortly divides into two ridges, one Turk Mtn., the other Sawmill Ridge. (Hikers will find 1.1 mi. side trip to top of Turk Mtn. via blue-blazed Turk Mtn. Trail, well worth the time.) In 250 ft., *AT* reaches crest and starts long gentle descent.

13.3 Cross to left of Skyline Drive, SDMP 95.3, in deep sag at north edge of Sawmill Run Parking Overlook. Trail now climbs. Looking backwards while ascending, there are views of Turk Mtn., Sawmill Ridge and city of Waynesboro.

13.8 Summit of unnamed hill (2,453 ft.). As Trail starts to descend, views to east of Bucks Elbow Mtn.

14.2 Cross grass-covered pipeline diagonally to right. Continue to descend.

14.7 South Fork of Moormans River, a small creek here; follow creek along west bank to source.

14.9 Cross Moormans River Fire Road. (Road leads right 0.1 mi. to Skyline Drive at Jarman Gap, SDMP 96.8 [2,173 ft.].) In 200 ft., pass *spring* on left, then climb.

15.1 Bucks Elbow Mtn. Fire Road, 100 yd. east of Skyline Drive, SDMP 96.9, and end of section. (To right, road leads to Skyline Drive at intersection with Moormans River Fire Road in Jarman Gap; left leads out of Park and along ridge of Bucks Elbow Mtn. to radio tower.)

Trail Description, South to North

0.0 Junction of *AT* and Bucks Elbow Mtn. Fire Road. Trail descends.

0.2 Pass *spring* on right of *AT*. In 100 yds. cross

Moormans River Fire Road. Continue descent along west bank of South Fork of Moormans River at its upper end.

0.4 *AT* leaves creek and ascends unnamed hill. Partway up it crosses a grass-covered pipeline area diagonally to right.

1.3 Summit of hill (2,453 ft.). Looking backwards, toward east, is view of Bucks Elbow Mtn. As Trail begins to descend, there are forward views of Turk Mtn., Sawmill Ridge, and city of Waynesboro.

1.8 *AT* crosses to left (west) of Skyline Drive, SDMP 95.3, in sag at north edge of Sawmill Run Parking Overlook.

3.2 Summit of knob (2,650 ft.); in 250 ft., Turk Mtn. Trail, blue-blazed, leads left 0.9 mi. to summit of Turk Mtn. (Worthwhile side trip.)

3.4 Turk Gap, SDMP 94.1 (2,625 ft). *AT* crosses to east side of Skyline Drive. Concrete post marks junction of *AT* with Turk Branch Trail. Trail ascends 400 ft., dips gently, then ascends second summit with about same elevation as first. (Backward views in winter of peaks in George Washington National Forest, Pedlar District, south of Rockfish Gap.) Trail now descends.

5.4 *AT* crosses to west of Skyline Drive, SDMP 92.4.

5.7 Junction with Wildcat Ridge Trail. (Wildcat Ridge and Riprap trails make 6.2 mi. loop with *AT*.) *AT* continues along western side of ridge crest, passing through one of few areas in SNP having Catawba rhododendron.

8.4 Trail ascends steeply 0.5 mi. around slope of Riprap Hollow.

8.5 Graded trail to right leads to Riprap Parking Area on Skyline Drive, SDMP 90.0.

8.8 Summit of knob (2,988 ft.). Riprap Trail comes in from left. *AT* descends.

9.5 In sag, cross to right of Skyline Drive, SDMP 88.9. *AT* climbs over small knob.

10.2 Trail comes into sag with Skyline Drive 150 ft. to

left. *AT* climbs second knob then descends steadily.

11.3 Cross Moormans River Fire Road in Blackrock Gap, SDMP 87.4 (2,321 ft.). Trail continues along east side of Drive for 0.25 mi.

11.5 *AT* crosses to left (west) of Drive, SDMP 87.2, ascends old road for 0.2 mi., then angles off slightly to left of road and parallels it.

12.0 Trail crosses to east of old road. In 100 ft., graded trail leads right, steeply down for 0.2 mi., to Blackrock Hut. (Hut for use of overnight hikers, located in very deep ravine. *Spring* 10 yds. in front of hut.) *AT* continues to ascend along eastern side of ridge. (Old road runs parallel on left.)

12.5 Junction with Trayfoot Mtn. Trail. In 300 ft. *AT* begins circling Blackrock (3,092 ft.). (Blackrock is reminiscent of terrain above tree-line on Mt. Washington, N.H. Views excellent.)

12.7 Graded trail leads left along ridge leading to Trayfoot Mtn.

13.0 *AT* and Trayfoot Mtn. Trail come within few feet of each other but do not cross. They are parallel about 0.1 mi. *AT* bears off to left. (Blue-blazed trail leads 750 ft. to Skyline Drive, SDMP 84.7. Parking for several cars.)

13.7 Cross to right side of Skyline Drive, SDMP 84.3. Trail passes through remnants of old apple orchard.

13.9 Junction with Jones Run Trail. (To left leads to Jones Run Parking Area, SDMP 84.1; to right descends Jones Run, then ascends Doyles River to rejoin *AT* in 4.7 mi.) *AT* continues with little change in elevation.

14.4 *AT* turns sharply to right; trail straight ahead leads to Dundo Picnic Area. (*Water* available May through October.) Beyond Dundo, Trail descends gently.

15.1 *AT* reaches Browns Gap where Skyline Drive intersects old Browns Gap Road, then crosses Drive, SDMP 82.9 (2,599 ft.).

SECTION 9
Jarman Gap to Rockfish Gap

8.0 miles — PATC Map #11

General Description: Except for a short distance over the northern summit of Calf Mtn., utilized by the *AT* with the owner's permission, the Appalachian Trail from Rockfish Gap to Jarman Gap is located entirely within a corridor of land originally part of the Blue Ridge Parkway. Views are excellent from summit of Calf Mtn. and Bear Den Mtn. Rock outcrops on the summits in this section consist of a green shale, rather than greenstone, the basaltic rock so predominant along the ridge crest in the SNP itself.

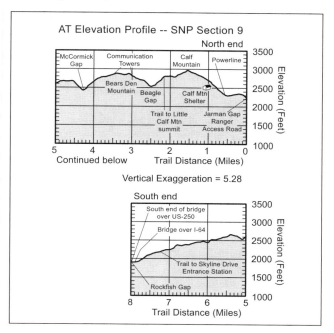

From Jarman Gap the *AT* climbs Calf Mtn., descends to Beagle Gap, where it crosses Skyline Drive, climbs over Bear Den Mtn., drops to McCormick Gap (where it recrosses the Drive), climbs up Scott Mtn., then slabs along the western side of the ridge as it drops gradually toward Rockfish Gap. Descending steeply to Skyline Drive just before reaching the Gap, it follows the Skyline Drive bridges over I-64/US 250, where the section ends, as does the Drive, at SDMP 105.4.

Trail Approaches: The northern end of this section begins at the Bucks Elbow Mtn. Fire Road, about 0.1 mile. east of Skyline Drive in Jarman Gap, SDMP 96.8. (Bucks Elbow Mtn. Fire Road is the more southerly of two roads that intersect at Skyline Drive. The other is Moormans River Fire Road.) Jarman Gap is 8.5 miles north of the I-64/US 250 entrance to Skyline Drive at Rockfish Gap.

The southern end is at the southern end of the Skyline Drive overpass of I-64/US 250 in Rockfish Gap, SDMP 105.4, on east side of Drive, where the *AT* leaves the sidewalk and goes down an earth embankment.

Side Trails: None other than old roads.

Accommodations: Gasoline, restaurant, and lodging facilities are available at Rockfish Gap and in Waynesboro, 4 mi. northwest via US 250. The Calf Mtn. Shelter, completed by PATC in 1984, is available for overnight use.

Trail Description, North to South

0.0 From Bucks Elbow Mtn. Fire Road in Jarman Gap, ascend southward.

0.4 *Spring* to left of Trail.

0.6 Pass under power lines.

1.0 Side trail leads right to *spring* in 0.2 mi. and Calf

Mtn. Shelter in 0.3 mi. (This is a PATC shelter, available for overnight use.)

1.3 Trail enters open area and follows pasture road through grass and staghorn sumac.

1.6 Trail passes below summit of Calf Mtn. (2,874 ft.). No views from summit. Continue along ridge.

1.7 Descend through pines and cross stone fence.

2.2 *AT* passes to left of Little Calf Mtn. (2,910 ft.). Unmarked trail leads right to summit with excellent view. Trail descends.

2.5 Cross Skyline Drive in Beagle Gap, SDMP 99.5 (2,523 ft.). Trail ascends open slopes of Bear Den Mtn.

3.0 Bare summit of Bear Den Mtn. (2,885 ft.). (Police radio installation here.) Continue past second summit (2,810 ft.).

4.3 Cross Skyline Drive in McCormick Gap, SDMP 102.1 (2,434 ft.). From Gap, cross stile and follow dirt road a few feet, then turn right from road and ascend steeply through brush and locust trees.

4.5 Trail ceases to climb and begins to slab western side of ridge, just below ridge crest.

5.6 Meet old trail and follow it south.

6.1 Come to another old trail and continue south.

6.3 Pass trail leading west.

7.2 Trail to right leads 0.2 mi. to southern entrance station of Skyline Drive.

7.7 Reach Skyline Drive and follow it south.

8.0 End of section at southern end of Skyline Drive, on bridge over I-64/US 250 in Rockfish Gap, SDMP 105.4 (1,902 ft.). For continuation, see *Guide to the Appalachian Trail in Central and Southwest Virginia* and PATC Map #12.

Trail Description, South to North

0.0 Skyline Drive at southern end of overpass over I-64/US 250 in Rockfish Gap. Trail follows footway along right (east) side of Drive.

0.1 Cross I-64/US 250, utilizing Skyline Drive overpass. Continue along right side of Drive.

0.3 At concrete post and *AT* trail marker, turn right away from Drive. Ascend steeply.

0.8 Trail leads left 0.2 mi. to southern entrance station of SNP. Backpackers can obtain camping permits at kiosk on trail.

1.7 Pass trail leading west.

1.9 At trail junction avoid right fork.

2.4 At another trail junction avoid right fork.

3.5 Trail starts to descend.

3.7 Cross stile and then Skyline Drive in McCormick Gap, SDMP 102.1 (2,434 ft.). Ascend through pine thicket, then across open land along ridge of Bear Den Mtn.

5.0 Bare summit of Bear Den Mtn. (2,885 ft.). (Police radio installation here.) Trail descends northeastward.

5.5 Cross Skyline Drive in Beagle Gap, SDMP 99.5 (2,532 ft.). Trail ascends Calf Mtn.

5.8 Pass slightly to right of Little Calf Mtn. (2,910 ft.). Unmarked trail leads left to summit with excellent view.

6.4 Trail passes below summit of Calf Mtn., (2,974 ft.). No view from summit.

7.0 Blue-blazed trail leads to *spring* in 0.2 mi. and Calf Mtn. Shelter in 0.3 mi.

7.4 Pass under two power lines.

7.6 *Spring* to right of Trail.

8.0 Bucks Elbow Mtn. Fire Road, 0.1 mi. east of Skyline drive at Jarman Gap, SDMP 96.8 (2,175 ft.).

Dappled fawn *Photo by Lee Sheaffer*

SUMMARY OF DISTANCES ALONG *AT*
South District

	Miles	
	N-S	**S-N**
Swift Run Gap	0.0	44.8
Hightop Hut	3.4+0.1	41.4+0.1
Smith Roach Gap, Skyline Drive crossing	4.6	40.2
Powell Gap, Skyline Drive crossing	6.2	38.6
Simmons Gap, Skyline Dr. crossing	9.5	35.3
Pinefield Hut	11.6+0.1	33.2+0.1
Ivy Creek Overlook, Skyline Drive	13.2	31.6
Loft Mtn. Camp Store	17.4	27.4
Doyles River Trail	19.6	25.2
Doyles River Cabin	19.6+0.3	25.2+0.3
Big Run Loop Trail, north end	19.6	25.2
Big Run Loop Trail, south end	21.1	23.7
Madison River Road	21.7	23.1
Browns Gap, Skyline Drive crossing	21.7	23.1
Jones Run Trail	23.0	21.8
Blackrock	24.2	20.6
Blackrock Hut	24.8+0.2	20.0+0.2
Blackrock Gap, Moormans River Fire Road	25.5	19.3
Riprap Trail	28.0	16.8
Wildcat Ridge Trail	31.1	13.7
Turk Gap, Skyline Drive crossing	33.4	11.4
Skyline Drive crossing, just north of Sawmill Ridge Overlook	35.0	9.8
Jarman Gap, 0.1 mi. east of Skyline Drive on Buck Elbow Fire Road	36.8	8.0
Calf Mtn. Shelter	37.8+0.3	7.0+0.3
Beagle Gap, Skyline Drive crossing	39.3	5.5
McCormick Gap, Skyline Drive crossing	41.1	3.7
Rockfish Gap, US 250/I-64	44.8	0.0

SUMMARY OF DISTANCES BY SKYLINE DRIVE
TO POINTS ON *AT*
South District

SDMP N-S		Miles S-N
65.5	Swift Run Gap	39.9
68.6	Smith Roach Gap	36.8
69.9	Powell Gap	35.5
73.2	Simmons Gap	32.2
75.2	Pinefield Gap	30.2
77.5	Ivy Creek Overlook	27.9
79.5	Loft Mtn. developed area (1.3 mi. to *AT*)	25.9
81.1	Doyles River Trail	24.3
81.9	Doyles River Parking Overlook	23.5
82.9	Browns Gap	22.5
84.1	Jones Run Trail (100 ft. to *AT*)	21.3
84.7	Trayfoot Mtn. Trail (0.1 mi. to *AT*)	20.7
87.4	Blackrock Gap	18.0
90.0	Riprap Trail Parking Area (300 ft. to *AT*)	15.4
92.1	Wildcat Ridge Trail Parking Area (0.1 mi. to *AT*)	13.3
94.1	Turk Gap	11.3
95.3	Sawmill Run Parking Overlook	10.1
96.8	Jarman Gap (0.1 mi. to *AT*)	8.6
99.5	Beagle Gap	5.9
102.1	McCormick Gap	3.3
105.4	Rockfish Gap	0.0

Columnar basalt, near Compton Peak

Photo by Tom Johnson

SIDE TRAILS
Shenandoah National Park

In addition to the AT, which traverses the Park from one end to the other, there are three other classes of trails in SNP. Blue-blazed trails are for foot-travelers only. Most of these, like the *AT* itself, are maintained by volunteers, members of the Potomac Appalachian Trail Club. Yellow-blazed trails, including fire roads, are classified as horse/foot trails; they are primarily maintained by Park personnel, although several equestrian groups have been assigned maintenance for specific trails. Park-maintained nature trails and stroller trails, usually quite short, may not be blazed.

For all trails, the trailheads and trail junctions are marked by concrete posts with aluminum bands that indicate direction and—usually—distance to the next trail junction or other landmark. It is wise, when hiking in a new area of the Park, to carry a guidebook or map with you, as the aluminum bands are sometimes removed by vandals.

Trail descriptions have been grouped according to area to facilitate planning of hikes. The PATC publication *Circuit Hikes in Shenandoah National Park* will also be useful in hike planning. The three PATC maps of the SNP (#9—North District, #10—Central District, #11—South District) are valuable for use in conjunction with the guide. USGS 7.5 min. quadrangle maps are available but are chiefly of value for bushwhacking and exploring.

In giving detailed trail data in this section, description is given in one direction only. The distances indicated on the left are those in the direction indicated. Those to the right are the distances in the reverse direction.

North District - Side Trails

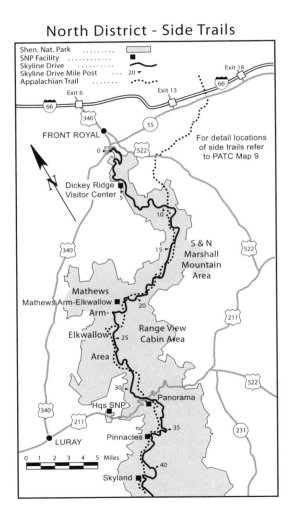

	Shen. Nat. Park	. . . .
	SNP Facility	. . . .
	Skyline Drive	. . . .
	Skyline Drive Mile Post	. . . 20
	Appalachian Trail	. . . .

Exit 18

Exit 6

Exit 13

66

Exit 6

340

FRONT ROYAL

55

522

For detail locations
of side trails refer
to PATC Map 9

0

N

Dickey Ridge
Visitor Center

5

10

340

15

S & N
Marshall
Mountain
Area

522

211

Mathews
Mathews Arm-Elkwallow

Arm-

20

Range View
Cabin Area

211

Elkwallow

25

Area

30

Hqs SNP

Panorama

522

340

211

LURAY

35

231

Pinnacles

0 1 2 3 4 5 Miles

40

Skyland

SIDE TRAILS
NORTH DISTRICT
Shenandoah National Park

View from Old Rag   *Photo by Lee Sheaffer*

DICKEY RIDGE TRAIL
9.2 miles — blue-blazed

This is a very popular trail because of its accessibility and gentle grade. The northern end is at the northern entrance to Skyline Drive. The trail parallels the Drive much of the way, crossing it at SDMP 2.1, again at Low Gap, and yet again at Lands Run Gap. The southern terminus is on the *AT* near Compton Gap, SDMP 10.4. Most of the climb along Dickey Ridge is between the northern end and the summit of Dickey Hill and involves a change in elevation of about 1,700 ft. The remainder of the route consists of gentle ups and downs.

There are few views from this trail. Where it climbs nearly to the top of Dickey Hill there are glimpses west of the Shenandoah Valley. (Summit has been cleared because of a federal navigational installation, VORTAC.) Near the southern end of the trail, the Fort Windham Rocks are of considerable interest.

Access: Northern terminus is on south side of US 340 at southern limits of Front Royal. Southern terminus is on *AT*, 0.3 mile north of Compton Gap, SDMP 10.4.

Trail Description: Front Royal to *AT* near Compton Gap

0.0-9.2 South side of US 340. Trail cuts across open area of Shenandoah Park's northern entrance and crosses to right side of Skyline Drive at Entrance Parking Area, SDMP 0.0. From here trail ascends very gently along small creek. Although close to Drive here, it is effectively isolated from it by trees and a jungle of Japanese honeysuckle. At about 1.4 mi. it turns sharply right away from creek and climbs more steeply.

1.9-7.3 Cross to left of Skyline Drive, SDMP 2.1. Continue to ascend. In about 0.5 mi. trail comes quite close to Drive at Shenandoah Valley Overlook, where there is good view of Front Royal and Signal Knob on Massanutten Mtn. Large patch of Virginia bluebells right on trail in this area, probably planted by a long-ago resident. (Bluebells bloom in latter part of April.)

4.0-5.2 Skyline Drive is slightly above and to right of trail here. Several side trails lead to Dickey Ridge Visitor Center, SDMP 4.6. Fox Hollow Trail, a Park interpretive trail, cuts across Dickey Ridge Trail directly below visitor center.

4.5-4.7 Cross Snead Farm Road (dirt). (To right, road leads few feet to Drive, just opposite exit road of Dickey Ridge Picnic Area, SDMP 5.1. To left, road leads into old apple orchard and site of Snead Farm.)

5.3-3.9 Trail skirts ridge, just below summit of Dickey Hill. Summit can be reached by a short scramble and offers sweeping views. From here trail descends gently.

5.7-3.5 Snead Farm Loop Trail enters on left. (Blue-blazed loop trail, 0.7 mi. long, has its lower end on Snead Farm Road, offering a nice circuit route.)

7.0-2.2 Low Gap, SDMP 7.9. Cross to right of Skyline Drive.

8.0-1.2 Lands Run Gap, SDMP 9.2. Cross to left of Drive.

8.6-0.6 Yellow-blazed Springhouse Road. (Trail leads left for 0.7 mi. to join Compton Gap Road and *AT* 0.3 mi. north of point where Dickey Ridge Trail itself joins *AT*.)

9.0-0.2 Pass Fort Windham Rocks on left. They are interesting to climb upon.

9.2-0.0 Junction with *AT*, which is here coincident with Compton Gap Road, at a point on *AT* 0.3 mi. from Compton Gap, SDMP 10.4. (*AT* follows road for another 1.2 mi. then turns left and descends into Harmony Hollow, reaching US 522 in 3.8 additional miles. Compton Gap Horse Trail leads down to Park boundary. As SR 610 it continues to US 522 at Chester Gap. Distance from Dickey Ridge Trail to Chester Gap via this route, 3.7 mi.)

FOX HOLLOW TRAIL
1 mile — blue-blazed

Attention: Pets are not allowed on this trail.

The interpretive trail starts from Skyline Drive directly across from the Dickey Ridge Visitor Center. It descends about 0.5 mi. then ascends through the former Fox Farm to complete the circuit. See PATC Map #9, inset on back, or check map displayed outside visitor center. A self-guiding booklet, with map, can be purchased at the visitor center or at the trailhead.

SNEAD FARM ROAD
0.7 mile — blue-blazed

A leisurely *circuit hike* of 2.5 mi. can be made with this road, along with the Snead Farm Loop Trail and a segment of Dickey Ridge Trail, starting at Dickey Ridge Picnic Area.

Trail Description

0.0 Snead Farm Road leaves Skyline Drive, SDMP 5.0, just across from exit road of Dickey Ridge Picnic Area.

0.3 Road leads left, downhill, from Snead Farm Road, soon coming to dead-end.

0.7 Snead home site at end of road. House is gone but barn is still standing. Concrete post at road's end marks lower end of Snead Farm Loop Trail.

SNEAD FARM LOOP TRAIL
0.7 mile — blue-blazed

Lower end of this trail is at end of Snead Farm Road. Upper end is on Dickey Ridge Trail, joining latter about 0.3 mi. south of summit of Dickey Hill. From here via Dickey Ridge Trail it is 1.2 mi. north (right) to return to Snead Farm Road and Skyline Drive.

LANDS RUN GAP ROAD
2.0 miles — yellow-blazed

Lands Run Gap Road leaves Skyline Drive, SDMP 9.2, in Lands Run Gap and descends west side of Blue Ridge to Park boundary, where it connects with SR 622. About 0.5 mi. from Skyline Drive road crosses Lands Run. Creek immediately below road here is very pretty, falling rapidly in a series of cascades.

Access: Upper end is on Skyline Drive, SDMP 9.2, in Lands Run Gap.

To reach lower end, drive to Browntown (which is about 6 mi. east of Bentonville via SR 613 and 7 mi. southwest of Front Royal on SR 649). Turn east in Browntown onto SR 634. In 1 mi. turn left onto SR 622. Reach fire road in 1 mi. from this junction.

HICKERSON HOLLOW TRAIL
1.2 miles — yellow-blazed

This trail leads from Lands Run Gap, SDMP 9.2, northward down one of the branches of Happy Creek into Harmony Hollow. It ends outside Park, where it meets SR 600 about 0.5 mi. from SR 604, main road through Harmony Hollow. (Land is posted along stretch of trail between Park boundary and SR 600.)

A *circuit hike* could include the *AT* from SR 601 in Harmony Hollow, uphill to its junction with Dickey Ridge Trail; that trail to Lands Run Gap, then Hickerson Hollow Trail back down mountain; then road walk down SR 600 and SR 604 and up SR 601 to start, for total distance of about 7 mi.

JENKINS GAP TRAIL
1.0 mile — yellow-blazed

From end of SR 634, about 2 mi. east of Browntown, trail climbs west side of Blue Ridge, and ends on the west side of Skyline Drive, SDMP 12.3. Across the drive from the parking lot, and a few yards south, is Jenkins Gap Overlook.

This section has nice gradient and is particularly attractive in early June, when the mountain laurel is in bloom. Lowest 0.2 mi. is outside Park. Remember that access to Park boundary across private land depends upon goodwill of landowner. Posted trail closures must be respected. Trail intersects *AT* about 0.1 mi. west of Drive.

Hikers wishing to continue down east side of Blue Ridge must follow Skyline Drive south for 0.3 mi. to start of Mt. Marshall Trail.

BROWNTOWN TRAIL
3.4 miles — yellow-blazed

This trail utilizes western portion of route of pre-Park Browntown-Harris Hollow Road. From Gravel Springs Gap, it runs down west side of Blue Ridge, descending in switchbacks. Grade is gentle and there are occasional glimpses of Hogback Mtn. and Gimlet Ridge through the trees.

Access: Upper trailhead is on Skyline Drive at Gravel Springs Gap, SDMP 17.7. In 50 ft. it intersects *AT*.

Lower end of trail can be reached by driving to Browntown (6 mi. east of Bentonville via SR 613 and 7 mi. southwest of Front Royal via SR 649). From Browntown follow SR 631 for about 1 mi. Where SR 631 turns sharply right, old Browntown Road is straight ahead. Room for two cars to park. *Do not* drive up old Browntown Road but start hiking here.

Trail Description: SR 631 to Skyline Drive

0.0-3.4 Junction with SR 631. Follow old road along creek, Phils Arm Run. Land is posted on both sides of road so stay on road.

0.2-3.2 Take right fork and immediately cross creek.

(Left fork leads through gate into field.)

0.8-2.6 Where road forks, take right fork straight ahead. In few yards road forks again; take right fork straight ahead. (Avoid other roads to right which are gated.) Road soon begins to climb.

1.1-2.3 Cross into SNP. Road, now trail, is gated here. Continue to climb and soon begin series of switchbacks. Occasional views of Hogback Mtn. and Gimlet Ridge.

3.4-0.0 Pass gate. In few feet intersect *AT* and a few feet farther reach Skyline Drive, SDMP 17.7.

COMPTON GAP FIRE ROAD-COMPTON GAP HORSE TRAIL-SR 610
4.0 miles — white (*AT* portion) and yellow-blazed

This fire road/horse trail leads northeast along the Blue Ridge crest from Compton Gap for 2.2 mi. Here it leaves the Park and becomes SR 610, which continues another 1.8 mi. to Chester Gap, where US 522 crosses the mountain (the last 340 ft. of road is SR 665). The *AT*, until 1974, followed this route from Compton Gap to Chester Gap and continued across US 522, following at first near the mountain crest, then on through woods to reach Mosby Shelter in another 2.5 mi. The present route of the *AT* follows the fire road from Compton Gap for 1.7 mi. then turns north away from it.

Access: Upper end of fire road is on Skyline Drive, SDMP 10.4 in Compton Gap.

Lower end is on US 522 in Chester Gap, 3.2 mi. east of junction of US 522 and VA 55 in Front Royal.

Trail Description: Compton Gap to US 522

0.0-4.0 Junction with Skyline Drive, SDMP 10.4 (2,415 ft.). *AT* hikers traveling north cross Drive at this junction after descending Compton Mtn. From here *AT* and fire road/horse trail are coincident for next 1.7 mi.

0.3-3.7 Dickey Ridge Trail leads left to Windham Rocks in 0.2 mi. then continues to Skyline Drive. To right is service road leading 0.4 mi. to the PATC Indian Run Maintenance Building. Spring is 250 ft. from road, on left, about 0.1 mi. before reaching building.

0.6-3.4 Yellow-blazed Springhouse Road leads left 0.7 mi. coming into Dickey Ridge Trail 6 mi. north of its junction with fire road. Beyond this point horse trail is blocked to motorized vehicles.

1.7-2.3 *AT* turns left, away from horse trail. Beyond this junction horse trail is yellow-blazed only.

2.2-1.8 Pass gate and leave Park. Beyond this point road is SR 610, paved and blue-blazed.

3.9-0.1 Take left fork of road, SR 665, and descend short distance.

4.0-0.0 US 522 in Chester Gap. To left along US 522 it is 1.5 mi. to *AT* crossing.

SIDE TRAILS IN NORTH AND SOUTH MARSHALL MOUNTAINS AREA

This group of trails includes the Mt. Marshall Trail, Bluff Trail, Jordan River Trail, Big Devils Stairs Trail and Harris Hollow Trail.

Access: From *Skyline Drive* there are two points of access. Yellow-blazed Mt. Marshall Trail enters Drive at SDMP 12.6, just south of Jenkins Gap Overlook.

At Gravel Springs Gap, SDMP 17.7, yellow-blazed Harris Hollow Trail descends eastward, paralleling *AT* for a short distance, and in 0.4 mi. intersects Bluff Trail near Gravel Springs. One can also follow *AT* from gap and reach start of Bluff Trail in 0.2 mi.

From *east*, main access to area is through town of Washington, VA. From main corner of town go north one block on SR 628, then turn left on SR 622. *To reach Mt. Marshall Trail* follow SR 622 for 2.4 mi. then turn right onto SR 625 and follow it about 1 mi. to end of state maintenance. Small parking area for three to four cars here. Sign and blue arrow mark trail which leads right from road. In about 250 yds. turn left onto old roadbed. Trail is not blazed until it enters Park. *To reach bottom of Harris Hollow Trail* follow SR 622 for about 5 mi. from Washington to the head of Harris Hollow. Trail starts just before reaching highest elevation of SR 622. There is a small sign saying "Trail" but no blazes outside Park. *Lower end of Jordan River Trail* is reached by taking US 522 to Flint Hill and turning west onto SR 641. In about 1 mi. continue straight ahead onto SR 606 for about 1 mi., then turn right onto SR 628 and, at a "T," turn left on graveled road, SR 629. Follow SR 629 up Jordan River to gate. Park here and continue up road on foot. In about 0.1 mi. enter SNP.

Trail access across private property depends upon goodwill of landowners. Posted trail closures must be observed.

MT. MARSHALL TRAIL
5.7 miles — yellow-blazed

This trail is valuable in providing access to the Bluff Trail and the Jordan River Trail, also for use in several circuit hikes. The upper 4 mi. are almost level. The trail is not blazed outside the Park but is marked at its lower end on SR 625.

Trail Description: Skyline Drive to Harris Hollow (SR 625)

0.0-5.7 Intersection with Skyline Drive, SDMP 12.6, just south of Jenkins Gap Overlook.

0.9-4.8 Trail enters wilderness area.

3.5-2.2 Junction with yellow-blazed Bluff Trail. (Bluff

Trail leads right 3.8 mi. to end on *AT* near Gravel Springs Gap.)

3.9-1.8 Jordan River Trail, yellow-blazed, leads down mountain 1.3 mi. following branch of Jordan River to SR 629.

5.1-0.6 Pass chain across road near Park boundary. Yellow blazes end here. Travel across private land beyond this point depends upon goodwill of landowner. Posted closures must be respected.

5.3-0.4 Pass through wooden gate.

5.7-0.0 Trail junction with SR 625 at end of state maintenance. From here it is 1 mi. via SR 625 to main road through Harris Hollow, SR 622.

BLUFF TRAIL
3.8 miles — first 0.3 mi. blue-blazed,
remainder yellow-blazed

"Bluff" was a local name for Mt. Marshall. The trail slabs southern and eastern slopes of mountain with a very gentle grade. It provides access to Big Devils Stairs Trail and is also useful in circuit hikes. There are nice winter views through trees to east along this stretch of trail.

Trail Description: *AT* to Mt. Marshall Trail (S to N)

0.0-3.8 Junction with *AT*, 0.2 mi. south of Gravel Springs Gap, SDMP 17.7.

0.2-3.6 Intersection with access road for Gravel Springs Hut. Hut, for use of overnight hikers, is 100 ft. to right.

0.3-3.5 Harris Hollow Trail enters from left. At this junction blue blazes end, yellow blazes start. Bluff Trail and Harris Hollow Trail are concurrent here.

0.4-3.4 Bluff Trail bends sharply left as Harris Hollow Trail continues straight ahead.

1.6-2.2 Junction with Big Devils Stairs Trail, which leads right, downhill to Park boundary. (No access from

Harris Hollow.)

3.4-0.4 Trail turns sharply right, soon followed by sharp turn to left.

3.8-0.0 Mt. Marshall Trail. (To left it is 3.5 mi. to Skyline Drive, SDMP 12.5, at Jenkins Gap; to right it is 0.4 mi. to Jordan River Trail and 2.2 mi. to lower end of Mt. Marshall Trail on SR 625.)

JORDAN RIVER TRAIL
1.3 miles — yellow-blazed

Although this trail is primarily used by horsemen, it is a pleasant walk for hikers along an abandoned road. About 0.1 mi. inside Park boundary are two very tall chimneys just across river, all that is left of what was once a large home. Much higher on the trail there are ruins of a simpler home.

Access: To reach lower end of trail first take US 522 to Flint Hill and turn west onto SR 641. In about 1 mi. continue straight ahead on SR 606 for about 1 mi., then turn right onto SR 628 and, at a "T," turn left on graveled road, SR 629. Follow SR 629 up Jordan River to gate and park. Continue beyond gate on foot. Access to Park boundary across private land depends upon goodwill of landowner. Posted trail closures must be respected. In about 0.1 mi. enter SNP.

Upper end of trail is on Mt. Marshall Trail in Thorofare Gap. To north it is 0.4 mi. to Bluff Trail and 3.5 mi. to Skyline Drive.

BIG DEVILS STAIRS TRAIL
1.6 miles — blue-blazed

The Big Devils Stairs canyon is one of the most impressive features of SNP. Originally, the trail followed through the canyon. Due to flooding, which obliterated the trail on a regular basis, a relocation was performed which situated the trail on east rim of the canyon. With caution, one can climb along the stream all the way through. The old route up the canyon is not recommended due to the rough going and lack of maintenance. The present trail should be traveled with caution due to the sheer cliffs along the east rim which follow the trail for most of its length.

There is no access to this trail from its lower end.

Trail Description: Bluff Trail to Park boundary

0.0-2.3 Junction with Bluff Trail, 1.6 mi. from *AT* and Gravel Springs Gap.

0.2-2.1 Trail follows eastern rim of canyon above creek (a branch of Rush River).

0.6-1.7 Trail continues along rim, following close to cliff edge. Excellent views across canyon and toward south. Once past cliffs, trail descends by switchbacks.

1.6-0.7 Cross creek and in a few feet reach Park boundary.

HARRIS HOLLOW TRAIL
2.8 miles — yellow-blazed

If starting at the lower end of the Harris Hollow Trail, park along SR 622 wherever there is room to pull off. *Please do not block a private driveway.* Trail is not blazed outside the Park but a small sign on SR 622 says "Trail." Where it leaves the gravel road it is again marked by a similar sign. Remember, access to the Park boundary across private land depends on the goodwill of the landowner. Trail closures must be respected.

Trail Description: Skyline Drive to SR 622

0.0-2.8 Junction with Skyline Drive at Gravel Springs Gap, SDMP 17.7. Trail follows access road toward Gravel Springs Hut.

0.3-2.5 Turn left off access road.

0.4-2.4 Bluff Trail. Follow it left for 0.1 mi.

0.5-2.3 Continue straight ahead where Bluff Trail bends sharply to left.

0.7-2.1 Reach roadbed of former Harris Hollow Road and turn left along it. (To right, Gravel Springs Hut trail leads 0.1 mi. up to Gravel Springs Hut. Hut for use of overnight hikers.)

1.4-1.4 Cross Park boundary. No blazes beyond this point. Continue down old road. Land is posted on both sides so stay on road.

2.6-0.2 Follow gravel road to right. Where gravel road bends left, continue straight ahead on old rutted road.

2.8-0.0 Junction with SR 622, 5 mi. from Washington, Va.

TRAILS IN THE RANGE VIEW CABIN AREA EAST OF SKYLINE DRIVE

The Keyser Run Fire Road, Piney Branch Trail and Hull School Trail are the major routes in the area. Trails that intersect one or more of these include Piney Ridge Trail, Little Devils Stairs Trail, Pole Bridge Link, Fork Mtn. Trail, Thornton Hollow Trail, and the *AT*. Many different circuit routes are possible.

Range View Cabin is ideally situated for campers who wish to hike in this area or in the adjacent Mathews Arm-Elkwallow area. Cabin reservations must be made in advance at PATC Headquarters; see "Shelters, Huts and Cabins."

Access from Skyline Drive:

1. *SDMP 19.4:* Here is upper end of Keyser Run Fire Road. Also at this milepost, but across Drive from fire road, a short trail goes west to connect with *AT* in 100 ft. One mile down fire road is Fourway, the point where Little Devils Stairs Trail goes to left (east) and Pole Bridge Link

Trail goes to right.

2. *SDMP 21.9*: *AT* crosses Drive here, just south of Rattlesnake Point Overlook. Follow *AT* south for 0.4 mi. to reach upper end of Piney Branch Trail and another 0.4 mi. to reach intersection with service road to Range View Cabin.

3. *SDMP 22.1*: Here a service road (gated) leads by Piney River Maintenance Office and on east to Range View Cabin, intersecting *AT*. Both Piney Branch Trail and Piney Ridge Trail have their upper ends on this road (and on or near *AT*). Upper end of Piney Ridge Trail is a few feet down road from this intersection.

4. *SDMP 25.4:* Thornton River Trail crosses the Drive.

5. *SDMP 28.1:* Hull School Trail descends eastward from Beahms Gap.

Access from the Piedmont north of Sperryville:

1. *Lower end of Piney Branch Trail:* To reach this point turn northwest from US 522/211 onto SR 612 just north of Thornton River bridge north of town. In 1.3 mi. continue ahead on SR 600, following Piney River. Reach junction with SR 653, which enters from left, when 3.3 mi. from US 522/211. Park car near this junction. Continue along SR 600 on foot to its end, about 0.1 mi. Here Piney Branch Trail leads left, crossing Piney River, then continuing up river for 0.6 mi. before entering Park. Fords of Piney River along lower stretch of Piney Branch Trail may be difficult in wet weather. Hull School Trail and lower end of Piney Ridge Trail are easily reached by this access route.

2. *Lower end of Thornton River Trail:* Turn off US 522/211 as described above but continue on SR 612 where it forks left at its junction with SR 600. About 3.2 mi. from junction reach end of state maintenance and park. Continue up road on foot and, in 0.1 mi., enter Park. This road, now Thornton River Trail, here yellow-blazed, con-

tinues up North Fork of river for 1.4 mi. to its junction with Hull School Trail. One can then follow Hull School Trail, right, to reach Fork Mtn. Trail, Piney Branch Trail and Keyser Run Fire Road. Using this route there are no fords of creeks except where Hull School Trail crosses Piney River. Above Hull School Trail, Thornton River Trail is blue-blazed.

3. *Lower ends of Little Devils Stairs Trail and Keyser Run Road:* From US 522/211 at southwest side of bridge over Covington River, about 2.5 mi. north of Sperryville, turn west onto SR 622. Follow SR 622 for 2 mi. to just past bridge over Covington River. Take left fork which is SR 614 and follow it about 3 mi. to start of Little Devils Stairs Trail and a parking area. There is a registration booth and a fee charged to hike this trail. If you hold a Shenandoah Pass, Golden Eagle Pass or Interagency Pass, the fee is waived. Keyser Run Fire Road is a continuation of SR 614 and is gated about 0.2 mi. beyond parking area.

KEYSER RUN FIRE ROAD
4.5 miles — yellow-blazed

This is a pleasant road to hike with an easy grade most of the way. It is also an important route as it offers access to Little Devils Stairs Trail, Pole Bridge Link, Piney Branch Trail and other trails in area. Across Drive from its upper end a short spur trail leads west to *AT*, thus extending the number of circuit hikes for which the fire road can be used.

Access: Upper end starts at Skyline Drive, SDMP 19.4, at east base of Little Hogback Mtn. A short trail (100 ft.) between *AT* and Drive directly opposite fire road gives access from *AT*.

Access from US 522-211 is via SR 622 and SR 614. (See "Access" under "Trails in the Range View Cabin Area.")

Trail Description: Skyline Drive to SR 614

0.0-4.5 From south or "east" side of Skyline Drive, SDMP 19.4, fire road drops very gradually, passing around head of hollow containing Little Devils Stairs.

1.0-3.5 Reach Fourway. To left, Little Devils Stairs Trail leads 2 mi. down to SR 614. To right, Pole Bridge Link leads 0.8 mi. to Piney Branch Trail.

3.3-1.2 Hull School Trail leads right, reaching Piney Branch Trail in 0.4 mi. and crossing Piney River 0.1 mi. farther. On left of Keyser Run Fire Road is walled-in Bolen Cemetery.

4.3-0.2 Road is gated.

4.5-0.0 Reach SR 614 at end of state maintenance. Little Devils Stairs trailhead is here at parking area.

LITTLE DEVILS STAIRS TRAIL
2.0 miles — blue-blazed

Note: A fee is charged to hike this trail from the lower parking lot.

This trail follows Keyser Run into the canyon known as Little Devils Stairs. The canyon area is steep, wild and picturesque. Its sheer cliffs are outstanding; they offer a challenge to rock climbers. Trail route is dangerous in wet or icy weather and even in good weather must be negotiated with care.

For a *circuit hike*, it is preferable to ascend the Little Devils Stairs Trail and to descend via the Keyser Run Fire Road or via the Pole Bridge Link to Piney Branch Trail, then the Hull School Trail.

Access: The trail's upper end is at Fourway on the Keyser Run Fire Road, 1 mi. from Skyline Drive and the *AT*.

Lower end is reached via SR 622 and 614 from US 522/211. (See "Access" under "Trails in the Range View Cabin Area.") There is a registration booth and a fee is charged to hike this trail.

Trail Description: SR 614 to Keyser Run Fire Road at Fourway

0.0-2.0 From parking area at end of state maintenance of SR 614 trail heads north, immediately crossing two small creeks. (SR 614 continues into Park as Keyser Run Fire Road and is gated 0.2 mi. beyond parking area.)

0.6-1.4 Trail approaches Keyser Run, stream that cut Little Devils Stairs canyon. Here is old rock wall, part of former dam or bridge. Trail crosses run frequently as it climbs steeply.

1.7-0.3 Trail makes sharp left turn and climbs steeply away from run.

1.8-0.2 Trail crosses rock-edged terrace, former home site.

2.0-0.0 Reach Keyser Run Fire Road at Fourway. (Directly across road is Pole Bridge Link, which joins Piney Branch Trail in 0.8 mi. To right, Keyser Run Fire Road leads 1 mi. to Skyline Drive and *AT*. To left, it leads 3.5 mi. to SR 614 at Little Devils Stairs trailhead.)

POLE BRIDGE LINK TRAIL
0.7 mile — blue-blazed

This trail links the Keyser Run Fire Road and Little Devils Stairs Trail with the Piney Branch Trail.

Trail Description: Keyser Run Fire Road to Piney Branch Trail

0.0-0.7 Four-way intersection on Keyser Run Fire Road, 1 mi. from Skyline Drive (and *AT*). Little Devils Stairs Trail starts here, from opposite side of fire road.

0.4-0.3 Intersection with Sugarloaf Trail. To right it is 1.4 mi. to *AT* near SDMP 20.8.

0.7-0.0 Intersection with Piney Branch Trail. (To right, via Piney Branch Trail, *AT* is 1.4 mi. and Range View Cabin 0.4 mi. farther. To left, Hull School Trail is 2.8 mi. and lower end of Piney Ridge Trail is 2.4 mi.)

PINEY BRANCH TRAIL
6.5 miles — blue-blazed between *AT* and
Hull School Trail, yellow-blazed from
Hull School Trail to Park boundary

This trail begins outside the Park at SR 600 and follows Piney River to its source, then continues on to *AT* and crest of Blue Ridge. Piney Branch is one of the more attractive streams in SNP. The middle portion of the trail narrows to a wide ravine with two waterfalls. Overnight campers should be certain to hang their food since this area is frequented by bear.

A *circuit hike* of 8 mi. can be made from Range View Cabin with this trail and Piney Ridge Trail. Another *circuit hike* could be: *AT* between Piney Ridge Trail junction and Keyser Run Road, fire road down to Fourway, then Pole Bridge Link and back up Piney Branch Trail to Range View Cabin. Another favorite *circuit hike* of 7.8 mi. starts from SR 614. Climb up Little Devils Stairs, then follow Pole Bridge Link, descend Piney Branch Trail to Hull School Trail. Follow Hull School Trail left and descend Keyser Run Fire Road to start. See PATC Map #9 for other possible circuits.

Access: Upper end of trail starts at Piney River Maintenance Area, SDMP 22.1. (See PATC Map #9 inset of Range View Cabin Area.) Adequate parking across Skyline Drive from Piney Branch Maintenance Building and beside entrance to Mathews Arm Campground.

Lower end of trail is on SR 600. See "Access" under "Trails in the Range View Cabin Area" for details.

Trail Description: *AT* to SR 600 and 653

0.0-6.5 Intersection with *AT*. Trail leads east at signpost and follows old road down mountain. Follow blue blazes.

1.3-5.2 Cross headwaters of Piney Branch.

1.4-5.1 Junction with Pole Bridge Link Trail which comes in from left. (Via Pole Bridge Link it is 0.8 mi. to Fourway on Keyser Run Fire Road.) Turn right at this junction.

4.0-2.5 Junction with Piney Ridge Trail, which enters from right. (Range View Cabin is 3.4 mi. from this junction via Piney Ridge Trail.)

4.3-2.2 Cross Piney Branch.

4.4-2.1 Junction with Hull School Trail. Blue blazes end here. Turn right. Piney Branch Trail and Hull School Trail are coincident for next 0.2 mi.

4.6-1.9 Cross Piney River, then turn left from Hull School Trail and descend old road along Piney River, following yellow blazes.

5.8-0.7 Leave Park and continue down road to SR 600.

6.5-0.0 Junction of SR 600 and SR 653.

PINEY RIDGE TRAIL
3.3 miles — blue-blazed

This trail, originally developed by PATC, can be used along with the Piney Branch Trail to provide a *circuit hike* from Range View Cabin. The trail follows a gentle downhill grade along the ridge until its intersection with the Fork Mountain Trail, where it turns left and drops moderately off the ridge down to Piney Branch Trail. The old Dwyer cemetery is located near the junction with the Fork Mountain Trail with gravesites dating from the late 1800s.

Access: Upper end of Piney Ridge Trail may be reached by following service road from Skyline Drive, SDMP 22.1, past Piney River Ranger Station south about 0.7 mi., crossing *AT* 30 ft. before reaching start of Piney Ridge Trail, which leads right from road. (Trailhead is nearly within sight of Range View Cabin at road's end.) One can also start at Rattlesnake Point Overlook and follow *AT* south for 0.8 mi. to its intersection with service road, then turn left onto road toward cabin and in 30 ft., reach start of Piney Ridge Trail.

Lower end of Piney Ridge Trail is on Piney Branch Trail 0.4 mi. above its junction with Hull School Trail.

Trail Description: Range View Cabin Service Road (near *AT*) to Piney Branch Trail

0.0-3.3 Junction with service road, just west of Range View Cabin. Trail bears south, descending along crest of ridge.

2.0-1.3 Pass old cemetery to right of trail; a few feet beyond take left (east) fork at trail intersection. (Straight ahead, blue-blazed Fork Mtn. Trail continues along ridge to Hull School Trail.)

2.3-1.0 Where stone piles mark old home site (hiking downhill), turn sharp right. Spring is 150 ft. to left in ravine below.

3.3-0.0 Reach Piney Branch Trail 0.4 mi. from its junction with Hull School Trail.

FORK MOUNTAIN TRAIL
1.2 miles — blue-blazed

This short trail leads along Fort Mtn. ridge from Piney Ridge Trail southeastward to its intersection with Hull School Trail. It makes a useful link in circuit hikes.

THORNTON RIVER TRAIL
5.2 miles — yellow-blazed east of
Hull School Trail, blue-blazed to west

From SR 612 trail follows an old road up the meandering North Fork of Thornton River to Hull School Trail. It continues up Thornton Hollow, passing through small hemlock stands. Near the headwaters, the trail follows along the edge of grassy fields of an old home site, now overgrown with young trees. As the trail heads away from the overgrown fields and up to Skyline Drive, the remnants of an old, Model A Ford can be seen. Crossing Skyline Drive on a diagonal at SDMP 25.4, the trail continues steeply uphill to the *AT*. During periods of drought, the North Fork of Thornton River may be almost dry. In early spring, the flowering redbud is beautiful and profuse along the lower half of the trail.

Trail Description: Junction of SR 612 and SR 653 to *AT*

0.0-5.2 From junction of SR 612 and SR 653, continue up SR 612 on foot.

0.6-4.6 State road maintenance ends.

0.7-4.5 Road gated at Park boundary. *Spring* to right of road just beyond gate. Trail is yellow-blazed from Park boundary to Hull School Trail.

2.0-3.2 Junction with Hull School Trail. Follow road a few feet beyond its sharp turn to right. Thornton River Trail (blue-blazed from here on) turns left away from road. Trail crosses river three times in next 0.6 mi. Difficult in wet weather.

3.4-1.8 Cross branch of river. Valley is wide here and there are numerous indications of old homesites, traces of old roads, and an old car.

3.6-1.6 From here trail climbs gently but steadily upward through open woods.

4.9-0.3 Skyline Drive, SDMP 25.4. Cross Drive diagonally to left.

5.2-0.0 Reach *AT* at point on *AT* 1.2 mi. north of Neighbor Mtn. Parking Area.

HULL SCHOOL TRAIL
4.4 miles — yellow-blazed

This trail makes use of a number of roads that existed before the Park was established—Beahms Gap Road, North Fork (of Thornton) Road, a bit of Keyser Run Road, and a short section long known as "PLD." The roads pass through deep and wild forest. One end is on Skyline Drive at Beahms Gap, SDMP 28.1; the lower end is on Keyser Run Road at Bolen Cemetery. Trails that intersect it include Thornton River Trail, Piney Branch Trail and Fork Mtn. Trail.

Trail Description: Skyline Drive to Keyser Run Fire Road

0.0-4.4 Skyline Drive, SDMP 28.1. Trail follows route of old Beahms Gap Road, occasionally detouring right or left of it where erosion has damaged old roadbed.

1.5-2.9 Enter area of old homesites. Find double daffodils in bloom first week of April.

1.9-2.5 Old home site on right. More daffodils.

2.2-2.2 Cross Thornton River and reach Thornton River Trail. Hull School Trail now follows route of former North Fork Road over ridge of Fork Mtn.

2.9-1.5 Summit of Fork Mtn. ridge. (Fork Mtn. Trail, blue-blazed, leads left about 1 mi. to end on Piney Ridge Trail.)

3.5-0.9 Junction with Piney Branch Trail. (To right, Piney Branch Trail, yellow-blazed, leads out of Park to SR 600.) Cross Piney River.

3.7-0.7 Piney Branch Trail, blue-blazed here, leads left 4.2 mi. to *AT.*

4.4-0.0 Keyser Run Fire Road. Just up fire road from junction is walled-in Bolen Cemetery. (To right, Keyser Run Road leads 1.2 mi. downhill to parking area for Little Devils Stairs Trail on SR 614. To left, fire road leads 3.3 mi. to Skyline Drive and *AT.*)

HOGBACK SPUR TRAIL
0.3 mile — blue-blazed

This short trail runs from Skyline Drive, SDMP 20.4, up to the *AT.* There is a *spring* near lower end. Upper terminus is less than 0.1 mi. north of hang glider launching area; main use of this trail is for hang glider enthusiasts.

SUGARLOAF TRAIL
1.4 miles — blue-blazed

This new trail in the area connects the *AT* to Pole Bridge Link, making possible several new circuit hikes. For most of its length it follows a pleasantly graded old road trace through mountain laurel. There are pretty stands of bluets wildflowers along this trail in early spring.

Trail Description: *AT* to Pole Bridge Link

0.0-1.4 Junction with *AT*, 100 ft. south of Skyline Drive, SDMP 20.8.

0.1-1.3 Bear right (southeast) onto old road trace.

1.0-0.4 Pass large flat area to right (west) of trail. Small stream 150 ft. to left of trail.

1.4-0.0 Junction with Pole Bridge Link. From here it is 0.5 mi. left to Fourway and Little Devils Stairs Trail and 0.4 mi. right to Piney Branch Trail.

MATHEWS ARM-ELKWALLOW AREA
(west of Skyline Drive)

This trail network includes about a dozen trails from the Tuscarora Trail and Mathews Arm Trail on the north to Neighbor Mountain Trail on the south. A study of PATC Map #9 will suggest a number of possible circuit hikes of varying lengths.

Note: Many of the trailheads in this section begin at Mathews Arm Campground. During the winter and certain other times the campground is closed and the access road is gated. These trailheads may be reached by parking at the parking lot on Skyline Drive, SDMP 22.2, and walking 0.5 mi. down the road to the campground registration station.

Historical note: Mathews Arm was part of a grant of land made by Lord Fairfax to Israel Mathews. Many of Israel's descendants still live in Warren County.

TUSCARORA TRAIL
7.6 miles — blue-blazed

The Tuscarora Trail extends 251 miles, with its southern terminus on the *AT* on Hogback Mountain in SNP and its northern terminus on the *AT* north of Carlisle, Pennsylvania. Originally, the Tuscarora Trail was envisioned as a new route for the *AT* to avoid growing population pressures in northern Virginia and Maryland. However, with permanent protection to the *AT* brought by the National Scenic Trails Act, an alternate *AT* route became less of a priority.

The trail was originally known as The Big Blue Trail and ran from its southern terminus here in the national park to Hancock, Maryland where it met the original Tuscarora Trail that continued on to the *AT* just north of Carlisle, Pennsylvania. This westward arc of this trail now serves as a worthwhile extended hiking/backpacking opportunity for the adventuresome seeking the more rural and wild scenery available in the Massanutten and Allegheny mountain ranges. The PATC maintains the entire length of the Tuscarora Trail. PATC guidebooks and a series of maps cover the Tuscarora route and are available from PATC sales office (and internet) and through many outdoor retailers. Hikers who either hike or backpack the entire Tuscarora Trail are entitled to purchase a "Tuscarora" patch from PATC.

For much of its length within SNP the Tuscarora follows Overall Run and is coincident with the Overall Run Trail. Just off the trail, 3.1 mi. from the *AT* and 4.6 mi. from US 340 via the Tuscarora Trail, is the beautiful cascade Overall Run Falls. This is one of the prettiest spots in the North District of the Park. The falls here are considered the highest in the Park. *Caution:* The Tuscarora Trail is extremely steep near here, and the side trail to the base of the falls is short and rough.

At the western boundary of SNP, at US 340, the

Tuscarora crosses the South Branch of Shenandoah River at the Bentonville low-water bridge, then climbs west over the ridges of the Massanutten, crosses the main Shenandoah Valley in the area of Toms Brook, climbs Little North Mountain and zigzags its way west to the Virginia-West Virginia state line, where it runs generally northeast.

Access: To reach southern end of Tuscarora Trail, follow *AT* south for 0.4 mi. from *AT* crossing of Skyline Drive at SDMP 21.1 or follow *AT* north 0.6 mi. from crossing of Drive at SDMP 21.9, just south of Rattlesnake Point Overlook (parking here). Concrete post on *AT* identifies trail here as Tuscarora Trail.

Trail Description: *AT* to US 340

0.0-7.6 Concrete post marks junction of *AT* and official southern terminus of Tuscarora Trail.

0.7-6.9 Concrete post, turn right. (Straight ahead, a short connecting trail leads 250 ft. to Traces Trail and beyond to northern part of Mathews Arm Campground. Follow Traces Trail to left 0.5 mi. to reach parking area and entrance road to campground.)

0.8-6.8 Pass to right of 12-foot diameter boulder.

1.2-6.4 Cross two small intermittent streams.

2.3-5.3 Concrete post. Continue straight ahead. Mathews Arm Trail bears to left. In another 90 yd. at another concrete marker, bear left on Tuscarora-Overall Run Trail as Mathews Arm Trail bears to right.

2.4-5.2 Come within 40 ft. of Overall Run, then turn right and travel parallel to run at a much higher elevation.

2.7-4.9 Rock outcrop about 15 ft. to left gives good view of Overall Run Valley.

2.8-4.8 Large rock outcropping, about 20 ft. to left. (Facing into valley there is an impressive view of Overall Run Falls to lower left, with 93-foot drop, highest in SNP.

Excellent views of Massanutten Mountain across valley to right.)

3.1-4.5 Cross intermittent tributary of Overall Run and descend its right bank

3.4-4.2 Near right bank of Overall Run.

3.6-4.0 Cross Overall Run and continue along left bank.

4.0-3.6 Cross Overall Run and continue along right bank. Cross minor tributaries flowing into run.

4.6-3.0 At concrete post, turn right heading uphill. (Overall Run Trail goes straight and downhill, which in 0.1 mi. passes a stretch of Overall Run with several small cascades and inviting pools.)

4.8-2.8 Turn left at concrete post. (Thompson Hollow Trail continues straight and in 0.4 mi. exits the Park at SR 630.)

5.4-2.2 Turn left off old road and descend into saddle and hills before rising to narrow ridge.

6.2-1.4 After 30 yd. of heading down a narrow ridge, turn left.

6.4-1.2 Bear right. Pass across head of drainage line, then bear left and continue sharply downhill.

6.6-1.0 Cross stream in Sandbank Hollow. In 50 yds. pass concrete post on left, marking Park boundary. For next mile to US 340, trail is on private land. *Stay on trail*.

6.7-0.9 Cross small drainage line flowing to left and immediately turn right on old road heading uphill.

6.8-0.8 Turn right on another old road and recross drainage line.

6.9-0.7 Briefly follow trees blazed red-orange to mark Park boundary on right, then turn left across relatively level stretch.

7.2-0.4 Turn left, heading down ridge road.

7.4-0.2 At blue-blazed post, turn right and leave ridge road.

7.5-0.1 Descend grassy ridge and cross gate at driveway of private land. Follow driveway through tunnel under Norfolk and Southern Railroad.

7.6-0.0 Reach US 340. Tuscarora Trail continues to right along US 340.

THOMPSON HOLLOW TRAIL
0.4 mile — blue-blazed

One end of this short trail is at Park boundary at end of SR 630 in Thompson Hollow south of Bentonville. Turn east on SR 613. In about 0.8 mi. turn south on SR 630 and drive to end of state maintenance. Paved parking for five cars on right. *Do not block road access.* Follow road extension, now a private driveway, staying to left at a mid-point intersection for about 0.3 mi. Immediately after crossing a stream turn right off driveway at an SNP trail post.

The upper, or southern, terminus of trail is on Tuscarora Trail at a point on latter 2.8 mi. from US 340 and 0.2 mi. from Overall Run.

The shortest approach to Overall Run Falls is by hiking Thompson Hollow Trail from SR 613, continuing straight for 0.2 mi. on Tuscarora Trail, turning left and ascending 2.1 mi. on Tuscarora-Overall Run Trail.

OVERALL RUN TRAIL
5.2 miles — blue-blazed

Most of what was earlier called the Overall Run Trail is now coincident with the Tuscarora Trail. Only the lowest section along the run, below the point where the Tuscarora turns away from it, remains separate. The trail ends 0.6 mi. below the turn-off for the Tuscarora Trail at the intersection of the Beecher-Overall Connecting Trail

A pleasant *circuit hike* can be made, starting at Mathews Arm Campground, by descending Mathews Arm Trail, going left on Beecher Ridge Trail and right on Beecher-Overall Connecting Trail, then ascending via Overall Run Trail, Tuscarora and Mathews Arm Trail.

Trail Description: East to West

0.0-5.2 See description of Tuscarora Trail for first 4.6 mi.

4.6-0.6 Overall Run Trail continues straight ahead. Tuscarora Trail turns right toward Thompson Hollow. (This point is 2.8 mi. from Mathews Arm Trail and 3 mi. from US 340 via Tuscarora Trail.)

4.7-0.5 Lower falls of Overall Run is few feet to left.

5.2-0.0 Lower end of trail. For continuation of circuit opportunities, turn left onto blue-blazed Beecher-Overall Connecting Trail for 0.7 mi. to reach Beecher Ridge Trail.

BEECHER-OVERALL CONNECTING TRAIL
0.7 mile — blue-blazed

Upper terminus of this trail is on Beecher Ridge Trail, 2.3 mi. down from its upper terminus on Mathews Arm Trail. Lower terminus is on Overall Run Trail at its lower end.

BEECHER RIDGE TRAIL
3.1 miles — yellow-blazed

This trail leaves Mathews Arm Trail 0.9 mi. from northern end of Mathews Arm Campground (1.4 mi. from campground registration station) and descends crest of Beecher Ridge following an old woods road. It comes into Heiskell Hollow Trail at a point on the latter 2.3 mi. below its upper terminus on Knob Mtn. Trail and 1.5 mi. from lower end on SR 697. At 2.3 mi. on right is Beecher-Overall Connecting Trail. This blue-blazed trail is 0.7 mi long and connects to lower end of Overall Run Trail.

A *circuit hike* can be made starting from Mathews Arm Campground registration station, using Beecher Ridge and Overall Run trails (9.5 mi.) or a shorter circuit using Beecher Ridge and Heiskell Hollow trails (7.5 mi.).

Backcountry camper   *Photo by John F. Mitchell*

MATHEWS ARM TRAIL
4.4 miles — yellow-blazed

This old road, most of which is now classified by the Park as trail, leads north from Mathews Arm Campground. After crossing Overall Run it continues on the long ridge, Mathews Arm, from which the campground takes its name, then descends to the Park boundary. It continues outside the Park but no parking is available. While the trail does continue outside of the Park boundary, its use is not recommended.

Access: From Skyline Drive, SDMP 22.2, drive down paved entrance road to Mathews Arm Campground and park in lot near registration station. In event that campground is closed, park at lot provided on Skyline Drive (SLMP 22.2) and walk 0.5 mi. down paved road to registration station. Walk through campground to far end chain gate at "tents only" section of B-loop. Distance from Drive to Tent Area B is 1.1 mi. One can follow abandoned section of Mathews Arm Road (kept clear for overhead power line) from Drive to registration station and avoid some paved road walking. Trail description below starts at camp road in Tent Area B.

Trail Description: Mathews Arm Campground to Park boundary

0.0 Mathews Arm Trail is gated as it leaves paved camp road in Tent Area B. Descend gently.

0.1 Traces Trail intersects road here.

0.4 Weddlewood Trail leads left to end on Heiskell Hollow trail in 1.3 mi.

0.9 Beecher Ridge Trail leads left down Beecher Ridge and over to Heiskell Hollow Trail.

1.3 Cross Overall Run and turn right.

1.4 Intersection with Tuscarora Trail. (To right it is 2.3 mi. to *AT*; to left it is 5.2 mi. to US 340.)

2.7 Trail descends steeply. In 0.6 mi. turn sharp left off ridge crest.

4.4 Park boundary.

THE TRACES TRAIL
1.7 miles — not blazed

Attention: Pets are not allowed on this trail.

This trail, which loops around Mathews Arm Campground, emphasizes the traces that remain of pre-Park days of this land. It starts at upper end of parking area (near registration station) and circles campground in a counterclockwise direction.

Trail Description:

0.0 Sign at edge of parking area.

0.5 Concrete post marks spur trail to campground. In 50 ft. second post marks spur trail which leads right 0.1 mi. to Tuscarora Trail.

1.1 Interpretive Trail intersects Mathews Arm Road at a point on latter about 0.1 mi. from northern end of campground.

1.3 Viewpoint on right.

1.6 Camp road at lower end of parking area.

1.7 Completion of loop at trail's start.

KNOB MOUNTAIN TRAIL
7.5 miles — yellow-blazed

The route over Knob Mountain is a fire road, forking from the Mathews Arm Campground at the north end of the Knob Mountain ridge for a distance of 4.3 mi to just below the summit of Knob Mtn., and becomes a foot trail from the summit down to Jeremys Run, a distance of 3.3 mi. A significant portion of the forest along this route was damaged or killed by gypsy moths. From the summit, the route drops 1,600 ft. to Jeremys Run, a mile away. Because of the steep descent into Jeremys Run, this trail is easier followed from north to south. There is an intermittent spring on the lower half of the trail, but no water along the fire road.

A *circuit hike* of 6 mi. would include 2.2 mi. of Knob Mtn. Trail, Knob Mtn. Cutoff Trail, upper portion of Jeremys Run Trail, the *AT* back to Elkwallow Gap, then Elkwallow Trail to Mathews Arm Campground.

Access: To reach upper end of trail and road, turn west from Skyline Drive, SDMP 22.2, onto entrance road to Mathews Arm Campground and drive 0.5 mi. to parking area at registration station. When entrance road to campground is closed, it is necessary to walk down from Skyline Drive. From parking area follow on foot the paved road leading left to yellow chain gate at far end of dump station turnaround. Continue past wastewater treatment plant and Heiskell Hollow Trail on right. Knob Mtn. Trail takes off to left at wooden sign just beyond Heiskell Hollow Trail. Start of trail is 0.9 mi. from Skyline Drive.

Lower end is reached via Jeremys Run Trail. See description of that trail.

Trail Description: Mathews Arm Campground to Jeremys Run

0.0-7.5 From loop of paved campground road, follow graveled road beyond chain.

0.4-7.1 Heiskell Hollow Trail junction, yellow-blazed, leads right 4 mi. to SR 697 near Compton.

2.2-5.3 To left, Knob Mtn. Cutoff Trail, blue-blazed, leads 0.5 mi. steeply down to Jeremys Run Trail at a point on latter 0.8 mi. from *AT*.

4.3-3.2 Trail continues as much narrower footway, immediately climbing over highest peak of Knob Mtn. (2,865 ft.), then descending along ridge crest, finally dropping steeply toward Jeremys Run.

7.5-0.0 Cross Jeremys Run and reach Jeremys Run

Trail in 50 ft. (From this junction it is 0.8 mi. right to Park boundary; to left it is 50 ft. to Neighbor Mtn. Trail. *AT* is 5.4 mi. via Jeremys Run Trail and 4.6 mi. via Neighbor Mtn. Trail.)

HEISKELL HOLLOW TRAIL
4.0 miles — yellow-blazed

This trail can be used in combination with others in the area—Mathews Arm Trail, Weddlewood Trail, Beecher Ridge Trail and the Tuscarora (Overall Run) Trail—for some excellent circuit hikes.

Access: To reach the "upper" or easternmost trailhead follow Knob Mtn. Trail from Mathews Arm Campground. In 0.5 mi. from registration station reach trailhead on right.

To reach "lower" or western trailhead follow US 340 to Compton, about 4.5 mi. south of Bentonville and 1.8 mi. north of Rileyville. Turn east on SR 662. In 0.4 mi. turn left onto SR 697 and follow it 0.6 mi. to its end. Room for parking here but don't block driveway. First 0.2 mi. of trail is on private property and necessitates passing through barnyard. Trail access to Park boundary depends upon goodwill of landowner. Trail closures must be observed. Trail roughly follows south side of Compton Run (or Dry Run) to Park boundary. Entry from SR 697 is open but it is not recommended.

Trail Description: Knob Mtn. Trail to SR 697

0.0-4.0 Trailhead on Knob Mtn. Trail, 0.5 mi. from Mathews Arm registration station. Descend.

0.7-3.3 Junction with yellow-blazed Weddlewood Trail. (To right leads 1.3 mi. to end on Mathews Arm Trail.)

2.5-1.5 Just after crossing Compton Run reach junction with Beecher Ridge Trail, also yellow-blazed. Within next mile trail crosses run four times.

3.8-0.2 Pass gate into pasture. Continue to parallel creek until reaching barnyard.

4.0-0.0 Reach SR 697.

WEDDLEWOOD TRAIL
1.3 miles — yellow-blazed

The eastern (upper) end of this short trail is on Mathews Arm Trail 0.5 mi. north of paved campground road (1 mi. north of campground registration station) and 1 mi. south of Tuscarora-Mathews Arm Trail junction. Its western (lower) terminus is on Heiskell Hollow Trail 0.7 mi. west of latter's upper end on Knob Mtn. Trail (and 1.2 mi. from Mathews Arm Campground registration station) and 3.3 mi. east of its end on SR 697. Weddlewood Trail utilizes an old roadbed and slope is a gentle one. Thanks to this trail, one can start outside Park using either Tuscarora or Heiskell Hollow Trail and make a circuit avoiding campground area.

KNOB MOUNTAIN (JEREMYS RUN) CUTOFF TRAIL
0.5 mile — blue-blazed

This is a short trail, steep in sections, that connects Jeremys Run Trail to Knob Mtn. Trail. It is useful in circuit hikes. One end is on Knob Mtn. Trail 2.2 mi. from Mathews Arm Campground; the other is on Jeremys Run Trail 0.8 mi. from its upper end on *AT* near Elkwallow Picnic Area.

ELKWALLOW TRAIL
2.0 miles — blue-blazed

This short trail leads from Elkwallow Wayside to registration area (and parking area) of Mathews Arm Campground, roughly paralleling Skyline Drive. It crosses *AT* near edge of wayside area. It is useful in circuit hikes.

One *circuit hike*, about 5 mi., would include *AT* from

Elkwallow Gap north 2.1 mi. to its junction with Tuscarora (Overall Run) Trail. Descend Tuscarora for 0.7 mi. Turn left on spur trail toward Mathews Arm Campground. Bear left along Traces Trail, entering paved entrance road to campground at upper end of parking area. Beginning of Elkwallow Trail, indicated by signpost, is directly across entrance road. Follow this back to Elkwallow Wayside. *Another possible circuit* would include upper portions of Jeremys Run and Knob Mtn. trails, Knob Mtn. Cutoff Trail and a short stretch of *AT*.

JEREMYS RUN TRAIL
6.5 miles — blue-blazed

Jeremys Run Trail is one of the more delightful routes in the Park. From Park boundary at base of western slope of Blue Ridge, it leads up Jeremys Run in a deep gorge between two projecting spurs, Knob Mtn. and Neighbor Mtn., to the *AT* at a point 0.3 mi. from Elkwallow Picnic Area. The whole of this valley is beautifully forested; the run itself is a continual series of cascades and pools. The hiking is generally easy, with a gentle rise in elevation and numerous crossings of the stream. The exception is one very steep stretch, the lowest 0.5 mi. to Park boundary. The valley abounds with wildlife. Deer are frequently seen and bear scat can be found on the trail. Jeremys Run is considered one of the finer trout streams in the Park. Sadly, the beautiful hemlock forest at the upper reaches of Jeremys Run is dying due to the woolly adelgid infestation in the Park. There are many stream crossings of Jeremys Run along this trail.

A *circuit hike* of about 6 mi. would include 0.8 mi. of Jeremys Run Trail, Knob Mtn. Cutoff Trail, upper portion of Knob Mtn. Trail, Elkwallow Trail and 0.6 mi. stretch of *AT*.

Access: Upper and northeast end of trail can be

reached by following *AT* south 0.6 mi. from Skyline Drive crossing in Elkwallow Gap, SDMP 23.9, or by following a short trail from Elkwallow Picnic Area to *AT* and then down *AT* 0.3 mi.

Lower end of the trail can be reached by turning onto SR 611 from US 340 at Rileyville. Follow SR 611 about 2.5 mi. to bridge crossing Jeremy's Run. There is limited shoulder parking just before bridge. First 0.5 mi. of this trail is through private property and trail closures must be respected.

Trail Description: *AT* to Park boundary
0.0-6.5 Junction with *AT*.
0.8-5.7 Junction with Knob Mtn. Cutoff Trail. In 100 yd. cross first of many fords of Jeremys Run.
3.1-3.4 Cross 11th ford of creek at halfway point of trail.
4.8-1.7 Pass largest waterfalls on Jeremys Run.
5.4-1.2 Junction with Neighbor Mtn. Trail, which enters from left. Knob Mtn. Trail enters from right in 50 ft.
5.5-1.0 Cross 16th and final ford.
6.2-0.3 Park boundary.
6.5-0.0 Trail continues through private land to SR 611.

NEIGHBOR MOUNTAIN TRAIL
5.6 miles — yellow-blazed

This trail follows a high, narrow spur to the very conspicuous conical peak of The Neighbor (2,736 ft.) and then leads steeply down to Jeremys Run. It offers a very delightful short walk from the *AT*. It involves only moderate climbing and leads through a very pleasing forest growth with fine views west and north over the deep gulch of Jeremys Run and Knob Mtn. The summit of The Neighbor is wooded. Those with sharp eyes might spot one of the few stands of white birch that occurs in the Park along the middle part of the ridge, looking north. This is one of the most southern occurrences of this species.

A *circuit hike* of 13.6 mi. can be made by following Neighbor Mtn. Trail to Jeremys Run Trail, then right (uphill) on Jeremys Run Trail to *AT* and *AT* south back to starting point.

Access: Upper end of this trail is on Skyline Drive, SDMP 28.1, directly across from Hull School Trail, also yellow-blazed. Hikers may prefer to park in grassy Neighbor Mtn. Trail Parking Area, SDMP 26.8, and either follow short spur trail to *AT* and thence south along *AT* for 0.3 mi. to Neighbor Mtn. Trail junction; or they can follow the "spur" horse trail, yellow-blazed, for 0.3 mi. from parking area to Neighbor Mtn. Trail.

Trail Description: Skyline Drive to Jeremys Run

0.0-5.6 From Skyline Drive, SDMP 28.1, opposite Hull School Trail, Neighbor Mtn. Trail follows service road toward Byrds Nest #4.

0.1-5.5 Blue-blazed trail leads left 0.1 mi. to *AT*.

0.4-5.2 Turn right off service road and circle east and north of Byrds Nest #4. Day use shelter; no camping.

0.9-4.7 Yellow-blazed spur trail leads 0.3 mi. to Neighbor Mtn. Trail Parking Area.

1.0-4.6 Concrete post marks intersection with *AT*. (Via *AT* it is 3.9 mi. north to Elkwallow Picnic Area and 1.2 mi. south to Beahms Gap.)

2.0-3.6 Pass curious rocks known as "The Gendarmes."

2.9-2.7 Peak of The Neighbor. Trail now descends steeply with switchbacks.

4.7-0.9 Spur trail leads right 50 ft. to Dripping Spring.

5.6-0.0 Jeremys Run Trail. (To left it is 0.8 mi. to Park boundary; to right it is 5.4 mi. to *AT*.)

ROCKY BRANCH TRAIL
3.2 miles — yellow-blazed

From its trailhead 50 ft. west of Skyline Drive, SDMP 28.1, on the Hull School Trail, this trail heads south, crossing the *AT* in 0.4 mi. Two miles from its start it crosses the Drive and descends eastward. It ends on SR 666 at a point on road where state maintenance begins.

To reach lower terminus, turn off US 211 just west of SNP Headquarters onto SR 674. Turn right in 0.2 mi. onto SR 658; in 0.4 mi. turn left onto SR 612. Follow SR 612 for 1.3 mi. then turn right onto SR 666 and continue to end of drivable road and park. (Room for one or two cars; do not block driveway.) Blazes begin in several hundred yards when trail enters Park.

PASS MOUNTAIN TRAIL
3.0 miles — blue-blazed

This trail starts on the *AT* 1.2 mi. north of Thornton Gap and furnishes access to Pass Mtn. Hut. It continues eastward following an old woods road, descending to a deep sag between Pass Mtn. and Oventop Mtn. Here it turns sharply right and descends to US 211, reaching it approximately 4.5 mi. west of Sperryville and 2.5 mi. east of Thornton Gap.

Trail Description: *AT* to US 211

0.0-3.0 Junction with *AT* 1.2 mi. north of Thornton Gap and 1.9 mi. south of Beahms Gap, SDMP 28.6.

0.2-2.8 Bear to right of Pass Mtn. Hut. (Hut is for use of overnight hikers.)

0.5-2.5 Come to old road and follow it downhill.

2.4-0.6 Trail turns 90 degrees to right. Pass Mtn. Trail now follows route of former Butterwood Branch Trail and descends along an old road.

3.0-0.0 End of trail at US 211.

Central District - Side Trails

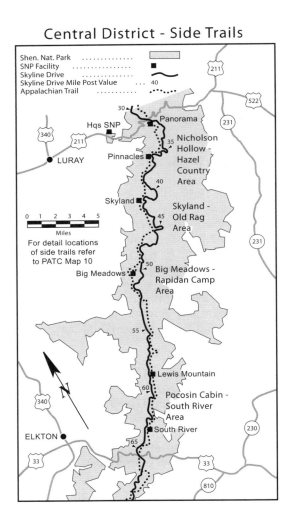

Shen. Nat. Park ....
SNP Facility ....
Skyline Drive ....
Skyline Drive Mile Post Value ... 40
Appalachian Trail ....

211

522

231

30

Panorama

Hqs SNP

340

211

Nicholson
Hollow -
Hazel
Country
Area

35

LURAY

Pinnacles

40

Skyland

Skyland -
Old Rag
Area

45

231

0 1 2 3 4 5

Miles

For detail locations
of side trails refer
to PATC Map 10

50

Big Meadows

Big Meadows -
Rapidan Camp
Area

55

N

Lewis Mountain

60

340

Pocosin Cabin -
South River
Area

65

ELKTON

South River

230

33

33

810

SIDE TRAILS
CENTRAL DISTRICT
Shenandoah National Park

View from Rattlesnake Point   *Photo by John F. Mitchell*

BUCK HOLLOW TRAIL
3.0 miles — blue-blazed

Frequently traveled due to its lower access from US 211, just 0.5 mi. inside Park boundary, trail for the most part follows several old roadbeds. After climbing about 500 ft. in elevation, and at midpoint of trail, path leads through a wild gorge where stream, flowing through Buck Hollow, cascades over and among large boulders. Second half of climb is more strenuous, rising another 1,300 ft. in elevation, before ending at a paved parking area on Skyline Drive (Meadow Spring Parking Area, SDMP 33.4). A *circuit hike* of 6.3 mi. can be made by hiking up this trail (3.0 mi.) and returning via Hazel Mountain Trail (0.4 mi.), Buck Ridge Trail (2.7 mi.), and retracing lower part of Buck Hollow Trail (0.2 mi.).

Access: Lower trailhead is on US 211, 3.4 mi. west of intersection of US 211 and US 522 in Sperryville; it is 4.6 mi. east of Thornton Gap.

Upper end is on Skyline Drive, SDMP 33.4. Park in Meadow Spring Parking Area on east side of Drive.

Trail Description: US 211 to *AT* (N to S)

0.0-3.0 From US 211 pass through flat brushy area.

0.1-2.9 Cross Thornton River and in 50 yd. cross Buck Hollow stream. Fords may be difficult just after heavy rains.

0.2-2.8 Buck Ridge Trail leads left 2.6 mi., climbing very steeply to Hazel Mtn. Trail and joining it 0.4 mi. from Skyline Drive.

0.4-2.6 Cross Buck Hollow stream. Trail now continues up valley at various distances from bank.

1.3-1.7 Cross Buck Hollow stream, and in continuing upstream along right bank, immediately cross a tributary. Next 250 yd. are gorge-like, with very steeply sloping mountainsides.

1.6-1.4 Trail turns left and climbs away from stream.

1.9-1.1 For next 0.6 mi. hemlocks, the predominant growth, died in the mid-1990s, so there is very little shade on sunny days.

2.6-0.4 Cross Buck Hollow stream (intermittent at this elevation).

3.0-0.0 South edge of Meadow Spring Parking Area, SDMP 33.4. (To reach *AT*, cross Drive diagonally to Meadow Spring Trail.)

MEADOW SPRING TRAIL
0.7 mile — blue-blazed

This short trail connects the *AT* and Skyline Drive at SDMP 33.4. From the *AT* it descends east steeply, levels out in the middle, passing Meadow Spring on the left, and continues its steep descent through mountain laurel to Skyline Drive across from the Meadow Spring Parking Area. The level portion of the trail has an old chimney, which was the site of a former PATC cabin that burned down in 1946.

BUCK RIDGE TRAIL
2.7 miles — blue-blazed

This trail has its lower end on the Buck Hollow Trail, about 0.2 mi. from the lower end of the latter on US 211. Its upper end is on the Hazel Mtn. Trail about 0.4 mi. from Skyline Drive, SDMP 33.4. Starting at Hazel Mountain Trail, the trail generally follows east through level forest, then bending northeast, descends steeply along an outlying ridge of "Hazel Country," occasionally passing through thick stands of mountain laurel. There is a restricted view to the east at the midpoint on this trail. Near the end of the ridge, the trail drops very steeply (35 degree incline in some places) to connect with the Buck Hollow Trail. There is no water along this route. It can be used along with the Buck Hollow and Hazel Mtn. trails for an excellent *circuit hike.*

LEADING RIDGE TRAIL
1.3 miles — blue-blazed

This trail leads northwest from Skyline Drive, SDMP 36.2, and crosses the *AT* in a few hundred feet. It then climbs to a small knob about 0.1 mi. west of the *AT* intersection before descending steeply along a ridge, finally coming into Jewell Hollow and passing through private property to reach SR 669. To reach the trail from the valley, turn south from US 211 about 1 mi. east of Park Headquarters and 2.5 mi. west of Thornton Gap. In 0.5 mi. turn left onto SR 669 and drive about 0.8 mi. Access across private land at the Park boundary is by goodwill of landowner. Posted closures must be respected.

CRUSHER RIDGE TRAIL
2.4 miles — blue-blazed

This trail starts on the Nicholson Hollow Trail a few feet west of Skyline Drive and heads north along Crusher Ridge, following an old road once known as Sours Lane. It crosses the *AT* about 0.1 mi. from the Drive. After 0.4 mi. it begins descent into Shaver Hollow, reaching the Park boundary 2.4 mi. from the start. The trail can be reached from PATC Tulip Tree Cabin and the Lambert Cabin 0.3 mi. beyond boundary.

NICHOLSON HOLLOW-HAZEL COUNTRY TRAIL NETWORK

This area was well populated before the creation of SNP. Now most of the old cabins are gone, but a few ruins can be seen along the trails. Corbin Cabin, on the Nicholson Hollow Trail, has been restored and is maintained in good condition by the PATC. It is available for use by hikers but reservations must be made in advance at PATC Headquarters. The cabin has been listed on the National Register of Historic Places. Its location is ideal for anyone wanting to explore the many trails of the area.

Most of the present trails were originally roads that served the mountain community. There are many other signs of the formerly well-populated area—small orchards, rock walls and the remains of chestnut rail fences, walled springs, even bits of rusting metal. Sometimes one discovers an old family cemetery, where the only markers are thin slabs of local rock set vertically into the ground. Very often periwinkle was planted around the graves, and its bright shiny greenery helps one spot the cemetery plots today.

Nicholson Hollow was named after the Nicholson clan that had homes along the Hughes River. It was also called "Free State" Hollow, reputedly because law enforcement officers avoided entering the hollow because of its ill-tempered and lawless inhabitants. George F. Pollock, in his book *Skyland*, gives a vivid if not entirely accurate description of some of the Nicholsons who lived here. (Recent studies of this area and the Nicholson clan suggest that they were quite different from the way G. F. Pollock describes them in his book and that the term "Free State" may have been a fabrication by Pollock to enhance the appeal of the area to his guests at Skyland.) The old USGS Stony Man quadrangle map, surveyed in 1927, indicated the location of many of the mountain cabins. A series of articles by H.T. Dockerty, published in the Washington Times and preserved in the PATC scrap books, recorded many legends of Nicholson (Free State) Hollow. All artifacts of former residents are protected by law. Please leave them undisturbed for future archaeological study.

Three major trails cross through the area—the Nicholson Hollow Trail that leads up the Hughes River, the Hannah Run Trail and the Hazel Mtn. Trail. Other trails in the area include the Catlett Mtn. Trail, Hot-Short Mtn. Trail, Sams Ridge Trail, Broad Hollow Trail, Corbin Cabin Cutoff Trail, Corbin Mtn. Trail, Catlett Spur Trail and Indian Run Trail, all blue-blazed; also White Rocks Trail,

Hazel River Trail and Pine Hill Gap Trail which are yellow-blazed horse/foot trails. See PATC Map #10 and PATC publication *Circuit Hikes in Shenandoah National Park.*

NICHOLSON HOLLOW TRAIL
5.8 miles — blue-blazed

This trail leads down through the hollow formed by the Hughes River. Corbin Cabin, located on the Nicholson Hollow Trail, was the pre-SNP home of George Corbin. The trail runs in a generally southeast direction to SR 600 at its junction with the old Weakley Hollow Road, following in a steady downhill slope until the trail reaches the confluence of the Hughes River and Brokenback Run. Wading may be required in crossing Brokenback Run and Hughes River fords when the water is high.

Trails connecting with the Nicholson Hollow Trail include: Hannah Run Trail, Hot-Short Mtn. Trail, Corbin Mtn. Trail, Indian Run Trail and Corbin Cabin Cutoff Trail, all blue-blazed.

Access: Upper end of Nicholson Hollow Trail is on east side of Skyline Drive at SDMP 38.4, and is marked by a concrete post. Parking is in Stony Man Overlook-Hughes River Gap Parking Area 0.2 mi. farther south.

Lower end is reached from VA 231. Turn west onto SR 601 or 602 then SR 707 to Nethers. Bear left onto SR 600 to 250-car Old Rag parking area on left. Continue on foot 0.4 mi. west on SR 600 to the Nicholson Hollow Trailhead. Area may be crowded on weekends. *Cars parked along the road or on private property are subject to towing.*

Trail Description: Skyline Drive to SR 600 (W to E)
0.0-5.8 From trailhead, descend bank and turn left along an old road which leads through area of scrub oak and laurel, then descends.
0.4-5.4 To right of trail is walled-in Dale Spring.

1.6-4.2 Cross creek.

1.7-4.1 Indian Run Trail leads right to Corbin Mtn. Trail. Nicholson Hollow Trail continues downhill, soon following Hughes River.

1.8-4.0 Corbin Cabin Cutoff Trail leads left 1.4 mi. to Skyline Drive, SDMP 37.9. (Corbin Cabin is to right.)

1.9-3.9 Pass overgrown field on right. This was once site of Madison Corbin's cabin.

2.0-3.8 Old road leads left to Hughes River. Just below road, across river, are ruins of Aaron Nicholson's cabin.

3.4-2.4 Cross to left side of Hughes River at base of deep pool.

3.9-1.9 Hannah Run Trail leads left 3.7 mi. to Skyline Drive, SDMP 35.1.

4.0-1.8 Cross Hannah Run.

4.1-1.7 Hot-Short Mtn. Trail, left, follows old road up valley between Short Mtn. and Hot Mtn. reaching Hazel Mtn. Trail in 2.1 mi.

4.5-1.3 Corbin Mtn. Trail leads right across Hughes River, then climbs 4.4 mi. to end at Old Rag Fire Road.

5.0-0.8 Walled-in spring to left of trail.

5.5-0.3 Leave SNP. The next 0.5 mi. is on private property. Stay on the trail.

5.7-0.1 Cross to right of Hughes River and 150 ft. farther cross Brokenback Run. Beyond, turn left onto dirt road.

5.8-0.0 SR 600, at its intersection with Weakley Hollow Road.

HANNAH RUN TRAIL
3.8 miles — blue-blazed

This trail descends steeply from Skyline Drive to the Nicholson Hollow Trail on the Hughes River. All told, the trail drops a total of about 2,000 ft. over its length. It passes the ruins of several old mountain cabins along the lower half. A *circuit hike* can be made by using the Catlett Mtn. Trail, Hazel Mtn. Trail, Hot-Short Mtn. Trail and

Nicholson Hollow Trail. *Another circuit* may be started by leaving car at Pinnacles Overlook and following trail down to Nicholson Hollow Trail. Follow Nicholson Hollow Trail 2.1 mi. to Corbin Cabin then take Corbin Cabin Cutoff Trail 1.5 mi. to Drive. Directly across Drive short spur trail connects with *AT*. Follow *AT* north 1.2 mi., turning off on spur trail, which leads few feet to Jewell Hollow Parking Overlook. From here it is 1.3 mi. along Drive to your car, for total distance of just under 10 mi.

Access: Upper terminus is on east side of Skyline Drive, SDMP 35.1, at Pinnacles Overlook Parking Area.

Lower terminus is on Nicholson Hollow Trail, 1.9 mi. from its lower end on SR 600.

Trail Description: Skyline Drive to Nicholson Hollow Trail

0.0-3.8 Pinnacles Overlook Parking Area. Trail descends steeply with switchbacks. Wintertime views to east over Hazel Country, with Hazel Mtn. as dominant feature.

1.3-2.5 Trail intersection in deep sag, with low knob ahead. Catlett Mtn. Trail leads 1.2 mi. to Hazel Mtn. Trail. Hannah Run Trail turns sharply right and again descends.

1.7-2.1 Trail is exceedingly steep, dropping 500 ft. in 0.2 mi.

1.9-1.9 Cross Hannah Run. After climbing out of ravine, pass ruins of cabin on right.

2.3-1.5 Pass between ruins of cabins. *Spring* and an old apple orchard on right. Trail descends along Hannah Run but does not cross it.

3.8-0.0 Cross small stream; in 200 ft. reach Nicholson Hollow Trail. (To left via Nicholson Hollow Trail it is 0.2 mi. to Hot-Short Mtn. Trail, 0.6 mi. to Corbin Mtn. Trail and 1.9 mi. to its lower end at SR 600. To right it is 2.1 mi. to Corbin Cabin and 1.8 mi. farther to Skyline Drive; via Corbin Cabin Cutoff Trail it is 1.5 mi. to Drive.)

HAZEL MOUNTAIN TRAIL
4.1 miles — yellow-blazed

For the first 2 mi. the trail descends gently along one branch of the Hazel River, passing the Buck Ridge Trail and White Rocks Trail along the way. It then curves south, crossing the end of a small ridge, and drops down to a crossing of Runyon Run and intersection with the Catlett Spur Trail. Curving southeast, the trail then begins a steady ascent along a spur branch of the Hazel River, passing the Hazel River Trail. The trail eventually tops out near the Sams Ridge Trail on the Hazel plateau as it curves to the southwest. The old Hazel School which served the area in pre-Shenandoah National Park days was situated near this trail intersection. From here, the trail is basically level for another 1.5 mi. as it follows through beautiful forest on the Hazel plateau. Note the stands of dead oak that were killed by the gypsy moths in this area. Also, those with good eyes might spot pink lady's slippers along this stretch in season.

Access: Upper end is on Skyline Drive, SDMP 33.4. Trail begins at south end of Meadow Spring Parking Area on east side of Drive, marked with concrete post.

Lower end is at junction of Hot-Short Mountain Trail and Pine Hill Gap Trail. To reach lower end via Pine Hill Gap Trail, from VA 231 turn west onto SR 681 or SR 707 from Nethers. Drive as far as you can drive, then continue on foot through private land to Gap.

Trail Description: Skyline Drive to Pine Hill Gap Trail and Hot-Short Mountain Trail

0.0-4.1 Skyline Drive, SDMP 33.4. Trail gated at Drive.

0.4-3.7 Where trail turns sharply to right, Buck Ridge Trail leads northeast down ridge to Buck Hollow Trail.

1.6-2.5 At fork, take right branch. (Left fork is White Rocks Trail leading to Hazel River Trail.)

1.7-2.4 Cross branch of Hazel River.

2.2-1.9 Junction with Catlett Spur Trail leading right to Catlett Mtn. Trail. Immediately beyond junction, ford Runyon Run, then in 250 ft. ford a second creek; both are branches of Hazel River. Old road now climbs, paralleling last creek.

2.9-1.2 Junction with Hazel River Trail leading left to Park boundary. Beyond junction, trail passes to right of bulk of Hazel Mtn.

3.1-1.0 Concrete post marks junction with Sams Ridge-Broad Hollow trails, which are coincident here. (Sams Ridge Trail leads east to SR 600; Broad Hollow Trail leads southeast to SR 681.)

3.6-0.5 Junction with Catlett Mtn. Trail, leading right to Hannah Run Trail.

4.1-0.0 Junction with Hot-Short Mtn. Trail leading to right, and Pine Hill Gap Trail continuing straight ahead.

CORBIN CABIN CUTOFF TRAIL
1.4 miles — blue-blazed

This is the shortest route from Skyline Drive to Corbin Cabin. It is an old, old trail used by the mountain residents in Nicholson Hollow long before there was a Skyline Drive. The trail is quite steep, descending 1,000 ft. in 1.4 mi.

Access: Trail begins on Skyline Drive, directly across from Corbin Cabin Parking Area, SDMP 37.9.

Lower end is on Nicholson Hollow Trail.

Trail Description: Skyline Drive to Nicholson Hollow Trail

0.0-1.4 From Skyline Drive, descend along blue-blazed trail.

0.5-0.9 Trail turns sharply to left.

0.7-0.7 Trail switchbacks to right. Footway is rough and rocky for next 250 ft.

1.1-0.3 Path leads right 180 ft. to graveyard. Only

unmarked, upended stones mark graves, as is true of most old family cemeteries in Park.

1.4-0.0 Cross Hughes River and come to Nicholson Hollow Trail just below Corbin Cabin, which is to right. (Corbin Cabin was once home of George Corbin and is typical of mountain cabins [though one of the smallest] which were once numerous in hollows. It has been restored by PATC and may be rented by hikers.)

SAMS RIDGE TRAIL
2.2 miles — blue-blazed

This trail is one of the trails leading into Hazel Country from east of the mountains. For its entire length, it follows an old woods road. The eastern half of the trail is quite steep. Those wishing an easier *circuit hike* can use the Hazel River Trail and Hazel Mountain Trail to reach the western end of the trail. There are a few old homesites and overgrown fields along the trail, and the middle portion has a number of dead stands of oaks due to gypsy moth damage. There are very nice wintertime views of Hazel Mountain and the Hazel River drainage as you descend the ridge.

A short *circuit hike* can be made by using this trail in combination with either Broad Hollow Trail, Hazel River Trail or Pine Hill Gap Trail, all of which have their upper ends on the Hazel Mtn. Trail and their lower ends on either SR 681 or SR 600, which forks from SR 681.

Access: From VA 231 turn west onto SR 681 just north of bridge over Hazel River. Follow SR 681 about 1 mi. to road fork. Take right fork, which is SR 600, and continue about 1 mi. to where SR 600 crosses Hazel River. Walking begins here.

Trail Description: SR 600 to Hazel Mtn Trail (E to W) **0.0-2.2** From SR 600 follow old road up south side of

Hazel River. "No Trespassing" signs are for property to left, not road, which may be used by equestrians and hikers.

0.4-1.8 Park boundary. Trail turns left away from road. (Road inside Park becomes Hazel River Trail, yellow-blazed.) Trail now tends away from Park, climbing slope of ridge through private property, then following crest of ridge.

0.6-1.6 Enter Park, continuing up Sams Ridge.

1.5-0.7 Pass site of mountaineer home. Stone foundation, scattered apple trees and rose bushes are only evidence of former habitation. Good view north of Hazel River Valley. *Spring* 200 ft. to left of trail.

2.0-0.2 Junction with Broad Hollow Trail coming in from left. From here two trails are coincident.

2.2-0.0 Junction of Sams Ridge-Broad Hollow Trail with Hazel Mtn. Trail. (To left it is 0.5 mi. to Catlett Mtn. Trail, 1 mi. to Hot-Short Mtn. Trail and Pine Hill Gap Trail. To right it is 0.2 mi. to Hazel River Trail and 1.5 mi. to White Rocks Trail.) The old Hazel School was located near this junction. *Spring* is 200 ft. to right of junction down abandoned Sams Run Trail.

HAZEL RIVER TRAIL
3.4 miles — yellow-blazed

This horse/foot trail following an old road offers yet another route into Hazel Country from the east. It follows the Hazel River upstream, with its numerous tumbling cascades, for over 1 mi. Leaving the stream, it swings left up a branch of the Hazel River and climbs steadily, and in some places steeply, along an old woods road. The trail eventually levels out some before rising and crossing over a shoulder of Hazel Mtn. to reach its upper end on the Hazel Mtn. Trail. Be prepared to wade the river at trail crossings after heavy rains.

Access: From VA 231 turn west onto SR 681 to fork, then right onto SR 600. Drive about 1 mi. to crossing of

Hazel River. "No Trespassing" signs are for property to left, not road, which may be used by equestrians and hikers.

Trail Description: SR 600 to Hazel Mtn. Trail (E to W)

0.0-3.4 From Hazel River follow private road up south side of river. (Blazes do not begin until Park boundary.) Where road turns right and crosses river, *stay* on south side of river.

0.4-3.0 Enter Park. Sams Ridge Trail turns left just beyond here.

0.9-2.5 Within next 0.6 mi. trail crosses river four times (difficult when water is high).

1.8-1.6 Trail junction. At concrete marker, Hazel River Trail turns left up a side creek and climbs. (To the right is White Rocks Trail, which soon crosses river and climbs 2.4 mi. to end on Hazel Mtn. Trail.)

3.4-0.0 Junction with Hazel Mtn. Trail 0.2 mi. northwest of Sams Ridge-Broad Hollow Trail junction and 1.3 mi. south of junction with White Rocks Trail.

BROAD HOLLOW TRAIL
2.4 miles — blue-blazed

Like Sams Ridge Trail, this trail offers access into Hazel Country from the east. It ascends about 1,400 ft., with its lower end on SR 681 and its upper end coincident with Sams Ridge Trail. It passes several abandoned cabins along the route.

A *circuit hike* can be made when this trail is used in combination with Sams Ridge Trail, Hazel Mtn. Trail and Pine Hill Gap Trail.

Access: From VA 231 turn west onto SR 681, just north of bridge over Hazel River. Follow SR 681 about 2.5 mi. to trailhead on right of road, which is 20 yds. to right of a private driveway where SR 681 turns sharply to the left.

Trail Description: SR 681 to Hazel Mtn. Trail (E to W)

0.0-2.4 Junction with SR 681. In about 50 ft. trail crosses Broad Hollow Run. In another 250 ft. old road takes off to right of trail.

0.3-2.1 Trail crosses run.

0.5-1.9 Trail recrosses run, continuing up hollow.

0.7-1.7 Two old trails, about 250 ft. apart, lead left to remains of two log buildings. Continue to ascend steeply, with several sharp turns in trail.

1.0-1.4 Pass rocked-up *spring* and, 150 ft. beyond, a ruined cabin with shingled sides.

1.5-0.9 Pass roofless cabin and another in about 0.25 mi.

2.1-0.3 Unmarked trail leads left about 0.2 mi. to Hazel Mtn. Trail, coming into latter about 0.2 mi. north of Catlett Mtn. Trail junction.

2.2-0.2 Junction with Sams Ridge Trail coming in from right. Two trails coincide for next 0.2 mi.

2.4-0.0 Junction with Hazel Mtn. Trail near site of old Hazel School. (To left it is 0.5 mi. to Catlett Mtn. Trail, 1 mi. to Hot-Short Mtn. Trail and Pine Hill Gap Trail. To right it is 0.2 mi. to Hazel River Trail and 1.5 mi. to White Rocks Trail. *Spring* is 200 ft. to right of junction, down abandoned Sams Run Trail.)

PINE HILL GAP TRAIL
2.1 miles — yellow-blazed

This trail leads from Pine Hill Gap to the junction of Hazel Mtn. Trail and Hot-Short Mtn. Trail. To reach the lower end at Pine Hill Gap, drive up SR 681 and park at the Broad Hollow Trailhead. Walk along old road 0.6 mi. to trailhead. This trail is useful for circuit hikes.

HOT-SHORT MOUNTAIN TRAIL
2.1 miles — blue-blazed

This is an interesting stretch of trail along the valley between Hot and Short mountains. It connects the Nicholson Hollow Trail with the Hazel Mtn. Trail. From its lower end this trail involves a considerable climb, with a change in elevation of about 1,300 ft. It follows up a stream much of the way, utilizing old roads and passing several old homesites.

Trail Description: Nicholson Hollow Trail to Hazel Mtn. Trail

0.0-2.1 This trail begins on Nicholson Hollow Trail 1.7 mi. from latter's intersection with SR 600, where it is joined by Weakley Hollow Road.

0.1-2.0 Turn left and follow trail between stone walls. From here trail ascends.

0.4-1.7 Continue to ascend along a road, with ravine to left.

0.7-1.4 Outcropping of rocks with splendid view of Corbin Mtn. and Robertson Mtn. across Nicholson Hollow.

0.9-1.2 Notice old home site across stream to left. In 200 ft. cross stream and follow it up. In another 250 ft. turn sharp left and ascend steeply. Turn right and cross overgrown clearing.

1.3-0.8 Cross stream and continue to ascend.

1.4-0.7 Trail leads through overgrown field with apple trees. To right is view of Hot Mtn.

1.6-0.5 Cross stream again.

1.9-0.2 Old chimney worthy of notice about 100 ft. to right of trail.

2.0-0.1 Enter old road and continue through level section.

2.1-0.0 Junction, to left on Hazel Mtn. Trail. It is 0.5 mi. to Catlett Mtn. Trail, 1 mi. to Broad Hollow-Sams Ridge Trail and 4.1 mi. to Skyline Drive. To right onto

Pine Hill Gap Trail, it is 2.1 mi. to Park boundary and trails leading to SR 600.

CATLETT MOUNTAIN TRAIL
1.2 miles — blue-blazed

This trail connects the Hannah Run Trail with the Hazel Mtn. Trail. It affords a pleasant, fairly level walk along the north slope of Catlett Mtn. through woods, abandoned orchards and small clearings before dropping down to a branch of Runyon Run and climbing up to the Hazel Mountain Trail. Turkeys are present in the area, and if you listen closely, you might be lucky enough to hear one gobbling back in the woods.

A *circuit hike* of 10 mi. could start at end of SR 600, west of Nethers. Follow Nicholson Hollow Trail for 1.7 mi. then Hot-Short Mtn. Trail for 2.1 mi. Turn left on Hazel Mtn. Trail and follow it 0.5 mi. to Catlett Mtn. Trail. Follow Catlett Mtn. Trail 1.2 mi. to Hannah Run Trail, Hannah Run Trail 2.5 mi. to Nicholson Hollow Trail, then 1.9 mi. down this trail back to SR 600.

Trail Description: Hannah Run Trail to Hazel Mtn. Trail

0.0-1.2 Junction with Hannah Run Trail 1.2 mi. from Skyline Drive. Follow old roadbed, descending slightly. In 200 ft. reach another trail junction and turn right. (Catlett Spur Trail leads straight ahead to Hazel Mtn. Trail.)

0.1-1.1 Bear right around a pit; remnants of old stone wall to right of trail. Climb gently.

0.3-0.9 Cross worn road. For some distance trail is level; summit of Catlett Mtn. is to right of trail.

0.7-0.5 Trail crosses shoulder of Catlett Mtn. From here it descends gradually through pine and abandoned orchard.

1.0-0.2 Cross stream and ascend.

1.2-0.0 Junction with Hazel Mtn. Trail 0.5 mi. north of Hot-Short Mtn. Trail and 1.5 mi. southwest of junction with Sams Ridge-Broad Hollow Trail.

CATLETT SPUR TRAIL
1.1 miles — blue-blazed

One end of this trail is on the Catlett Mtn. Trail, a short distance from the Hannah Run Trail; the other is on the Hazel Mtn. Trail. The Catlett Spur Trail starts in mature oak forest and descends steadily from the Hanna Run Trail, following an old woods road. In places, old split rail fences may be seen, now long fallen. The lower half of the trail continues descending and, before reaching the Hazel Mountain Trail, passes the stone fences of an old home site on the right.

Follow Hannah Run Trail from Skyline Drive; reach junction with Catlett Mtn. Trail in 1.2 mi. (Hannah Run Trail turns right.) Follow Catlett Mtn. Trail straight ahead for about 200 ft. At trail junction, marked by metal post, Catlett Mtn. Trail turns right, whereas the Catlett Spur Trail goes straight ahead. It descends gently along Runyon Run, coming into the Hazel Mtn. Trail 2.2 mi. east of Skyline Drive. This end of the Catlett Spur Trail is 1.4 mi. nearer the Drive than the Catlett Mtn.-Hazel Mtn. Trail junction.

WHITE ROCKS TRAIL
2.4 miles — yellow-blazed

This horse/foot trail leads east from the Hazel Mtn. Trail. It is one of five routes down the mountain from the Hazel Mtn. Trail to the eastern Park boundary. A *circuit hike* can be made using this trail in combination with any one of the other four—Hazel River, Sams Ridge, Broad Hollow or Pine Hill Gap Trail.

Trail Description: Hazel Mtn. Trail to Hazel River Trail
0.0-2.4 Follow old roadbed (former Old Hazel Rd.).
0.9-1.5 Trail follows crest of White Rocks ridge.
1.4-1.0 White Rocks to right of trail. Continue along crest, then begin descent.
2.1-0.3 In gap, turn right and descend to Hazel River.

2.3-0.1 Cross Hazel River.

2.4-0.0 End of trail on Hazel River Trail.

TRAILS IN THE SKYLAND-OLD RAG AREA

Skyland is situated almost in the center of Shenandoah National Park. The story of Skyland's early days, from about 1888 to the formation of SNP in the 1935, and of its charismatic founder, George Freeman Pollock, has given the whole area around Skyland a romantic aura. Who can't help smiling at the thought of Pollock's guests, elegant Washingtonians, rubbing elbows with rough mountain characters such as those who lived in the mountain hollow once known as "Free State"? But what is Skyland today? Lodging units, dining hall, cottages and dormitories, a conference hall, stables and much, much more.

At the northern entrance to Skyland, Skyline Drive reaches its highest elevation, 3,680 ft. Surrounding Skyland is as great a variety of fascinating places to explore as one could ask for. To start, listing them in clockwise order, there is the "Free State" Hollow (Nicholson Hollow), which legend states, perhaps inaccurately, was once home of the reputedly fierce and lawless Corbins and Nicholsons; then unique Old Rag Mtn., with its ragged top and extraordinary views; next, magnificent Whiteoak Canyon, with its series of cascades; Hawksbill Mtn., which towers over the rest of the Park; fearsome Kettle Canyon, immediately below Skyland; and lastly, Stony Man Mtn., whose "profile" is visible when traveling south along the Drive. Small wonder that the Park's most popular trails are here.

STONY MAN TRAIL
(and *AT* to Little Stony Man)
1.3 miles plus 0.4-mile loop
marked by signs and white blazes of *AT*

Attention: Pets are not permitted on this trail except with long-distance AT hikers.

The Park Service has constructed a self-guiding trail leading from the Stony Man Trail Parking Area to Stony Man Mtn., where the trail loops around the summit and offers a view from the top of the cliffs that form the Stony Man's profile. The self-guiding trail and *AT* are coincident here.

The cliffs of Stony Man and Little Stony Man are the weathered remnants of ancient beds of lava. (See "Geology of SNP.") From 1845 to the turn of the century, a copper mine operated near the top of Stony Man Mtn. Overgrown culm banks and tree-masked workings on the cliff face, with green rock showing the presence of copper, mark the place. The ore was smelted at Furnace Spring, the site of which is on the Passamaquoddy Trail just north of Skyland. After operations were discontinued the mine was still a spot of much interest to visitors. The shaft, however, became a hazard and was filled in. There is now no trail to the spot.

A *circuit hike* can be made by starting at the Stony Man Trail Parking Area and following the self-guiding trail (also *AT*) to Stony Man. Continue on *AT* past Stony Man 0.6 mi. to Little Stony Man. Descend and branch left onto Passamaquoddy Trail. After 1 mi. turn left onto yellow-blazed Furnace Spring horse trail leading back to Stony Man Trail Parking Area.

Access: Stony Man Trail Parking Area is on Skyline Drive, SDMP 41.7, at northern entrance to Skyland. Northern approach is from Little Stony Man Parking area,

SDMP 39.1. Follow *AT*, white-blazed, 0.3 mi. to start of Little Stony Man Trail.

Trail Description: Trail Parking Area to Little Stony Man Parking Area (S to N)

0.0-1.3 Stony Man Trail Parking Area. Follow white blazes of *AT*.

0.4-0.9 Trail junction. Straight ahead self-guiding trail continues and in 250 ft. starts 0.4 mi. loop around summit of Stony Man Mtn. Turn right here to continue on toward Little Stony Man, following white blazes.

0.8-0.5 Cliffs of Little Stony Man Mtn. Passamaquoddy Trail is directly below cliffs. From here trail descends steeply by switchbacks.

1.0-0.3 Junction with Passamaquoddy Trail. Follow white-blazed *AT* to parking area.

1.3-0.0 Little Stony Man Parking Area, SDMP 39.1.

PASSAMAQUODDY TRAIL
1.2 miles — blue-blazed

This is a slight relocation of the original Passamaquoddy Trail laid out by George Freeman Pollock in 1932. Until 1990 it was used as the route for the *AT*. (Passamaquoddy is a Maine Indian word meaning "abounding in pollock.")

The northern end is on the *AT*, 0.3 mi. south of Little Stony Man Parking Area, SDMP 39.1. Passamaquoddy Trail takes right fork at concrete post, then follows base of rocky cliffs. Its southern end is at end of pavement behind Skyland Dining Room.

Trail Description: North to South

0.0-1.2 From intersection with *AT*, take right fork at concrete post. Follow ledge below Little Stony Man cliffs, with excellent views.

0.9-0.3 Pass Skyland power line and housed Furnace

Spring 25 ft. to left of trail. In 200 ft. turn left onto former Skyland Road. Yellow-blazed Furnace Spring Trail bears left here.

1.0-0.2 Turn left off road at signpost. Ascend through woods.

1.1-0.1 Cross paved Skyland Road and continue through woods.

1.2-0.0 Follow paved path to left, uphill, to Skyland Dining Hall.

STONY MAN HORSE TRAIL
0.6 mile — yellow-blazed

This trail begins just beyond the Stony Man Trail Parking Area, SDMP 41.7, at northern entrance to Skyland, and climbs to the top of Stony Man Mtn.

MILLERS HEAD TRAIL
0.8 mile — blue-blazed

This short but rewarding trail leads over Bushytop Mtn. and out the ridge to a lower peak known as Millers Head. The ridge forms the southern wall of the deep Kettle Canyon. A stone platform on Millers Head offers a superb view of the Shenandoah Valley, Massanutten Mtn. and mountains farther west, Kettle Canyon, the buildings of Skyland, and, to the southwest, Buracher Hollow. No trails link up with Millers Head, so the hike is an "in and out."

Access: Park at southern entrance to Skyland, SDMP 42.5 and walk up Skyland road toward stables (left fork) only a few feet to reach *AT*. Follow *AT* to right until it crosses paved Skyland Road. Turn left along road for 200 ft. Sign indicates start of Millers Head Trail.

Trail Description: Skyland Road to Millers Head

0.0 Trail sign on paved Skyland Road. (Gravel road to left of trail rejoins trail on summit of Bushytop, where it ends.)

0.2 Summit of Bushytop. (Microwave installation here.) For excellent viewpoint to right, continue 100 ft. farther along trail. Kettle Canyon is below and the Skyland buildings are quite visible above canyon.

0.8 Reach Millers Head.

SKYLAND FIRE ROAD
3.2 miles — yellow-blazed

As one walks this road it is fun to imagine what a trip to the "top of the mountain" was like in Pollock's day, when it was barely usable for horse-drawn vehicles. The road climbs 2,200 ft., following up the ridge between Kettle Canyon and Dry Run Hollow. It is gated at the Park boundary and again just below Furnace Spring, located at the head of Dry Run.

Access: To reach lower end from Luray, head south on US 340. Just south of town turn left onto SR 642. Follow SR 642 about 1.6 mi., then turn right onto SR 689 and follow it another 2 mi. Turn left onto SR 668 for 0.9 mi. then right on SR 672. State maintenance ends in 0.6 mi. and road continues as Skyland Road, soon entering the Park.

FURNACE SPRING TRAIL
0.5 mile — yellow-blazed

The upper end of the trail is on the Stony Man Horse Trail just north of the northern entrance to Skyland and west of the parking area for the Stony Man self-guiding trail. The horse trail zigzags down toward the northwest, ending on Old Skyland Road Trail, just above where it is gated (and where the Passamaquoddy and Old Skyland Road Trail merge, a few feet from Furnace Spring).

Hikers making the circuit using the Stony Man, *AT* and Passamaquoddy trails may find this short trail a pleasant way to return to the parking area, rather than walking up the paved road.

WHITEOAK CANYON TRAIL
5.2 miles — blue-blazed

Note: A fee is charged to hike this trail from lower parking lot.

Whiteoak Canyon is one of the scenic gems of SNP. Whiteoak Run gathers waters from a number of streamlets gushing from as many springs located just below Skyline Drive in the Skyland area. The broad area where these headwaters gather was once covered with a virgin hemlock forest and is still called the "Limberlost," the name given to it by Mr. Pollock, as it reminded him of the locale of Gene Stratton Porter's novel, *Girl of the Limberlost*. When this forest was threatened with logging, Addie Narin Pollock paid ten dollars per tree for one hundred trees—for a total of one thousand dollars—then an exorbitant price. The woolly adelgid has killed these trees in recent years.

Below the Limberlost, Whiteoak Run has cut a deep canyon in its rush to Old Rag valley far below. There are six cascades, each more than 40 ft. high, along its route. (See waterfall chart, p. 83.) The falls occur between layers of the ancient lava beds, now tilted vertically, because the less resistant rock could withstand the creek's erosive powers much less than the basaltic rock. From the start of the Whiteoak Canyon Trail to the base of the sixth or lowest cascade there is a loss in elevation of 2,000 ft. The trail drops another 350 ft. before reaching Berry Hollow Road (SR 600).

The canyon is lined with towering trees—white oak, hemlock, tulip and ash. This is a heavily used trail, and you can expect to see people here regardless of the weather or time of year. *Backcountry camping is not allowed within 0.5 mi. of the canyon.*

A few miles to the south, Cedar Run forms a canyon paralleling Whiteoak Canyon. A very popular *circuit hike* includes a trip down one canyon and up the other. See Cedar Run Trail for description.

Access: Upper end of trail is at parking area east of Drive, almost directly across Skyline Drive from southern entrance to Skyland, SDMP 42.5. Parking may be difficult during holiday weekends and during fall color.

To reach lower end by car, follow VA 231 to about 5 mi. north of Madison and turn west onto SR 670, which passes through community of Criglersville. 5 mi. beyond Criglersville, at Syria, turn right onto SR 643. In 0.8 mi. turn left onto SR 600. (One can also reach this point by turning west off VA 231 at Etlan onto SR 643 and reaching junction of SR 600 in about 4 mi.) Follow SR 600 north, up Robinson River, for 3.6 mi. Just beyond fording of Cedar Run turn left into large parking area divided into two sections by Cedar Run but connected by a low-water bridge. Trailhead is at end of parking area most distant from SR 600. A fee is charged to hike this trail from the lower parking lot. The lower trailhead is staffed on weekends and holidays from spring to fall. There are also portable restroom facilities located near the lower trailhead.

Trail Description: Skyline Drive to SR 600

0.0-5.2 From parking area trail descends.

0.5-4.7 Cross branch of Whiteoak Run, then cross Limberlost Trail.

0.6-4.6 Cross Old Rag Fire Road. (To right road leads 0.2 mi. to a parking area and 0.1 mi. farther to Skyline Drive. To left it leads down mountain.) Trail soon enters Limberlost area.

0.8-4.4 Junction with Limberlost Trail. (To right, it is 0.8 mi. to parking area near beginning of Old Rag Fire Road. To left, trail leads 0.1 mi. to Old Rag Fire Road.) Whiteoak Canyon Trail descends more and more steeply from here.

2.2-3.0 Turn sharp left and cross footbridge over Whiteoak Run. (Just below present bridge is location of Mr. Pollock's "Middle Bridge" This was site of his famous barbecues in old "Skyland Days" and a favorite spot of his Skyland guests.) A few feet farther trail intersects Skyland-Big Meadows Horse Trail. (Horses must ford run. West of run horse trail follows Whiteoak Fire Road up mountain to Skyline Drive, SDMP 45.0.)

2.3-2.9 To right is excellent viewpoint over upper Whiteoak Falls, first of six cascades in canyon. From here trail descends very steeply.

2.4-2.8 Spur trail on right leads 250 ft. along Whiteoak Run to near base of upper falls. Canyon trail continues its steep descent, remaining on northeast side of run. Occasional views of various falls as trail switchbacks down canyon.

3.7-1.5 Cross side creek. (Falls on this creek visible from trail.) Trail now comes quite close to Whiteoak Run, just below lowest cascade.

4.3-0.9 Junction with Cedar Run-Whiteoak Link Trail which leads right, fording Whiteoak Run, then continuing almost level until it reaches Cedar Run Trail in 0.8 mi. (It is another 2.7 mi. via Cedar Run Trail to Skyline Drive at Hawksbill Gap.)

4.8-0.4 Cross Whiteoak Run.

5.0-0.2 Cedar Run Trail leads right, soon crossing Cedar Run and climbing 3.1 mi. to Skyline Drive, SDMP 45.6, at Hawksbill Gap.

5.1-0.1 Cross Cedar Run.

5.2-0.0 Parking area, just off SR 600.

CEDAR RUN TRAIL
3.1 miles — blue-blazed
Note: A fee is charged to hike this trail from lower parking lot.

Cedar Run flows southeast, paralleling Whiteoak Run, which it joins near the Berry Hollow Road, SR 600. The two canyons are separated by a high ridge along which the former Halfmile Cliffs Trail extended. Cedar Run Canyon is deep and wild with tall trees. While the stream has a lesser flow of water than Whiteoak Run, it has several high falls, sheer cliffs and deep pools. This is a popular trail used by many people.

A *circuit hike* is often made using Cedar Run Trail and Whiteoak Canyon Trail. The full circuit, starting at Hawksbill Gap, would be to descend Cedar Run Trail, follow Cedar Run-Whiteoak Link Trail, ascend Whiteoak Canyon Trail all the way to the Drive, cross to *AT* and follow it back to Hawksbill Gap, a distance of 10.5 mi. A *shorter circuit* which would still include the deep canyon area of Whiteoak Canyon Trail would be to descend as before, then ascend Whiteoak Trail to just above Upper Falls; turn left across the Run and follow Whiteoak Fire Road up mountain to Drive; then walk along Drive 0.5 mi. back to Hawksbill Gap, for total distance of 7.8 mi. If starting the hike from SR 600 it is necessary to add 0.8 mi. to distance.

Access: Upper end of Cedar Run Trail is on east side of Drive, directly across from Hawksbill Gap Parking Area, SDMP 45.6.

Lower end of trail is reached from Berry Hollow by following Whiteoak Canyon Trail from parking area near SR 600 for 0.2 mi. A fee is charged for those hiking from lower parking. Lower trailhead is also staffed on weekends and holidays from spring to fall. Hikers who hold a

Shenandoah, Golden Eagle or Interagency Pass are exempt from fee.

Trail Description: Hawksbill Gap to Berry Hollow
0.0-3.1 Hawksbill Gap Parking Area.
0.1-3.0 Cross Skyland-Big Meadows Horse Trail; trail soon descends along north side of Cedar Run.
1.1-2.0 To right is uppermost cascade of Cedar Run.
1.6-1.5 Cross to right of Cedar Run and swing away from it.
1.8-1.3 Trail again comes near Cedar Run near its highest falls. Sheer Halfmile Cliffs are across creek.
2.5-0.6 Trail turns left and fords run immediately below a falls. (Old road which follows down right side of run passes through private property to reach SR 600.)
2.7-0.4 At trail fork, bear right. (To left is Cedar Run-Whiteoak Link Trail which leads 0.8 mi. to Whiteoak Canyon Trail, joining it just below lowest falls.)
3.1-0.0 Reach lower end on Whiteoak Canyon Road, about 0.2 mi. west of parking area near SR 600.

CEDAR RUN-WHITEOAK LINK TRAIL
0.8 mile — blue-blazed

This trail connects the Whiteoak Canyon Trail and Cedar Run Trail near their lower ends. It is almost level. Northern terminus is on Whiteoak Canyon Trail just below lowest falls and about 0.9 mi. from its lower end at parking area near SR 600. Southern end is on Cedar Run Trail, 0.4 mi. from its lower end.

This trail is part of the popular Cedar Run-Whiteoak Canyon circuit hike. See Cedar Run Trail.

WEAKLEY HOLLOW FIRE ROAD
2.5 miles — yellow-blazed
and
BERRY HOLLOW FIRE ROAD
0.8 mile — yellow-blazed

Prior to the establishment of SNP, Old Rag valley was an extensive mountain community. The state road that is now SR 600 went from the village of Nethers through this valley and out to Syria. Many buildings, including the Old Rag Post Office, were located at the highest spot on this road, at its junction with a road coming down the Blue Ridge from Skyland. The section of the old highway now in the Park, that lies northeast of the junction, is now known as the Weakley Hollow Fire Road, whereas southwest of the junction it is called the Berry Hollow Fire Road. These two fire roads along with their extensions outside the Park (SR 600 in both directions) are very valuable for access purposes; both the Ridge Trail and Saddle Trail start from here, the lower termini of the Whiteoak Canyon Trail (and access to Cedar Run Trail) and Nicholson Hollow Trail are on this old route, as is the Old Rag Fire Road. The Robertson Mtn. Trail and the Corbin Hollow Trail also have their lower ends on the former state road.

The Weakley Hollow Fire Road is an important link for completing a circuit of Old Rag Mtn. It is very heavily used by hikers. Parking is just outside the Park boundary 0.8 mi. from the trailhead on SR 600. This parking lot can hold more than 200 cars and a fee is charged to use parking lot and trail. There are also portable restroom facilities at this parking lot. *Note: Parking is limited and no parking is permitted along the road or on private property.*

A *circuit hike* can be made using this road, along with the Whiteoak Canyon Trail and the Old Rag Fire Road.

Access: To reach Weakley Hollow Fire Road turn west off VA 231 (south of Sperryville) onto SR 602 just south of bridge over Hughes River. Continue up river on SR 707 where SR 602 ends. About 4 mi. from VA 231, where SR 707 turns right and crosses river, continue on paved SR 600 another 0.6 mi. to large 250-car parking lot on left.

To reach Berry Hollow Road, turn west off VA 231 onto SR 670 about 5 mi. north of Madison. Continue on SR 670 through Criglersville and Syria, about 3.5 mi., then turn right onto SR 643 and very shortly turn left onto SR 600. Follow SR 600 up Robinson River and Berry Hollow 4.8 mi. to Park boundary. Parking space is very limited along road. Park at lower end of Whiteoak Canyon Trail.

Trail Description: Northeast to Southwest

0.0-3.3 End of SR 600 and Park boundary gate. (Ridge Trail over Old Rag Mtn. leads south from here.)

1.2-2.1 Corbin Hollow Trail leads right, crossing Brokenback Run then following up creek.

1.3-2.0 Robertson Mtn. Trail leads to right up ridge.

2.5-0.8 Road junction. (To right, Old Rag Fire Road leads to Skyline Drive, SDMP 43.0. To left, Saddle Trail leads 1.9 mi. to summit of Old Rag Mtn., passing Old Rag Shelter in 0.4 mi. and Byrds Nest #1 in 1.5 mi.) Berry Hollow Fire Road continues straight ahead and descends.

3.3-0.0 Park boundary and SR 600. (Lower end of Whiteoak Canyon Trail is 0.9 mi. farther down SR 600.)

OLD RAG FIRE ROAD
5.0 miles — yellow-blazed

In pre-SNP days, a road led from Skyland down the east slope of the Blue Ridge to the Old Rag valley, coming into the road through the valley at its highest point. The Old Rag Post Office was located at this junction. Now the building that served as post office is gone, as is the community it served. But the lower 4 mi. of the present fire road follows much the same route as the old road down the mountain. Above Comer's Deadening, the present road continues almost due west and reaches Skyline Drive about 1 mi. southwest of spot where original road crossed the Drive.

From Skyline Drive fire road is shortest route to start of Saddle Trail up Old Rag Mtn. Fire road also serves as access to Corbin Mtn. Trail, Corbin Hollow Trail and Robertson Mtn. Trail.

A *circuit hike* of about 11.5 mi. can be made using this road in conjunction with Whiteoak Canyon Trail and Berry Hollow Fire Road.

Access: Skyline Drive, SDMP 43.0. Fire road leads east, with parking 0.1 mi. on left.

From parking area at Park boundary at foot of Weakley Hollow Fire Road it is 2.5 mi. to junction with Old Rag Fire Road; from parking area on Berry Hollow Fire Road it is 0.8 mi. (See Weakley Hollow and Berry Hollow fire roads for travel directions.)

Trail Description: Skyline Drive to Weakley Hollow and Berry Hollow fire roads

0.0-5.0 Skyline Drive (3,360 ft.). Fire road leads eastward.

0.1-4.9 Parking area to left of road. (To right of road is upper end of Limberlost Trail, leading 0.8 mi. to Whiteoak Canyon Trail.) Ahead, fire road is gated. Just beyond gate, Skyland-Big Meadows Horse Trail enters road from left and follows it.

0.3-4.7 Whiteoak Canyon Trail crosses fire road. (To left it is 0.6 mi. to Skyline Drive at southern entrance to Skyland, SDMP 42.5. To right it is 0. 2 mi. to lower end of Limberlost Trail, 1.6 mi. to viewpoint above upper falls and 4.5 mi. to SR 600 in Berry Hollow.)

0.5-4.5 Spur trail leads right 0.1 mi. to junction of Whiteoak Canyon and Limberlost trails.

0.7-4.3 Cross Whiteoak Run.

1.0-4.0 Area known as Comer's Deadening. (Skyland-Big Meadows Horse Trail turns right, leaving fire road and reaching Whiteoak Run just above upper falls in 1.7 mi. Along fire road 100 ft., horse trail, marked with concrete post, comes in from left and leads about 1 mi. to Skyline Drive just opposite northern entrance to Skyland.)

1.1-3.9 Pass ranger cabin on right. Beyond here, fire road descends steadily.

1.8-3.2 Corbin Mtn. Trail leads left 4.4 mi. to Nicholson Hollow Trail.

2.3-2.7 Corbin Hollow Trail leads left 2 mi. to Weakley Hollow Fire Road, 1.2 mi. above parking area at SR 600.

2.4-2.6 Robertson Mtn. Trail leads left 2.4 mi., climbing over Robertson Mtn. (3,296 ft.), then descending to Weakley Hollow Fire Road.

5.0-0.0 Junction with Weakley Hollow and Berry Hollow fire roads, at top of gap between Old Rag Mtn. and main Blue Ridge (1,913 ft.). Directly ahead is start of Saddle Trail.

LIMBERLOST TRAIL
1.3 miles — blue-blazed

Attention: Pets are not permitted on this trail.
Note: Portions of this trail are handicapped accessible.

This trail leads through a once beautiful forest of virgin hemlock and some spruce, called by George Freeman Pollock the "Limberlost" because of its supposed similarity to the woods in the novel by Gene Stratton Porter entitled *Girl of the Limberlost*. These trees were killed by the woolly adelgid. There is little change in elevation on this trail. It is frequently used by hikers.

For a *circuit hike* of about 4 mi., include upper 0.4 mi. of Limberlost Trail, Crescent Rock Trail, *AT* back to Skyland, and short section of Skyland-Big Meadows Horse Trail between *AT* and Limberlost Parking Area. (See

Crescent Rock Trail for slightly different circuit.)

Access: Skyline Drive, SDMP 43.0. Follow Old Rag Fire Road (unpaved) 0.1 mi. east to Limberlost Trail Parking Area.

Trail Description: This trail is a 1.3-mile circuit, starting from southeast side of parking lot.

0.0 Follow Limberlost Trail, which is a gravel trail to right of concrete post.

0.5 Turn left to stay on Limberlost Trail where Crescent Rock Trail enters on right.

0.9 Whiteoak Canyon Trail on left.

1.0 Cross Old Rag Fire Rd.

1.3 Arrive back at Limberlost Parking Area.

CORBIN MOUNTAIN TRAIL
4.4 miles — blue-blazed

This trail has one terminus low on the Nicholson Hollow Trail; its other is on the Old Rag Fire Road. There is a change in elevation of over 1,800 ft., most of which is at the very steep eastern end. If seclusion is what you seek, then the Corbin Mountain Trail does not disappoint. The middle portion of the trail route passes through a once-populated area and one can find house ruins and other indications of past human occupancy.

Good all-day *circuit trips* can be made utilizing this trail. Start from SR 600 (above Nethers) and hike up Nicholson Hollow Trail for 1.3 mi. to reach this trail, then follow Corbin Mtn. Trail, which ascends long and steep for 1 mi. One return route is via Indian Run and Nicholson Hollow trails, about 11 mi. A shorter return route is via Old Rag Fire Road, Corbin Hollow Trail and Weakley Hollow Fire Road, about 9.5 mi.

Trail Description: Nicholson Hollow Trail to Old Rag Fire Road

0.0-4.4 Trailhead marked with concrete post on Nicholson Hollow Trail 0.4 mi. below Hot-Short Mtn. Trail junction and 1.3 mi. northwest of SR 600. Cross Hughes River (be prepared to wade) and ascend along small tributary. (At first bend to right, faint trail leads left to very pretty waterfall.)

1.2-3.2 Pass ruins of house. Trail crosses run just beyond ruins.

3.8-0.6 In sag just below summit of Thorofare Mtn. trail turns sharply left. At turn, Indian Run Trail leads right, reaching Nicholson Hollow Trail 0.1 mi. above Corbin Cabin in 1.7 mi.

4.4-0.0 Old Rag Fire Road. Skyline Drive is 1.8 mi. right via fire road; upper end of Corbin Hollow Trail is 0.5 mi. to left. *Water* can be found along this stretch.

INDIAN RUN TRAIL
1.4 miles — blue-blazed

This short trail connecting Nicholson Hollow Trail with the Corbin Mtn. Trail and, via the latter, with Old Rag Fire Road, widens the hiking opportunities for users of Corbin Cabin. Several *circuit routes* are possible using Indian Run Trail as a segment. From Skyline Drive, SDMP 43.0, follow Old Rag Fire Road 1.8 mi. to reach upper end of Corbin Mtn. Trail. Follow latter 0.6 mi. to sag where that trail makes sharp right turn. Here a post marks upper end of Indian Run Trail. Lower end is on Nicholson Hollow Trail 0.1 mi. west of Corbin Cabin and 1.7 mi. east of Skyline Drive (or 1.8 mi. east of *AT*). The trail drops steadily on its way down to Nicholson Hollow, passing through a very nice mixed hardwood forest. Indian Run may be dry during times of drought.

CORBIN HOLLOW TRAIL
2.0 miles — blue-blazed

Upper end is on the Old Rag Fire Road, 2.3 mi. from Skyline Drive, SDMP 43.0, and 2.7 mi. on fire road from Weakley Hollow Fire Road. Lower end is on Weakley Hollow Fire Road, 1.3 mi. on that road northeast of its junction with Old Rag Fire Road and 1.2 mi. southwest of parking area at Park boundary. Trail follows an old road along Brokenback Run through quiet and secluded Corbin Hollow. This area was the location of a mountain community.

Upper terminus of this trail is 0.5 mi. east of upper end of Corbin Mtn. Trail and 0.1 mi. west of upper end of Robertson Mtn. Trail. It can be used with either of these for a *circuit route*.

ROBERTSON MOUNTAIN TRAIL
2.4 miles — blue-blazed

This trail offers some excellent views of Corbin Hollow and Old Rag Mtn. by bushwhacking off the highest point of the Robertson Mountain Trail to the summit. While the views are not as exposed or as extensive as those on Old Rag, they are still very worthwhile. This, linked to the fact that the trail is significantly less populated by hikers, makes it a worthwhile second choice to Old Rag. (The summit of Robertson is actually higher than Old Rag.)

Upper end of trail is on Old Rag Fire Road 2.4 mi. east of Skyline Drive, SDMP 43.0, via fire road, and 2.6 mi. northwest of Weakley Hollow Fire Road. Lower end is on Weakley Hollow Fire Road 1.3 mi. up road from SR 600 at Park boundary (and parking area) and 1.2 mi. down road from its junction with Old Rag Fire Road. Upper and lower ends of Robertson Mtn. Trail and Corbin Hollow Trail are each about 0.1 mi. apart.

From Old Rag Fire Road starting at an elevation of about 2,800 ft., trail climbs for 0.8 mi. with many switchbacks to a point just below the summit of Robertson Mtn. (3,296 ft.). Summit and corresponding views can be reached by turning right on high point of trail and bush-whacking for a short distance to top of ridge. Short climb to ridge can be a challenge when there is snow on the ground. On ridge, turn right again and walk a short distance to views.

From high point, trail descends steeply eastward, again with many switchbacks. Where it joins Weakley Hollow Road elevation is only 1,532 ft. Those wishing an easier hike should take route starting at Old Rag Fire Road. Route from Weakley Hollow Fire Road can be a long grind, especially during hot weather. There is no water along this trail.

WHITEOAK CANYON FIRE ROAD
1.6 miles — yellow-blazed

The chief use of this road, for hikers, is as a link to complete the circuit when descending Cedar Run Trail and ascending Whiteoak Canyon as far as the upper falls. The Skyland-Big Meadows Horse Trail also utilizes this road, following it from Whiteoak Run to just short of Skyline Drive. Lower end of this road is at Whiteoak Run, just above upper falls at site of G.F. Pollock's Middle Bridge. Upper end is on Skyline Drive, SDMP 45.0, about 0.6 mi. "north" of Hawksbill Gap and the upper end of Cedar Run Trail.

OLD RAG MOUNTAIN CIRCUIT
8.8 miles
Ridge Trail, 2.8 mi. — blue-blazed
SR 600 parking to trailhead, 0.8 mi.
Saddle Trail, 1.9 mi. — blue-blazed
Weakley Hollow Fire Road, 2.5 mi. — yellow-blazed
Park boundary to SR 600 parking, 0.8 mi.

Note: A fee is charged to hike this trail from the Weakley Hollow parking area.

Attention: Pets are not permitted on either the Ridge Trail or the Saddle Trail. No exceptions!

To hikers, Old Rag Mtn. has a very special character. The only other mountains in the east that can compete with it are Katahdin in Maine and Grandfather Mtn. in North Carolina. Of the three, Old Rag has the advantage, or disadvantage, of being the most accessible. Old Rag is the favorite hike of many Washington-area organizations, so that every weekend finds one or more large groups camping in the area or hiking on the mountain, as well as family groups, novice hikers, and veteran walkers. Those who survive the steep climb up the Ridge Trail or the shorter, easier climb up the Saddle Trail are rewarded by the fascinating walk over and around the tremendous rocks and by the outstanding open views, first in one direction, then another.

Old Rag stands apart from the main Blue Ridge, separated from it by the narrow Old Rag valley. It consists of a long, rocky ridge composed primarily of granite. However, long ago, lava welled up in cracks in the granite and formed a series of basaltic dikes, varying in thickness from a few feet to fifty. This basaltic material has weathered more rapidly than the surrounding granite, creating some of the rock features that give the mountain its ragged appearance. At one place on the Ridge Trail there is a regular staircase, with high vertical walls of granite and "steps" formed by the characteristic weathering of columnar basalt in blocks.

In wintertime, when snow and ice make the trails on Old Rag too difficult and dangerous for most hikers, there is still a special breed of walker who enjoys the challenge this mountain has to offer. He or she comes equipped with proper clothing for exposure to cold and wind, and uses crampons when traveling over icy spots.

It is advisable to carry water when hiking up Old Rag. There is no water at Byrds Nest #1 (shelter for day use only) which is situated in the saddle, about 0.4 mi. from summit, along the Saddle Trail. The other day-use shelter, Old Rag Shelter, is much lower down on the Saddle Trail and a *spring* is located there. *(No camping is allowed on Old Rag above 2,800 ft. elevation.)*

Access: From VA 231 south of Sperryville, turn west onto SR 602 just south of bridge over Hughes River. Stay on south side of river, first on SR 602, then SR 707, then SR 600 for about 0.6 mi. to the parking lot for Old Rag. On the left there is a registration station, which is staffed part-time by the Park Service, and parking for over 200 cars. A fee is collected at this point from all hikers who do not have a Shenandoah, Golden Eagle or Interagency Annual Pass. No parking is permitted along the road or on private property.

Ridge Trail starts at the end of SR 600 and the park boundary. To reach lower end of Saddle Trail, walk 2.5 mi. up Weakley Hollow Fire Road to its junction with Berry Hollow Fire Road and Old Rag Fire Road.

Note: The Park Service has provided portable restroom facilities at both main parking lot and at Ridge Trail trailhead.

Trail Description: Circuit described in clockwise direction, starting with Ridge Trail.

0.0-8.8. From parking area, follow SR 600 0.8 mi. west to Park boundary.

0.8-8.0 Bear left unto Ridge Trail.

2.2-6.6 Pass wet weather spring, to right of trail, close under steep side of ridge.

2.3-6.5 Crest of ridge in broad wooded saddle; turn sharply right.

2.5-6.3 Emerge from woods onto rocks.

3.8-5.0 End of Ridge Trail. To right are projecting rocks forming summit of Old Rag (3,291 ft.). Trail, now Saddle Trail, descends south along ridge crest.

4.2-4.6 Reach the "Saddle" and Byrds Nest #1. *No camping; day use only.* A portion of this shelter is a search and rescue cache to aid emergency response to the many injuries that occur on Old Rag. Trail turns sharply right, leaving ridge, and descends steadily by switchbacks along northwest slopes of mountain.

5.3-3.5 Old Rag Shelter (*no camping; day use only*) is 100 ft. ahead. Trail turns right onto blue-blazed dirt road and continues to descend.

5.7-3.1 Junction of three fire roads, all yellow-blazed—Weakley Hollow, Berry Hollow and Old Rag—at site of former Old Rag Post Office. Turn right on Weakley Hollow Fire Road and descend. (From fire road junction it is 5 mi. to Skyline Drive, SDMP 43.0, via Old Rag Fire Road and 1.6 mi. left via Berry Hollow Fire Road to foot of Whiteoak Canyon Trail.)

8.0-0.8 Park boundary and SR 600 just beyond.

8.8-0.0 Parking area.

SKYLAND-BIG MEADOWS HORSE TRAIL
11.0 miles — yellow-blazed

From the east side of Skyline Drive this trail leads to Old Rag Fire Road, which it follows down to Comer's Deadening. Here it turns right and enters Whiteoak Canyon. It crosses Whiteoak Run just above the upper falls, then follows the Whiteoak Fire Road almost to its junction with Skyline Drive, SDMP 45.0. From here it parallels the Drive until beyond the Upper Hawksbill Parking Area; it then descends along the southwest slope of Spitler Hill and circles the head of Rose River Canyon. It again crosses the Drive just south of Fishers Gap and then parallels the Drive to reach Big Meadows maintenance area. The trail has posts marking the half miles.

The section of horse trail between Whiteoak Canyon Trail and Fishers Gap gets very little horse traffic so is pleasant walking. The part near Rose River is quite scenic. Hikers should remember to yield right-of-way to equestrians should they meet.

Access: Northern end of trail is on Skyline Drive, SDMP 41.7, across from northern entrance to Skyland; southern end is at Big Meadows, SDMP 51.2.

Trail Description: Skyland to Big Meadows

0.0-11.0 East side of Skyline Drive. Trail parallels Drive.

0.4-10.6 Come to Old Rag Fire Road and follow it to left. (A parking area is 200 ft. to right along road. Skyline Drive is 0.1 mi. farther.)

1.3-9.7 Horse trail turns sharply right away from fire road at signpost and heads toward Whiteoak Canyon. This area is known as Comer's Deadening. Horse trail follows old road.

2.5-8.5 Ford Whiteoak Run just above upper falls. From here horse trail follows Whiteoak Fire Road.

4.1-6.9 About 0.1 mi. from Skyline Drive, horse trail

turns left and parallels Drive.

4.6-6.4 Intersection with Cedar Run Trail. (To right it is few feet to Skyline Drive at Hawksbill Gap.)

6.0-5.0 Horse trail comes into old farm road near summit of Spitler Hill and follows road to left. (To right, road leads to Skyline Drive just south of Upper Hawksbill Parking Area, SDMP 46.7.) Lady's tresses, a type of orchid, may be found here, blooming in September and October. For over 0.5 mi. trail passes through old fields, now quite overgrown. Old road gradually narrows into trail.

7.8-3.2 Cross stream, branch of Rose River.

8.3-2.7 Cross second branch of Rose River.

8.9-2.1 Dark Hollow Falls-Rose River Loop Trail enters from left and follows horse trail.

9.4-1.6 Cross Rose River Fire Road just east of Fishers Gap, SDMP 49.3. In 0.1 mi. cross to right (west) of Skyline Drive. Horse trail swings out of sight of Drive, then turns to parallel it.

10.8-0.2 Intersection with Story of Forest Trail.

11.0-0.0 Big Meadows stables, SDMP 51.2.

CRESCENT ROCK TRAIL
1.1 miles — blue-blazed

This short trail runs from Skyline Drive, SDMP 44.4, across from the Crescent Rock Overlook (look for concrete post just south of north entrance) down to Limberlost Trail, with a gentle downgrade all the way.

A pleasant half-day *circuit hike*, 4.5 mi., can be made by following this trail from the overlook, turning right onto Limberlost Trail and following it 0.4 mi., then ascending Whiteoak Canyon Trail to Skyline Drive. Cross Drive and, a few yards up road toward Skyland stables, turn left onto *AT* and follow it for 2 mi. A short spur trail, marked with concrete post, leads to north end of Crescent Rock Overlook.

HAWKSBILL MOUNTAIN TRAIL
1.8 miles — blue-blazed

Hawksbill Mtn. is the highest mountain in SNP. Native spruce and balsam are found on its upper slopes. An observation platform at the summit (4,050 ft.) provides excellent views of Timber Hollow to the north and Page Valley and Massanutten Mtn. to the west.

Byrds Nest #2 is a three-sided shelter situated just off the summit of Hawksbill. *No camping permitted.* Water is available from *spring* 0.8 mi. downhill. Cliffs near summit shelter offer fine views of the Shenandoah Valley to the west.

This trail begins at Upper Hawksbill Parking Area, SDMP 46.7, and ascends to Hawksbill Service Road in 0.6 mi. It turns right and follows service road 0.3 mi. to summit of Hawksbill, then descends northeastward 0.9 mi. to end in Hawksbill Gap, SDMP 45.6, where there is another parking area.

A *circuit hike* over Hawksbill could include the Hawksbill Trail from Hawksbill Gap to summit, 0.9 mi., Salamander Trail down to *AT*, 0.7 mi., and *AT* back to Hawksbill Gap.

SALAMANDER TRAIL
0.7 mile — blue-blazed

The Salamander Trail leaves the *AT* just north of Rock Spring Hut and leads east to the top of Hawksbill. It can be reached via the *AT* by hiking north from Rock Spring Cabin Parking/Spitler Knoll Overlook, SDMP 48.0. In 1 mi. Salamander Trail (no sign) leads right 0.8 mi. to summit of Hawksbill. It can also be approached via the *AT* from Hawksbill Gap.

SERVICE ROAD TO BYRDS NEST #2
0.9 mile — not blazed

This service road leaves Skyline Drive at SDMP 47.1 and climbs to Byrds Nest #2 near the summit of Hawksbill. There is little or no parking at its beginning on Skyline Drive.

TRAILS IN THE BIG MEADOWS-RAPIDAN CAMP (CAMP HOOVER) AREA

The Big Meadows developed area includes the Byrd Visitor Center, a wayside, lodge, cabins, restaurant, camp store, gift shop, picnic area and the largest campground in the Park.

Big Meadows is located on a very broad, flat area of the Blue Ridge. Many geologists believe that this area is the remnant of an old, high peneplain. Because of its surprising flatness water does not run off easily and some of the area is quite boggy. There are several plants growing here uncommon to Virginia; Canadian burnet is one. A network of trails and fire roads provides the camper with many miles of good walking. There are a number of *circuit hikes* possible in the area, some quite short, others that can provide a full day of hiking. Hikers using trails maintained primarily for equestrians should yield the right-of-way.

Rapidan Camp (formally known as Camp Hoover), situated within the Park on the Rapidan River, was originally built as a presidential hideaway for Herbert Hoover while he was president. Later he donated the camp to the Commonwealth of Virginia to be included in the future park, for use by future presidents and their guests. The Park Service administers the property and welcomes visitors on the grounds of the camp. Only three of the original buildings—the President's Cabin, the Prime Minister's Cabin and "The Creel"—remain today. The camp buildings and landscape have been restored to their original 1930 condition.

Access to Rapidan Camp from east is via Rapidan Fire Road and SR 649. Refer to write-up for this road. From Skyline Drive one can (1) follow the Rapidan Fire Road from Big Meadows, SDMP 51.3; (2) descend Mill Prong Trail from Milam Gap, SDMP 52.8; or (3) follow *AT* north from Bootens Gap, SDMP 55.1, to reach Laurel Prong Trail and descend latter.

RED GATE FIRE ROAD
4.8 miles — yellow-blazed

This road, gated at both ends, leads from the base of the mountains 4 mi. east of Stanley to Skyline Drive at Fishers Gap, SDMP 49.3. (This road is the western portion of the old Gordonsville Pike. It continues on the east slope of the Blue Ridge as the Rose River Fire Road.) The Red Gate Fire Road climbs with a gentle grade and has many switchbacks to gain 1,500 ft. of elevation. It offers a pleasant walk except that one does have to beware of cars as Park and concessionaire personnel use this road to reach Big Meadows.

To reach the lower end of the Red Gate Fire Road, turn east from US 340 in Stanley onto either SR 624 or SR 689. Beyond junction of these roads, follow SR 689 eastward for about 1 mi. then continue straight on SR 611 where SR 689 turns sharply left. Continue on SR 611 to Park boundary, where road becomes Red Gate Fire Road and is gated.

STORY OF THE FOREST TRAIL
1.8 miles — not blazed
Attention: Pets are not permitted on this trail.
The trail begins at the Byrd Visitor Center, SDMP 51.0.

Trail Description:
0.0 From visitor center head east and cross lovely stone bridge.

0.3 Spur trail on right leads down 300 ft. to Skyline

Drive directly opposite Dark Hollow Falls Trail.

0.8 Trail turns sharply left. (Straight ahead leads to campground.)

0.9 Paved road leading to picnic and camping areas of Big Meadows. Trail turns left here and follows paved path along road back to visitor center. To reach Amphitheater Parking Area and *AT*, turn right on paved path as far as campground registration office, then walk along road to picnic area, keeping left at road fork (wrong way for cars). Look for trail, just left of parking area, that leads on to *AT*.

1.8 Big Meadows Wayside and Byrd Visitor Center.

LEWIS SPRING FALLS TRAIL
1.8 miles — blue-blazed

This trail leads from the *AT* immediately below Big Meadows Lodge, SDMP 51.0, to Lewis Spring Falls and ends on the *AT* at Lewis Spring. To reach start of trail find path between Amphitheater Parking Area and lodge. Follow it north about 0.1 mi. to *AT* intersection, marked by signpost. (*AT* leads south to Lewis Spring and north to Big Meadows Campground.) Lewis Spring Falls Trail is directly across from here.

For a *circuit hike* of 2.7 mi., follow this trail, then turn left onto *AT* for return to Big Meadows.

Trail Description: Big Meadows Lodge to Lewis Spring

0.0 Trail descends.

1.2 Trail leads right 150 ft. to stone-walled overlook at head of falls. Trail now ascends steeply.

1.7 Lewis Spring service road.

1.8 End at *AT*.

DARK HOLLOW FALLS-
ROSE RIVER LOOP TRAIL
3.5 miles — first 2.6 mi. blue-blazed
last 0.9 mi. — yellow-blazed

The Dark Hollow Falls Trail, 0.8 mi. in length, is the most popular trail in the Park. It leads to a very lovely cascading waterfall on the Hogcamp Branch of the Rose River. For a very short trip, park at Dark Hollow Falls Parking Area on Skyline Drive, SDMP 50.7.

For a somewhat longer trip park at the Amphitheater Parking Area of Big Meadows (follow road signs). On foot, follow the exit road as far as campground registration office. Then walk, going to right, along paved path which follows road. In 0.1 mi., at concrete post, turn left onto Story of the Forest Trail and continue on it for about 0.6 mi. At an intersection marked by a concrete post continue straight ahead (Story of the Forest Trail bears right) and in 300 ft. reach Skyline Drive directly across from Dark Hollow Falls Trail Parking Area.

A *circuit hike* of about 6 mi. can be made by starting at Amphitheater Parking Area. Proceed to Dark Hollow Falls Trail as described above and descend; continue along Rose River Loop Trail (which is very scenic and passes a falls on Rose River) to Fishers Gap. Cross Drive and follow Red Gate Fire Road few feet to *AT*. Turn left and return to Big Meadows via *AT*.

Access: Northern end of trail is in Fishers Gap, SDMP 49.3; southern end is at Dark Hollow Falls Parking Area, SDMP 50.7.

Trail Description: Dark Hollow Falls Parking Area to Fishers Gap

0.0-3.5 From northern end of parking area trail descends steadily with stream on right.

0.6-2.9 Top of Dark Hollow Falls, a series of terraced

cascades. From here trail descends very steeply.

0.8-2.7 Rose River Fire Road. (This is a portion of old Gordonsville Pike. To left it is 1.1 mi. to Fishers Gap.) Turn right onto road and cross bridge over Hogcamp Branch. 50 ft. beyond bridge, at sign, turn left off road and follow Rose River Loop Trail down creek.

1.7-1.8 At junction, turn sharply left and cross Hogcamp Branch. In 250 ft. cross small stream. In 50 ft. pass site of old copper mine to left of trail. Trail soon approaches main branch of Rose River, turns left at sign pointing to Rose River Falls and climbs along west bank of river.

2.3-1.2 Pass waterfall.

2.6-0.9 Turn left, uphill, onto old road, now route of Big Meadows-Skyland Horse Trail (yellow-blazed).

3.5-0.0 Turn right onto Rose River Fire Road and in few feet reach Skyline Drive, SDMP 49.3, at Fishers Gap.

ROSE RIVER FIRE ROAD
6.5 miles — yellow-blazed

From Fishers Gap, SDMP 49.3, this old road winds its way down to SR 670 west of Syria. In pre-Park days it was known as the Gordonsville Pike and many hikers still refer to it by that name. (West of Skyline Drive the road continues as the Red Gate Fire Road.)

Access: From VA 231 about 16 mi. south of US 522 near Sperryville and 5 mi. north of Madison, turn west onto SR 670. Follow SR 670 through Criglersville and Syria to Park boundary. Parking space near end of SR 670 is very limited. From boundary continue up road on foot, with river to right of road in deep gorge.

Trail Description: Fishers Gap to SR 670
0.0-6.5 Skyline Drive at Fishers Gap, SDMP 49.3.
1.1-5.4 Dark Hollow Falls Trail, marked by post, leads

to right 0.8 mi. uphill to Skyline Drive. Just beyond junction, road crosses Hogcamp Branch. In 50 ft. post marks Rose River Loop Trail, which leads left down Hogcamp Branch.

2.0-4.5 Stony Mtn. Trail leads right 1.1 mi. to Rapidan Fire Road.

5.2-1.3 Post on right marks Upper Dark Hollow Trail, which leads 2.2 mi. to Rapidan Road at Broyles Gap.

6.5-0.0 Park boundary, where road becomes SR 670.

STONY MOUNTAIN TRAIL
1.1 miles — yellow-blazed

This trail follows an old road that connects the Rose River Fire Road (Gordonsville Pike) and the Rapidan Fire Road. Its northern end is 2 mi. down Rose River Fire Road from Skyline Drive. Southern end is 2.9 mi. down Rapidan Fire Road from Drive.

UPPER DARK HOLLOW TRAIL
2.2 miles — yellow-blazed

This trail route connects the Rose River Fire Road and the Rapidan Fire Road. Its lower end is about 1.3 mi. up the Rose River Fire Road from the Park boundary (at end of SR 670). The trail route involves a climb of about 1,250 ft. to reach its upper end on the Rapidan Fire Road at Broyles Gap. The lower portion of the trail passes through a once beautiful hemlock forest. For the upper half of its route the trail utilizes an old roadbed, so it offers easy walking.

For a *circuit hike* of about 9 mi., start at lower end of Rose River Fire Road, walk up road for about 4 mi. to Stony Mtn. Trail. Follow this trail about 1 mi. to Rapidan Fire Road. Descend the Rapidan Road for about 1 mi. to Broyles Gap, then descend Upper Dark Hollow Trail back to Rose River Fire Road and descend to car.

TANNERS RIDGE HORSE TRAIL
0.9 mile — yellow-blazed

This trail connects the Big Meadows maintenance area to Tanners Ridge Rd.

TANNERS RIDGE ADMINISTRATIVE ROAD
1.4 miles within SNP — yellow-blazed

This road, gated at the Drive and at Park boundary, leads west from Skyline Drive, SDMP 51.6, for 1.4 mi. to Park boundary, where it becomes SR 682 (about 6 mi. from Stanley). There is a cemetery, still being used for burials, at junction of this road with *AT*, about 0.3 mi. from the Drive.

RAPIDAN FIRE ROAD-SR 649
10.0 miles — yellow-blazed

This fire road is gated at Skyline Drive (Big Meadows) and at the "first" Park boundary, just below the junction with Rapidan Camp Road. The upper portion of this road is used as a horse trail and also by hikers. The road continues east of the gate through Rapidan Wildlife Management Area and descends along the Rapidan River. It then reenters SNP. After another mile along the river the road climbs to the top of Chapman Mtn. ridge before reaching the easternmost Park boundary. Although there is some traffic on this part of the road, it is light and the road is not unpleasant for walking. The road passes through the very scenic Rapidan River drainage used by President Hoover and many members of his cabinet for trout fishing. There is a good swimming hole on the river at the junction of this road and the Graves Mill Trail and Lower Rapidan Road.

A *circuit hike* can be made using this trail in conjunction with the Mill Prong Trail and the *AT*.

Access: Upper end is on Skyline Drive, SDMP 51.3, across from Big Meadows Wayside, where there is ample parking.

To reach road from east, turn west off VA 231 onto SR 670 about 16 mi. south of US 522 near Sperryville and 5 mi. north of Madison. Follow SR 670 for about 1 mi. beyond Criglersville. Turn left onto SR 649, crossing the Rose River and following up a side stream toward Chapman Mtn. Road is narrow but driveable over Chapman Mtn. and on beyond junction with SR 662 on Rapidan River to just below Rapidan Camp access road, where it reenters SNP. Here it is gated.

Trail Description: Skyline Drive to easternmost Park boundary. (Mileages estimated.)

0.0-10.0 Junction with Skyline Drive, SDMP 51.3, across from Big Meadows Wayside.

1.2-8.8 Mill Prong Horse Spur Trail leads right 1.8 mi. to Rapidan Camp.

2.9-7.1 Stony Mtn. Trail leads left to Rose River Fire Road.

3.8-6.2 Upper Dark Hollow Trail leads left to Rose River Fire Road.

5.4-4.6 At road junction, fire road continues straight ahead. Road to right leads up Rapidan River for about 0.8 mi. to Rapidan Camp.

5.8-4.2 Reach Park boundary, where road is gated, and enter Rapidan Wildlife Management Area, where road becomes SR 649 and is open to automobile traffic.

7.5-2.5 At road fork, SR 649 continues straight ahead, descending along Rapidan River. (Fork Mtn. Road, gated, goes right to radio tower on Fork Mtn.)

7.6-2.4 Reenter SNP.

8.8-1.2 At road junction take left fork and climb, leaving river. (Right fork is Graves Mill Horse Trail, which follows down Rapidan River to Park boundary in 1.7 mi.)

9.4-0.6 At road junction on top of Chapman Mtn. ridge, continue straight ahead. (To right, a Virginia forest road leads out Blakey Ridge past Utz Hightop Lookout Tower.

Gated road to left is access road to private land.)

10.0-0.0 Road leaves Park. (From here it is 3 mi. to SR 670.)

MILL PRONG TRAIL
1.0 mile — blue-blazed

This trail leads from the *AT* in Milam Gap east to the Mill Prong Horse Trail. A good *circuit hike* of 7 mi. can be made using these two trails, along with Laurel Prong Trail and *AT*. A *longer circuit*, 12 mi., includes Mill Prong Trail, Mill Prong Horse Trail, Rapidan Fire Road, Rapidan Camp Road and *AT*.

Trail Description: Milam Gap to Mill Prong Horse Trail

0.0-1.0 Junction with *AT*, a few feet south of Skyline Drive crossing at Milam Gap, SDMP 52.8. Trail descends gently through old field and orchard, now overgrown.

0.6-0.4 Cross main branch of Mill Prong. Trail now descends through tall trees and fern-covered forest floor.

1.0-0.0 Cross another branch of Mill Prong and bear right, reaching junction with Mill Prong Horse Trail, which comes in from left. (Via Horse Trail it is 1 mi. north to Rapidan Fire Road and 1.2 mi. farther along fire road to Skyline Drive at Big Meadows Wayside.)

MILL PRONG HORSE TRAIL
1.8 miles — yellow-blazed

A *circuit hike* to Rapidan Camp (formally known as Camp Hoover) can be made using this trail, along with the Mill Prong Trail and *AT*; distance about 8 mi.

Access: Upper end of this trail is on Rapidan Fire Road, 1.2 mi. from Skyline Drive at Big Meadows, SDMP 51.3.

Lower end is at Rapidan Camp just west of road bridge

over Mill Prong Trail.

Trail Description: Rapidan Fire Road to Rapidan Camp Road

0.0-1.8 Rapidan Fire Road. Horse trail heads south.

1.0-0.8 Mill Prong Trail leads right for 1 mi. to *AT* in Milam Gap. Trail now descends along creek.

1.5-0.3 Cross to right of creek just below Big Rock Falls. Crossing is easy to miss.

1.8-0.0 Junction with Rapidan Camp Road 100 ft. west of bridge over Mill Prong.

LAUREL PRONG TRAIL
2.8 miles — blue-blazed

This trail starts from the *AT* near Bootens Gap, descends very gently along the southern slope of Hazeltop Mtn. with good wintertime views of the valley below, to Laurel Gap. The trail then turns left and descends more steeply through an area of much mountain laurel. For the final mile it leads through the valley of Laurel Prong. To the right of the trail, in several locations along the creek, one can find the great laurel or rosebay rhododendron which blooms here in late June or early July. In some places a carpet of false lily-of-the-valley, blooming in late May, carpets the ground; in other places running cedar, a type of club moss, acts as a ground cover.

Access: From Bootens Gap, SDMP 55.1, follow *AT* north for 0.6 mi. Concrete post marks trailhead.

To reach lower end, follow directions for getting to Rapidan Camp from east (Rapidan Fire Road). Laurel Prong trailhead is near end of access road to Rapidan Camp, about 300 ft. west of bridge over Mill Prong.

Trail Description: *AT* to Rapidan Camp

0.0-2.8 Junction with *AT*.

1.0-1.8 Laurel Gap. (Concrete post marks start of Cat

Knob Trail, leading right to Jones Mtn. Trail.) Turn left and continue to descend.

2.2-0.6 Concrete post marks Fork Mtn. Trail, which leads right 1.5 mi. to "The Sag" and Fork Mtn. Fire Rd. (Upper end of Fork Mtn. Trail also connects with Staunton River Trail and Jones Mtn. Trail.)

2.8-0.0 Rapidan Camp. To reach Mill Prong Horse Trail, follow access road left for 250 ft.

CAT KNOB TRAIL
0.5 mile — blue-blazed

This is a short trail that connects Laurel Prong and Jones Mtn. trails. The shortest route to Jones Mtn. Cabin from Skyline Drive, 5.7 mi., would use this "short cut," along with the *AT*, Laurel Prong Trail, Jones Mtn. Trail and Jones Mtn. Cabin Trail.

GRAVES MILL HORSE TRAIL
2.1 miles — yellow-blazed

Portions of this road were severely impacted by the flood of June 27, 1995.

Trail Description: Rapidan Road to Park boundary

0.0-2.1 Trail begins at concrete post at Rapidan Rd. Parking Area.

0.6-1.5 Cross Rapidan River.

1.5-0.6 Junction with Staunton River Trail.

0.0-2.1 Trail ends at Park boundary and SR 662.

FORK MOUNTAIN ROAD
4.5 miles (approx.) — blue-blazed

This road is gated. It leads from the Rapidan Fire Road about 2 mi. southeast of Rapidan Camp up the eastern and southern slopes of Fork Mtn., winding in and out of SNP. It reaches "The Sag," the divide between the Staunton River drainage area and that of Laurel Prong, then climbs to the tower on top of Fork Mtn. (3,840 ft.). Where the road crosses the upper reaches of the Staunton River the Staunton River Trail enters from the left. At "The Sag" the Fork Mtn. Trail leads west 1.3 mi. to Laurel Prong Trail and the Jones Mtn. Trail leads south to Cat Knob and then descends the Jones Mtn. ridge.

STAUNTON RIVER TRAIL
4.3 miles (approx.) — blue-blazed

This trail follows up the deep woods and secluded drainage of the Staunton River from SR 662 at the junction of the Staunton and Rapidan rivers, to the Fork Mtn. Fire Road. Fork Mtn. Fire Road continues on for 0.8 mi. to "The Sag," where a connection can be made with the upper ends of the Jones Mtn. Trail and the Fork Mtn. Trail leading down to the Laurel Prong Trail.

The lower half of the trail follows an old road which was improved during WW II for mountain training of U.S. Army troops. Staunton River is always close by, tumbling over rocks and rushing into deep pools along its course. The old woods road ends after crossing the Staunton River for the first time at an area known as Hundley's Ford, near a large pile of chestnut boards (they were lumbered at the request of the Park Service after the chestnut blight). The trail continues on as a footpath after crossing the Staunton River a second time and ascending at a steeper rate, passing a nice swimming hole on the right. The trail connects with the Fork Mtn. Fire Road.

An outstanding *circuit hike* can be made from Jones Mtn. Cabin by hiking the very secluded Jones Mtn. Trail and returning via the Staunton River Trail (and including the McDaniel Hollow Trail if so desired) for a distance of 7.5 mi.

Access: To reach lower end of this trail follow VA 230 west from US 29 south of Madison for 4 mi. to Wolftown (or follow VA 230 northeast from US 33 in Stanardsville). Turn north onto SR 662 and continue on paved road as far as Graves Mill, 5.5 mi. At road junction, take right fork, still SR 662, which crosses Kinsey Run and follows up Rapidan River, soon entering SNP as Graves Mill Horse Trail. Junction of Staunton and Rapidan rivers is 2 mi. beyond Graves Mill. Road inside Park is rough, so parking is recommended just outside Park boundary, where there is room for five cars. There is room for a few cars on fire road. One small parking area is reserved for cabin users at trailhead.

Trail Description: SR 662 to the Fork Mountain Road

0.0-4.3 SR 662 near junction of Staunton and Rapidan rivers. Trail follows old woods road along southwest side of Staunton River.

2.0-2.3 Jones Mtn. Trail leads left, steeply uphill, passing Bear Church Rock. It passes side trail to Jones Mtn. Cabin in 0.8 mi.

2.4-1.9 McDaniel Hollow Trail leads southeast to join Jones Mtn. Trail in 0.5 mi.

4.3-0.0 Reach Fork Mtn. Fire Road.

FORK MOUNTAIN TRAIL
1.4 miles (approx.) — yellow-blazed

This very lovely trail has its lower end on the Laurel Prong Trail 0.6 mi. from Rapidan Camp. The Fork Mtn. Trail crosses Laurel Prong in an area with much rosebay rhododendron. As trail gradually climbs Fork Mtn. the rhododendron is replaced by mountain laurel. The route of the trail follows an old farm road as it switchbacks up the mountain to reach "The Sag," where it meets the Fork Mtn. Fire Road, Jones Mtn. Trail and Staunton River Trail.

JONES MOUNTAIN TRAIL
4.8 miles — blue-blazed

The Jones Mountain Trail passes next to Bear Church Rock, which offers an excellent view of the upper Staunton River valley to the northwest. This is also the access route to PATC Jones Mtn. Cabin (available for rental from PATC.) The main attraction of the Jones Mountain Trail is the extraordinary seclusion it offers the hiker. When linked with the Mill Prong-Laurel Prong-Cat Knob trails, and the Staunton River Trail, an excellent overnight trip is possible, with few people seen along the way. Originally, this was grazing land for beef and dairy cattle, but now, fully overgrown with trees, it offers a quiet refuge from crowds using the other, more "popular" trails in the Park. There is no water along this trail.

Access: Lower end of this trail is on Staunton River Trail 2 mi. from its junction with Graves Mill Horse Trail, extension of SR 662 within Park. Trail's upper end is at "The Sag" on Fork Mtn.

Trail Description: Staunton River Trail to "The Sag"

0.0-4.8 Junction with Staunton River Trail 2 mi. west of SR 662. Trail climbs steeply uphill.

0.5-4.3 McDaniel Hollow Trail leads right 0.5 mi. to Staunton River Trail.

0.7-4.1 Jones Mtn. Cabin Trail leads left (east) 0.2 mi. to cabin.

1.2-3.6 Short "opening" to exposed Bear Church Rock; excellent views northwest.

1.3-3.5 Reach highest point. Trail now follows narrow ridge of Jones Mtn.

2.2-2.6 Trail turns northwestward where ridge from Bear Church Rock and Bluff Mtn. join.

3.4-1.4 Slight sag between Jones Mtn. and Cat Knob.

4.0-0.8 Summit of Cat Knob. Trail now swings sharply

to northeast over almost level ground. (Cat Knob Trail leads left to end on Laurel Prong Trail in 0.5 mi.)

4.8-0.0 Reach "The Sag" and junction with Fork Mtn. Fire Road and upper ends of Fork Mtn. Trail.

McDANIEL HOLLOW TRAIL
0.5 mile — blue-blazed

This short trail has one end on the Jones Mtn. Trail and the other on the Staunton River Trail. It follows the route of an old mountain road across McDaniel Hollow and affords a short-cut for hikers making a circuit using the Staunton River and Jones Mtn. trails.

POWELL MOUNTAIN TRAIL
3.6 miles — blue-blazed

This trail leads from Skyline Drive at the Hazeltop Ridge Overlook, SDMP 54.4, to the summit of Powell Mtn. in 2 mi. It descends westward following an old road, and along the way passes a number of overgrown fields. The trail drops more steeply as it heads down to Big Creek and SR 759 for a total elevation loss of 1,800 ft. The trail is infrequently used and is a good choice for hikers seeking solitude.

A *circuit hike* of under 10 mi. uses this trail, the upper stretch of SR 759, the Meadow School Trail and the *AT*.

MEADOW SCHOOL TRAIL
1.5 miles (approx.) — yellow-blazed

This former fire road, now a horse/foot trail, is gated at Skyline Drive and at Park boundary. Its upper end is on Skyline Drive, SDMP 56.8, directly opposite Slaughter Fire Road. From here it steeply descends western slope of the Blue Ridge for a total elevation loss of 900 ft. Outside Park, Meadow School Trail becomes SR 759.

POCOSIN CABIN-SOUTH RIVER AREA

LEWIS MOUNTAIN EAST TRAIL
1.0 mile — blue-blazed

One end of this trail is on the *AT* at the southern edge of the Lewis Mountain Campground. The trail rises slightly over the southern peak of Lewis Mountain, then drops steeply down to a saddle along the ridge. Beyond the saddle, the trail disappears. For the more adventuresome, hikers can bushwhack northeast from the saddle along an old and rather indistinct woods road (unmarked), dropping down to the Slaughter Trail after a short distance. This route is recommended **only** for hikers with map and compass, and experience in traveling off-trail routes in the Park.

CONWAY RIVER FIRE ROAD
1.4 miles within Park — yellow-blazed

This road, gated at the top and at the Park boundary, leads from Skyline Drive, SDMP 55.1, to the edge of the Park, about 1.4 mi., then continues for another 2.8 mi. through open land set aside as a Virginia Wildlife Area. From here it continues as SR 615 down the valley to Graves Mill on the Rapidan River. Logging was conducted in some areas of the Virginia Wildlife Area.

BEARFENCE MOUNTAIN LOOP TRAIL
0.3 mile — blue-blazed

Attention: Pets are not permitted on this trail.

A very short but very scenic trail leads from the *AT* up over the rocky ridge top of Bearfence Mtn., then back down to the *AT*. In addition, a very rough trail—more rock scramble than a real trail—continues north along the ridge top for another 0.2 mi., then swings downhill, crossing the *AT* and continuing on for another 0.1 mi. to Bearfence Mtn. Parking Area on Skyline Drive, SDMP 56.4. There are excellent views along the route, and the trail is heavily used by hikers. The Park Service conducts nature hikes here during the summer.

A *circuit hike* can be made using the Bearfence Mtn. loops and the *AT*. Southernmost junction of loop trail with *AT* is 0.6 mi. north of access road to Bearfence Mtn. Hut via *AT*. Northernmost junction is 0.4 mi. farther north along *AT*.

SLAUGHTER ROAD
4.0 miles — yellow-blazed

From the Drive the trail first follows the service road to Bearfence Mtn. Hut for 0.1 mi., crossing the *AT* a few feet from the Drive. The first 1.5 mi. is pleasant walking and should be particularly lovely in early June, as there is much mountain laurel in bloom along the trail as it descends along the Devils Ditch.

A long *circuit hike* can be made by descending Pocosin Fire Road and Pocosin Hollow Trail, continuing outside Park to SR 667, then following up SR 667 and Slaughter Trail, finally following *AT* south to Pocosin Fire Road; total distance about 13 mi.

Access: Upper end of this former fire road is on Skyline Drive, SDMP 56.8, and is just across the Drive from the Meadow School Trail.

Lower end is near Conway River on SR 667, roughly 7.5 mi. north of VA 230 (and an additional 3 mi. from Stanardsville). *Note: There is no parking on SR 667.*

POCOSIN FIRE ROAD
2.5 miles — yellow-blazed

From Skyline Drive, SDMP 59.5, this road leads south-eastward passing Pocosin Cabin, a locked structure available for use with advance reservations from PATC. It becomes SR 637 outside the Park and is gated at both Skyline Drive and the Park boundary.

Trail Description: Skyline Drive to Park boundary

0.0-2.5 Skyline Drive, SDMP 59.5.

0.2-2.3 Intersection with *AT*. (Via *AT* it is 2.8 mi. south to South River Fire Road and 0.5 mi. farther to South River Falls Trail.)

0.3-2.2 Pocosin Cabin to right of road.

1.1-1.4 Pocosin Trail leads right 1.3 mi. to South River Fire Road. (Via fire road it is 1.2 mi. to South River Falls Trail and 0.8 mi. farther to *AT*.) Just beyond junction and to right of road are interesting ruins of former Upper Pocosin Mission.

1.3-1.2 To left, Pocosin Hollow Trail leads north.

1.8-0.6 Entry Run Trail to right. (This trail leads past PATC Johns Rest Cabin and PATC Rosser-Lamb Cabin to SR 643.

2.5-0.0 Park boundary. Road continues outside Park and becomes SR 637 farther east.

ENTRY RUN TRAIL
2.4 miles — blue-blazed

This trail connects the Pocosin Fire Road inside the Park and SR 643 adjacent to the Johns Rest Cabin. It also passes the side trail leading to the PATC Rosser-Lamb Cabin.

Trail Description: SR 643 to Pocosin Fire Road

0.0-2.4 SR 643 ends at small, rough parking lot and trail.

0.1-2.3 Trail junction on left. Johns Rest Cabin to right.

1.1-1.3 Side trail leads to PATC Rosser-Lamb Cabin.

1.5-0.9 Park boundary.

2.4-0.0 Intersection with Pocosin Fire Road.

POCOSIN TRAIL
1.3 miles — yellow-blazed

This trail connects the Pocosin Fire Road and the South River Fire Road (no public access from SR 642). At the junction of the trail with the Pocosin Fire Road one can examine the ruins of the old Upper Pocosin Mission. On the trail about 0.1 mi. from its end on the South River Fire Road a side road leads east, passing the interesting, periwinkle-covered South River Cemetery in 0.1 mi.

POCOSIN HOLLOW TRAIL
2.8 miles — blue-blazed

Pocosin Hollow, like Nicholson Hollow and "Hazel Country" farther north, was once well populated. When bushwhacking, one sees remnants of old farm roads, rock walls and chestnut log fences, old homesites and at least one quite large cemetery with fieldstone grave markers.

The Pocosin Hollow Trail has its upper end on the Pocosin Fire Road, 1.3 mi. from Skyline Drive, SDMP 59.5. Heading north from road junction, trail follows along side of a ridge, then curves to east, eventually dropping down a small hollow to stream. Crossing stream, trail climbs uphill and connects with an old woods road that leads to Park boundary. After first crossing, hollow narrows considerably, revealing numerous small waterfalls and pools along boulder-choked streambed. At Park boundary, trail ends on a private road (not posted) which leads 0.7 mi. to SR 667. (This point is about 6 mi. from VA 230 and 3 mi. farther from Stanardsville.) Pocosin Hollow is a secluded valley, and hemlock forest along lower portion of trail was one of prettiest in Park; however, woolly adelgid infestation has killed many of the trees, leaving towering bare snags. Many of the old homesites are up the hollow from the spot where the trail first crosses the run.)

SOUTH RIVER FALLS TRAIL
1.9 miles — blue-blazed

This scenic trail leads from the South River Picnic Area, SDMP 62.8, down into the deep wooded gorge of South River. It continues to the foot of the very lovely

South River Falls. From top to bottom the trail loses 1,000 ft. of elevation. The cascading falls are about 70 ft. high. This is a popular trail used by many hikers. During the hotter months, hikers frequently use the pool at the base of the falls for wading.

For a *circuit hike*, follow South River Falls Trail to base of falls, then backtrack 0.7 mi. to point where South River Falls Trail turns left off road. Continue straight ahead here for another 0.4 mi. to South River Fire Road. Follow fire road uphill about 0.8 mi. to *AT*. Turn left onto *AT* and follow it 0.5 mi. to South River Falls Trail.

Trail Description: Skyline Drive to base of falls

0.0 Trailhead is on road that loops through South River Picnic Area at point where road is farthest to east.

0.1 Intersection with *AT*. (Via *AT* it is 3 mi. south to Swift Run Gap and 3.3 mi. north to Pocosin Cabin.)

1.0 Pass observation point near top of falls.

1.2 Old road leads left to South River Fire Road. Stay right.

1.8 Reach South River about 500 ft. below falls. Go upstream on foot trail.

1.9 Base of falls.

SOUTH RIVER FIRE ROAD
2.1 miles described — yellow-blazed

This road leads east from Skyline Drive, SDMP 62.7, just north of South River Overlook. Road continues to left and into Rapidan Wildlife Management Area (RWMA). Road ends at "No Trespassing" signs at boundary of RWMA. There is no public access from other side of RWMA.

Trail Description: Skyline Drive to Boundary of RWMA

0.0 Skyline Drive, SDMP 62.7, just north of South River Overlook.

0.3 Intersection with *AT*. (Via *AT* it is 0.5 mi. south to South River Falls Trail and 2.8 mi. north to Pocosin Cabin.)

1.1 Junction with old road, branch of South River Falls Trail.

1.5 Cross gate.

2.0 Old road leads uphill on left.

2.1 Road is blocked with several "No Trespassing" signs and posted letters from Virginia Game Warden warning of prosecution to the fullest extent of the law for trespassing. Please honor private land closings.

SADDLEBACK MOUNTAIN TRAIL
1.4 miles — blue-blazed

This trail runs from the *AT* to the *AT* passing the South River Maintenance Bldg. (no camping). To reach northern trailhead, park in South River Picnic Area and follow South River Falls Trail 0.1 mi. to *AT*. Follow *AT* south (right) for 0.5 mi. Southern trailhead is 1.1 mi. farther south along *AT*. This is a very secluded trail following an old woods road through deep woods past some old cleared fields. There is a *spring* along trail (which might be dry during times of drought) not too distant from trail connection with *AT*. Total distance for loop trail is 3.5 mi. There are no hard climbs, making this walk ideal for families with small children.

DRY RUN FALLS FIRE ROAD
2.8 miles — yellow-blazed

This fire road, gated at Skyline Drive and near Park boundary, leads from the Drive, SDMP 62.6, down west side of the Blue Ridge. Near lower end a faint trace of an old road leads left to Dry Run, a few hundred feet up creek from Dry Run Falls. These falls are well worth seeing after a period of wet weather.

Lower end of fire road is on SR 625, 3.1 mi. from SR 759 and 2.6 mi. farther from Elkton on US 340. To right it is 1.1 mi. to Hensley Church.

Bear peek-a-boo in the Park   *Photo by Lee Sheaffer*

South District - Side Trails

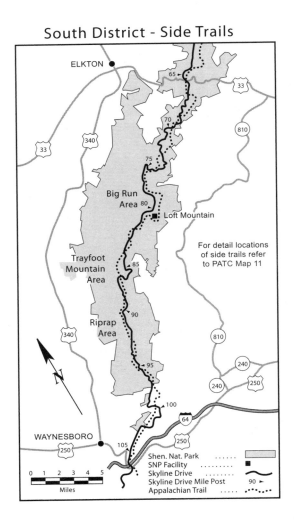

ELKTON

33

810

33   340

Big Run
Area

Loft Mountain

For detail locations
of side trails refer
to PATC Map 11

Trayfoot
Mountain
Area

Riprap
Area

340

810

240

250

WAYNESBORO

250

100

64

105

250

N

Shen. Nat. Park	......
SNP Facility	....
Skyline Drive	....
Skyline Drive Mile Post	90 ▶
Appalachian Trail	.....

0 1 2 3 4 5
Miles

SIDE TRAILS
SOUTH DISTRICT
Shenandoah National Park

Rock Spring Hut   *Photo by Lee Sheaffer*

HIGHTOP HUT ROAD
0.7 mile — blue-blazed

This road leads from the Smith Roach Gap Fire Road, 0.8 mi. from Skyline Drive, SDMP 68.6, and continues to Hightop Hut, crossing the *AT* 0.2 mi. before reaching hut.

For a short *circuit hike*, one can follow *AT* from Smith Roach Gap to summit of Hightop, then descend by backtracking as far as Hightop Hut, following Hightop Hut Road to Smith Roach Gap Fire Road and fire road back to Smith Roach Gap.

SMITH ROACH GAP FIRE ROAD/HORSE TRAIL
1.0 mile within Park — yellow-blazed

This road leads southeastward from Skyline Drive at Smith Roach Gap, SDMP 68.6, to the Park boundary. The access road to Hightop Hut leads left from fire road about 0.8 mi. from Drive. Beyond this point and also at Park boundary, road is blocked to vehicular traffic as well as at Park boundary. A short way beyond Park boundary, road divides. Left fork, SR 626, descends gradually, skirting head of Whiteoak Spring Branch, then descends a ridge extending from Hightop Mtn. and finally coming into SR 630 very near SR 810. Right fork leads south over private land, following a long ridge toward Slaters Mountain, eventually coming into SR 631.

SIMMONS GAP FIRE ROAD
1.0 mile east of Skyline Drive — yellow-blazed
1.5 miles west of Skyline Drive, within Park — yellow-blazed

This road leads from western Park boundary in Beldor Hollow as a continuation of SR 628, crosses Skyline Drive at Simmons Gap, SDMP 73.2, then descends to eastern Park boundary where it becomes SR 628 again. Road is gated at both boundaries and on both sides of Drive. Western portion is also known as Beldor Road.

ROCKY MOUNT TRAIL
5.4 miles — blue-blazed

In the South District of the Park there is a Rocky Mount, a Rocky Mountain and a Rockytop. Rocky Mount is the most northern of these. The Rocky Mount Trail starts at Skyline Drive, SDMP 76.1, and is marked by a concrete post. It leads along a northward-bearing side ridge, reaching the peak of Rocky Mount (2,741 ft.) in 3.4 mi. From the peak it descends very steeply 400 feet to Gap Run.

A *circuit hike* of 10 mi. begins by descending Rocky Mount Trail, turning right, following Gap Run Trail to its upper end on Rocky Mount Trail and returning to start via Rocky Mount Trail.

Trail Description: Skyline Drive to Gap Run

0.0-5.4 Skyline Drive, SDMP 76.1. Follow ridge which extends northward. Many good views.

2.2-3.2 Gap Run Trail leads down Gap Run to rejoin Rocky Mount Trail at its lower end.

3.4-2.0 Summit of Rocky Mount (2,741 ft.). From here trail descends rather steeply. In about 1 mi. trail turns right off ridge, descends to creek and follows it down.

5.4-0.0 End of Rocky Mount Trail. Gap Run Trail leads right, rejoining Rocky Mount Trail in 2.3 mi.

GAP RUN TRAIL
2.3 miles — blue-blazed

This trail starts from the Rocky Mount Trail 2.2 mi. from Skyline Drive and leads down along Gap Run to rejoin the Rocky Mount Trail at its lower end in the gap. The Gap Run Trail is often used along with the Rocky Mount Trail for a *circuit hike*.

ONEMILE RUN TRAIL
3.7 miles — blue-blazed

This trail leads north from Skyline Drive and follows

the narrow Twomile Ridge, which separates Twomile Run and Onemile Run. In 1 mi. it turns off the ridge and descends to Onemile Run, continuing down the run for nearly 2 mi. It swings north, crosses over to Twomile Run and ends on a private road just north of the run.

Access: To reach start of this trail, park at Twomile Run Overlook, SDMP 76.2, and walk south along Drive for about 0.1 mi. Trailhead is marked. (*AT* comes within 100 ft. of east side of Drive just south of here. Look for unmarked path.)

Trail Description: Skyline Drive to Park boundary
  0.0 From Skyline Drive, SDMP 76.3, trail heads northwest along Twomile Ridge.
  1.0 In sag, trail leaves ridge and descends westward.
  1.4 Reach Onemile Run and descend along run.
  2.9 Trail leaves Onemile Run and heads north.
  3.7 Park boundary.

IVY CREEK MAINTENANCE HUT ROAD
0.4 mile — not blazed

This short road, which runs from Skyline Drive, SDMP 79.4, to the PATC Ivy Creek Maintenance Hut (no camping) can be used by hikers as part of a short *circuit hike* which would include a climb up to Loft Mtn. ridge via the Frazier Discovery Trail, SDMP 79.5, then the *AT* between the Frazier Discovery Trail and PATC Ivy Creek Maintenance Bldg., return to Skyline Drive via service road, and a 0.1 mi. walk along the Drive for total distance of 2.1 mi. There is *water* about 100 ft. east of the hut, along the trail.

FRAZIER DISCOVERY TRAIL
1.3 mile circuit — blue-blazed

Attention: Pets are not permitted on this trail.

This is a short but very interesting Park Service discovery trail. It involves a fairly steep climb of 0.6 mi. from Skyline Drive to the *AT* on Loft Mtn., turns left on *AT* for 0.1 mi., then makes an equally steep descent. The trail starts on the east side of the Drive, at the entrance to Loft Mtn. developed area, SDMP 79.5.

DOYLES RIVER TRAIL–JONES RUN TRAIL
4.7 miles — blue-blazed

These lovely trails afford a most rewarding circuit on the east slope of the Blue Ridge from either the Skyline Drive or the *AT*. Originally constructed by the CCC in 1936-37, the trails' main features are the waterfalls on both Doyles River and Jones Run and the tall timber. The route involves a considerable descent of 1,500 ft. and ascent back up to the *AT* and Skyline Drive. Browns Cove to the east is an interesting mountain valley with much white pine. The main Doyles River and Jones Run are located in deep gorges, with broken precipitous cliffs and enormous timber. PATC Doyles River Cabin (a locked structure for use of hikers with advance reservations) is near the Doyles River Trail, 0.4 mi. from Skyline Drive.

A *circuit hike* of 8 mi. includes these two trails and a section of *AT*. For a *shorter circuit* of 6.5 mi., descend along Jones Run, ascend along Doyles River past upper falls, then follow Browns Gap Fire Road to *AT*. Complete circuit by proceeding south along *AT* to Jones Run Parking Area.

Access: Doyles River Trail has its upper end at Doyles River Parking Area on Skyline Drive, SDMP 81.1. Jones Run Trail has its upper end at Jones Run Parking Area, SDMP 83.8. Both trails have their lower ends at junction of Doyles River and Jones Run.

Trail Description: South (Jones Run) to North (Doyles River)

0.0-4.7 Jones Run Parking Area, Skyline Drive (2,700 ft.). Jones Run Trail crosses *AT* in 100 ft. then continues eastward, descending.

0.6-4.1 Trail crosses Jones Run.

1.5-3.2 Trail returns to run and follows south bank.

1.6-3.1 Base of sloping falls.

1.7-3.0 Top of upper falls. Short side trail affords good view of falls.

1.9-2.7 Top of lower falls.

2.5-2.2 Halfway point, junction of Jones Run and Doyles River. Jones Run Trail ends. Ascend on Doyles River Trail.

3.2-1.5 Top of lower falls of Doyles River, a two-step cascade between high rock cliffs.

3.5-1.2 Top of upper falls. This is a three-step cascade in lovely canyon.

3.8-0.9 Cross Browns Gap Fire Road. (Road leads west uphill 1.7 mi. to *AT* at Browns Gap. To east it leads to Browns Cove.)

4.4-0.3 Pass *spring* on right of trail. Spur trail leads right 0.1 mi. steeply up to Doyles River Cabin.

4.7-0.0 Cross *AT*. (To north it is 10 mi. to Simmons Gap, to south 2.2 mi. to Browns Gap and 3.4 mi. to Jones Run Trail.) In 200 ft. reach Skyline Drive at Doyles River Parking Area (2,800 ft.).

BROWNS GAP FIRE ROAD
3.5 miles in Park — yellow-blazed

This old road, the eastern extension of the Madison Run Road, leads from Skyline Drive at Browns Gap, SDMP 82.9, down the east slopes of the Blue Ridge to Browns Cove, crossing the Doyles River Trail and the Doyles River in 1.8 mi. The old road continues beyond the Park boundary for another 1 mi. where it becomes SR 629. The start of SR

629 is 0.8 mi. above the highway bridge over the Doyles River and 1.2 mi. from SR 810. One should park along or near SR 810, as SR 629 is only a one-track road above the bridge and there is almost no place to pull off road. (*Attention*: Lower access from SR 629 may be posted. Please respect "No Trespassing" signs on private land.)

The Browns Gap Road was used by Stonewall Jackson and his men during the Civil War. About 0.4 mi. down from Skyline Drive, to the left of road, a short footpath leads to the grave of William H. Howard, Co. F, 44 Va. Inf., C.S.A. Farther down the road but above the Doyles River is a tulip tree of tremendous girth. The stretch of old road between the Doyles River Trail intersection and the Park boundary is quite lovely. There are many large trees, including hemlock, and the road itself clings along the edge of a steep hillside with the river far below.

TRAILS IN THE BIG RUN AREA

The Big Run ravine is a wild, sheer-walled canyon of spectacular rock formations and talus slopes on the west slope of the Blue Ridge. It is of unusual interest and creates an extraordinary impression of isolation. The Big Run Portal Trail extends the length of this sheer-walled canyon, abruptly closed in at its northern end by the rock walls designated as "The Portal."

Big Run and its tributaries comprise the largest watershed in the Park. This area is contained in the largest of the Park's wilderness areas and is separated from the one just south of it only by the Madison Run Fire Road. The ten trails included in the Big Run Area are for the most part rugged but extremely scenic and isolated, and frequently offer outstanding views of the Shenandoah Valley, especially in the winter months. There are many circuit hikes that can be made, many ideal for backpackers.

BIG RUN PORTAL TRAIL
4.4 miles — yellow-blazed

This is the valley route through the canyon of Big Run, which flows from south to north. The trail follows an old fire road and has a very gentle grade from the Park boundary to its upper end on the Big Run Loop Trail, making for an easy and very pleasant walk. Despite the size of the Big Run drainage, most of the time the stream is smaller than expected, and flows slow and shallow due to the nearly level grade. However, after a storm or melt-off the crossing can be dangerously high. During the spring and summer months, hikers and overnight visitors should carry insect repellant to guard against the mosquitoes and biting gnats. The cliffs, talus slopes and gorge at "The Portal" just below the Big Run Portal Trail's bridge over Big Run are spectacular.

Access: Upper end can be reached from Big Run Loop Trail, following it "south" from Big Run Parking Overlook, SDMP 81.2, for 2.2 mi. to its lowest elevation, or by following Big Run Loop Trail north from its intersection with *AT* 0.6 mi. north of Browns Gap, SDMP 82.9. No access across private land at Park boundary.

Trail Description: Big Run Loop Tr. to Park boundary
0.0-4.4 Intersection with Big Run Loop Trail.
0.7-3.7 Ford side creek. While descending run, there are nine fords, seven of Big Run, the other two of side streams. When run is full, fording may be difficult.
0.9-3.5 Trail crosses to west bank, then recrosses again in 0.2 mi. and again in 0.3 mi.
2.3-2.1 Patterson Ridge Trail enters from right. In 250 yds. cross Rocky Mtn. Run, immediately come to fork and continue straight ahead. (To right is Rocky Mtn. Run Trail, which connects with Brown Mtn. Trail in 2.7 mi.)
2.7-1.7 After two more fords, reach deep pool. To right,

area is flat and shrubby where once there was a field.

3.7-0.7 Cross bridge over Big Run. Brown Mtn. Trail comes in on right 75 yds. before the bridge.

4.2-0.2 Junction with Rockytop Trail, which enters from left. (To right, one can bushwhack down to Big Run at "The Portal.")

4.4-0.0 Gate at Park boundary.

ROCKY MOUNTAIN RUN TRAIL
2.7 miles — blue-blazed

This trail runs from the Big Run Portal Trail up to Brown Mtn. Trail and offers a pleasant connector trail for *circuit hikes* in the area.

PATTERSON RIDGE TRAIL
3.1 miles — yellow-blazed

This trail leads from Skyline Drive, SDMP 79.4, opposite the service road leading to PATC Ivy Creek Maintenance Bldg., descending westward through beautiful forest along Patterson Ridge. It comes into the Big Run Portal Trail 0.1 mi. above the lower end of the Rocky Mtn. Run Trail and 1.5 mi. above the lower end of the Brown Mtn. Trail, 1,500 ft. below its starting point. It can be used for *circuit hikes*.

BIG RUN LOOP TRAIL
4.2 miles — blue- and yellow-blazed

This trail affords access to the upper end of Big Run. The Big Run Loop Trail together with the Big Run Portal Trail affords access to the lower ends of the Rockytop Trail and the Brown Mtn. Trail, as well as the Rocky Mtn. Run Trail and the Patterson Ridge Trail. The Big Run Loop Trail, at its southern end, links the *AT* with the Rockytop Trail.

An excellent *circuit hike* of 5.8 mi. can be made by using the *AT* in one direction and the Big Run Loop Trail in the other.

Access: Northern end of this trail is at Big Run Parking Overlook on Skyline Drive, SDMP 81.2.

Southern end is on *AT* 0.6 mi. north of Browns Gap, SDMP 82.9.

Trail Description: North to South

0.0-4.2 Big Run Parking Overlook. Trail (blue-blazed here) descends steeply by switchbacks.

0.7-3.5 Trail follows crest of ridge between branches of Big Run, then swings left down into main hollow.

2.2-2.0 Junction with Big Run Portal Trail (yellow-blazed). Turn left. This 1.3 mi. section is dual-blazed blue and yellow. Trail ascends steadily following above branch of Big Run.

3.0-1.2 Turn sharply right, away from ravine.

3.5-0.7 At trail junction in sag, Big Run Loop Trail (blue-blazed) turns left. (Rockytop Trail goes right, blue-blazed, and leads along ridge 5.7 mi. to Big Run Portal Trail. Madison Run Spur Trail, yellow-blazed, goes straight ahead to descend to Madison Run Road.)

4.2-0.0 Junction with *AT*. It is 0.3 mi. north to Skyline Drive, SDMP 82.2, and 0.6 mi. south to Browns Gap, SDMP 82.9.

MADISON RUN TRAIL
0.3 mile — yellow-blazed

This short trail runs from the junction of the Rockytop Trail with the Big Run Loop Trail down to Madison Fire Road, entering it 0.8 mi. west of Skyline Drive at Browns Gap.

BROWN MOUNTAIN TRAIL
5.3 miles — blue-blazed

Rocky Mtn. and Brown Mtn. comprise the ridge extending west from the main Blue Ridge along the north side of Big Run. The trail was initially constructed as a fire trail and has a narrow, graded tread. It lies along the crest of one of the spectacular east-west ridges of the South District of the Park. The location and type of forest growth make for extraordinary views. To the north of this ridge is the lower Twomile Ridge, with Rocky Mount in the background. To the south is the high, imposing ridge along which the Rockytop Trail runs. From Skyline Drive the trail leads west along the ridge, first crossing the twin summits of Rocky Mtn., then over Brown Mtn. before dropping steeply to the Big Run Portal Trail.

A *circuit hike* can be made by descending this trail and ascending the Big Run Portal Trail, then turning left onto the Big Run Loop Trail to Big Run Overlook. Walk north a few feet, cross Drive and descend to *AT*. Turn left (north) and follow *AT* to Ivy Creek Overlook. Walk north along Drive remaining distance to Brown Mtn. Overlook. Complete circuit is 18 mi. For a *shorter loop hike*, 11 mi., descend on Brown Mtn. Trail, ascend on Big Run Portal Trail, and turn left onto Big Run Loop Trail to Big Run Overlook. A *shorter circuit hike*, 9.3 mi. can be made by descending Brown Mtn. Trail, ascending Big Run Portal Trail for 1.3 mi., then turning onto Rocky Mtn. Run Trail and climbing along this trail for 2.7 mi. to its junction with Brown Mtn. Trail. Turn right to return to Brown Mtn. Overlook.

Access: Upper end of this trail begins at Brown Mtn. Parking Overlook on Skyline Drive, SDMP 76.9.
Lower access is from Big Run Portal Trail.

Trail Description: Skyline Drive to Big Run Portal
0.0-5.3 Brown Mtn. Parking Overlook, Skyline Drive,

SDMP 76.9.

0.7-4.6 Rocky Mtn. Run Trail leads left down to Big Run Portal Trail.

1.6-3.7 Reach crest of peak of Rocky Mtn. (2,800 ft.). Striking views of Massanutten Mtn. Footing is rough beyond this point.

2.2-3.1 Pass to right of second peak of Rocky Mtn. (2,864 ft.). Along trail from here to summit of Brown Mtn. there is much turkeybeard, a grass-like member of the lily family blooming in early June. Turkeybeard is a close relative of western beargrass.

3.1-2.2 Summit of Brown Mtn. (2,560 ft.). (The Brown Mtn. ridge, like Rockytop to southwest, consists of a sandstone streaked with fossil wormholes.) Descend along a ridge crest with magnificent views of Rockytop, Shenandoah Valley and southern end of Massanutten Mtn. Descend steeply toward Big Run.

5.3-0.0 Junction with Big Run Portal Trail at east end of bridge over Big Run. "The Portal" of Big Run is a short distance down creek from here. Upstream it is 1.4 mi. to lower end of Rocky Mtn. Run Trail and 3.7 mi. to Big Run Loop Trail. To right on Big Run Portal Trail it is 0.5 mi. to lower end of Rockytop Trail and 0.2 mi. farther to gate at Park boundary. There is no access at this boundary. Posted closures must be respected.

ROCKYTOP TRAIL
5.7 miles — blue-blazed

This trail extends along the crest of the ridge which forms the sheer southwest wall of Big Run Canyon. It takes its name from its outstanding feature, Rockytop. (Hikers prefer to call the more northern peak (2,856 ft.) the "real" Rockytop, rather than the one marked on USGS maps.) Where the trail skirts the western face of this highest peak it offers a superb view of the peaks to the southwest and of the Shenandoah Valley. In addition, the rocks of this part of the ridge are quite fascinating. An examination of them will show they contain long, slender cylindrical markings, perhaps an eighth inch in diameter. It is believed that these are fossils of wormholes now 500 million years old! (See "Geology of Shenandoah National Park.") For wildflower enthusiasts, the Rockytop Trail also offers an abundance of turkeybeard, the eastern version of beargrass found in profusion in the western U.S. You will find it in bloom in early June.

This trail has a rather narrow footway and is rough underfoot. However, its advantages far outweigh its disadvantages. It offers excellent views, and access to the Austin Mtn. Trail and the Lewis Peak Trail. A *circuit hike* is possible using the Rockytop Trail along with either of these trails.

Access: Upper end of Rockytop Trail is on Big Run Loop Trail. From Skyline Drive follow *AT* north from Browns Gap, SDMP 82.9, for 0.6 mi., turn left onto Big Run Loop Trail and follow it for 0.7 mi. Rockytop-Big Run Loop Trail junction is marked by concrete post.

Lower end of Rockytop Trail is on Big Run Portal Trail, 0.2 mi. east of gate at Park boundary (no access).

Trail Description: Big Run Loop Trail to Big Run Portal Trail

0.0-5.7 From junction with Big Run Loop Trail, marked by concrete post, Rockytop Trail ascends.

0.4-5.3 Take right fork here. (Left fork is Austin Mtn. Trail.) Trail now skirts right side of ridge for 0.6 mi. then swings to left side, crossing a talus slope with views of Austin Mtn. and Lewis Mtn.

2.2-3.5 Junction with Lewis Peak Trail, marked by concrete post. Rockytop Trail is right fork.

3.0-2.7 Sag at base of hikers' "Rockytop," highest peak of ridge. Ascend along its left side.

3.5-2.2 Cross talus slope with outstanding views of

Austin Mtn., Lewis Mtn. and Lewis Peak to southwest and Shenandoah Valley and Massanutten range farther north. Many of the rocks here and on smaller rock slopes beyond are full of "wormhole" fossils, giving rocks a striated appearance.

3.6-2.1 Bear right and ascend by switchbacks over crest of ridge bearing northwest. Descend along northbearing ridge. (Hangman Run splits main ridge here.)

5.7-0.0 Big Run Portal Trail, marked with concrete post. To left on Big Run Portal Trail it is 0.2 mi. to Park boundary, where it is gated. No access at this boundary.

AUSTIN MOUNTAIN TRAIL
3.2 miles — blue-blazed

This trail runs from Rockytop Trail across Austin Mtn. and down to Madison Run Fire Road. The Austin Mtn. Trail is the more southern of the parallel routes that lead westward from the high ridge of the Rockytop Trail to outlying conical peaks. The upper (eastern) end of the Austin Mtn. Trail begins on the Rockytop Trail near the upper end of the latter. It follows a side ridge between Deep Run and Madison Run to just short of the top of Austin Mtn. The trail slabs the south side of the mountain, then descends steeply to Madison Run Fire Road. Sections of this trail are rocky, steep and poorly graded. Heavy-duty foot gear is recommended.

A *circuit hike* of 9.5 mi. can be made from Browns Gap using the *AT*, Big Run Loop Trail, Rockytop Trail, Austin Mtn. Trail and Madison Run Fire Road.

Access: To reach upper end of this trail follow *AT* for 0.6 mi. north from Browns Gap, SDMP 82.9. Turn left onto Big Run Loop Trail and follow it for 0.7 mi. to its junction with Rockytop Trail. Follow Rockytop Trail (straight ahead at junction) for 0.4 mi. to Austin Mtn. Trail trailhead.

Lower end of Austin Mtn. Trail is on Madison Run Fire

Road 4.4 mi. from Skyline Drive at Browns Gap, SDMP 82.9. To reach trail from US 340 follow SR 663 from Grottoes (or SR 659 from just north of Grottoes) and continue on SR 663 beyond junction with SR 659, passing SR 708 on left and parking at junction of a second road, also entering from left. From here (about 2.5 mi. from US 340) continue up SR 663 on foot another 0.2 mi. to gate, then continue up fire road for 0.7 mi. to trailhead marked by concrete post.

Trail Description: Rockytop Trail to Madison Run Road

0.0-3.2 Junction with Rockytop Trail.

2.1-1.1 Trail descends steeply across rock slopes and under cliffs.

2.7-0.5 Sharp turn in trail. Steep descent continues.

3.2-0.0 Madison Run Road. To left it is 4.4 mi. to Skyline Drive at Browns Gap. To right it is 0.6 mi. to lower end of Furnace Mtn. Trail and 0.1 mi. farther to gate where road becomes SR 663.

LEWIS PEAK TRAIL
2.6 miles — blue-blazed

This trail is the more northern of the parallel routes leading west from the Rockytop Trail. It continues beyond Lewis Peak, descending to the Park boundary and then a short distance farther to a dirt road in the valley (no access). Lewis Peak itself is reached by a 0.3 mi. side trail. From the peak there are good views of the Shenandoah Valley and the Massanutten range to the northwest and west and the surrounding peaks of the Blue Ridge on the north, east and south.

Access: Upper end is reached via Rockytop Trail. Trailhead is 2.3 mi. from Rockytop Trail-Big Run Loop Trail junction and 3.4 mi. from Rockytop Trail-Big Run Portal Trail junction.

Lower end of this trail is posted at Park boundary. There is no access here.

Trail Description: Rockytop Trail to Shenandoah Valley

0.0-2.6 Junction with Rockytop Trail. Follow crest of ridge extending west between branches of Lewis Run.

0.7-1.9 Reach sag.

0.9-1.7 At junction, main trail goes left. (Right fork is 0.3 mi. spur trail leading to summit of Lewis Peak [2,760 ft.]. Panoramic view of Shenandoah Valley, Massanutten range and surrounding peaks.) Main trail descends toward west and northwest along ridge paralleling Upper Lewis Run.

2.4-0.2 Cross Upper Lewis Run. In 50 ft. turn right onto well-worn road, passing a cabin.

2.6-0.0 Come into private road where trail ends. Posted closures must be respected.

MADISON RUN FIRE ROAD
5.1 miles — yellow-blazed

This road, gated at each end, runs from Browns Gap down west side of Blue Ridge, becoming SR 663 outside Park. It can be used with either Austin Mtn. Trail or Furnace Mtn. Trail for a *circuit hike*. Upper end of this road starts at Browns Gap, SDMP 82.9 (2,599 ft.). Lower end can be reached by following SR 663 east until it becomes fire road, about 2.8 mi. from US 340 in Grottoes. Elevation at Park boundary is 1,360 ft. Madison Run Trail, 0.3 mi., connects fire road with Big Run Loop Trail.

STULL RUN FIRE ROAD
2 miles — yellow-blazed in Park

Starting near the junction of SR 663 and SR 629 east of Grottoes, the Stull Run Fire Road (yellow-blazed) leads south. In about 2 mi. it runs out of Park and continues as a private road. A bit farther south a short section of road, where it follows Stull Run, lies within Park but this portion is being abandoned and closed to vehicles. No trails connect with fire road but it offers bushwhackers access to wilderness area that includes Abbott Ridge and Hall Mountain.

TRAYFOOT MOUNTAIN AREA

TRAYFOOT MOUNTAIN TRAIL
5.4 miles — blue-blazed

This trail leads from Skyline Drive to the top of Trayfoot Mountain (3,374 ft.), then descends along a narrow ridge leading southwest and forming the divide between Paine Run and Stull Run. Along the route are some rock formations offering outstanding views. The trail's lower end on the Paine Run Trail is at an elevation of 1,440 ft.

A *circuit hike* of 10 mi. would include the Paine Run Trail and the stretch of *AT* between Blackrock Gap and the Trayfoot Mtn. Trail.

The Trayfoot Mtn. Trail offers the shortest route (about 0.5 mi.) to Blackrock from the Drive. There is parking space for several cars on the trail a few hundred feet from the Drive.

Access: Upper end is on Skyline Drive, SDMP 84.7, about 2 mi. south of Browns Gap.

To reach the lower terminus, turn east from US 340 just south of Grottoes onto SR 661. Park at turnaround at end of state maintenance. Continue up private road on foot to Paine Run. Paine Run Trail, blocked to vehicles at its lower end by large rocks, is just north of run. Follow it up run for 0.3 mi. to start of Trayfoot Mtn. Trail. Please help keep road and parking area free of trash. Access across private land at Park boundary is by goodwill of landowners. Posted closures must be respected.

Trail Description: Skyline Drive to Paine Run Trail

0.0-5.4 Trailhead on Skyline Drive, SDMP 84.7. Trail leads west, soon almost touching but not crossing *AT*. Trails run parallel for about 0.1 mi., then Trayfoot Mtn. Trail passes to south of Blackrock whereas *AT* circles through Blackrock area.

0.4-5.0 Intersection with *AT* just south of Blackrock.

0.5-4.9 Old road to left leads down southwestward ridge paralleling *AT*. (Road used as service road to Blackrock Hut.) Trayfoot Mtn. Trail continues straight ahead and enters largest wilderness area in Park.

0.9-4.5 Where trail reaches ridge crest, Blackrock Spur Trail leads right and back along ridge crest for 0.1 mi. to *AT* at Blackrock.

1.4-4.0 Where trail turns sharply to left climbing Trayfoot Mtn., Furnace Mtn. Trail leads north (straight ahead) to Madison Run Fire Road in 3.4 mi.

1.6-3.8 Just short of summit of Trayfoot Mtn. trail leaves old fire road and bears right, heading southwest along crest of long Trayfoot Mtn. ridge. Descend gradually, crossing numerous knobs. Views on both sides of trail.

4.8-0.6 Turn sharply left (east). Excellent view of Buzzard Rock peak across Paine Run.

5.1-0.3 Turn sharply right.

5.4-0.0 Junction with Paine Run Trail. (To left it leads to Skyline Drive in 3.4 mi. To right leads to Park boundary and SR 614.)

BLACKROCK SPUR TRAIL
0.1 mile — blue-blazed

From the *AT* at Blackrock this trail follows the ridge crest toward Trayfoot Mtn., coming into the Trayfoot Mtn. Trail where the latter reaches the ridge crest. This is a very short but useful connector trail.

FURNACE MOUNTAIN TRAIL
3.4 miles — blue-blazed

This trail, which has its upper end on the Trayfoot Mtn. Trail, leads down the long northwest-bearing ridge of Trayfoot Mtn. toward the peak of Furnace Mtn. From a sag at the base of this peak the main trail descends along the west slopes of the mountain, while a spur trail leads right 0.5 mi. over the summit to an excellent viewpoint. Almost the entire trail lies within a wilderness area and is in one of the more remote sections of the Park. The lower end of the trail is on the Madison Run Fire Road.

Access: To reach lower end of trail, follow SR 663 east from US 340 in Grottoes (or from US 340 north of Grottoes turn onto SR 659 and follow it to SR 663) and continue up road to Park boundary, where road is gated. Continue up road (Madison Run Fire Road) on foot 0.1 mi. to concrete post marking start of Furnace Mtn. Trail on south side. It crosses Madison Run, then heads *downstream* for a hundred feet or so before starting to climb.

To reach upper end follow Trayfoot Mtn. Trail from Drive, SDMP 84.7, for 1.4 mi. to point where latter makes sharp bend to left before ascending toward summit of Trayfoot Mtn. Trailhead is right at bend, to right of road. One may also reach trailhead by following *AT* 1.1 mi. from its crossing of Skyline Drive, SDMP 84.3, to Blackrock, then Blackrock Spur Trail 0.1 mi. to Trayfoot Mtn. Trail. Continue out ridge for 0.6 mi. to sharp bend described above.

Trail Description: Trayfoot Mtn. Trail to Madison Run Fire Road

0.0-3.4 Junction with Trayfoot Mtn. Trail. Follow ridge leading north-northwest.

0.7-2.7 Trail turns sharply right.

1.8-1.6 Take left fork at junction. (To right leads 0.5 mi.

to beyond summit of Furnace Mtn., ending on ledge with excellent view over Madison Run.)

3.4-0.0 Madison Run Fire Road. (To right is lower end of Austin Mtn. Trail in 0.6 mi. To left is Park boundary, where road is gated and becomes SR 663 leading to US 340.)

PAINE RUN TRAIL
3.7 miles — yellow-blazed

This trail, formerly a fire road, leads west from Skyline Drive at Blackrock Gap, SDMP 87.4. In about 1 mi. it passes near Blackrock Springs, site of a former hotel. Below the springs the trail descends along Paine Run, finally passing through a narrow gorge between the southeast end of the Trayfoot Mtn. ridge and a sharp peak, Buzzard Rock. About 0.3 mi. before its lower end, the Trayfoot Mtn. Trail branches to the north to Skyline Drive in 5.4 mi.

A *circuit hike* of 9.5 mi. can be made from Blackrock Gap by following the *AT* north to Blackrock, the Blackrock Trail to Trayfoot Mtn. Trail, west and south on Trayfoot Mtn. Trail to Paine Run Trail and then ascending the latter back to Blackrock Gap.

RIPRAP AREA

RIPRAP TRAIL
4.5 miles — blue-blazed

This is a very picturesque route. From its northern trailhead on the *AT* it swings west and climbs along Calvary Rocks with excellent views, then continues on to Chimney Rocks with more views. Along the upper half of the Riprap Trail you may notice evidence of a forest fire, which burned 1,400 acres in October 1998. The fire originated near Calvary Rocks, then burned toward Paine Run to the north and Riprap Hollow to the south before it was brought under control. The Riprap Trail was also closed for a time in late April and early May of 1999 due to the Shop Run Fire. This fire was extensive and closed a large part of the South District. Riprap Trail descends Cold Spring Hollow and on to Riprap Hollow. This is one of the few areas of the Park where one can find the Catawba rhododendron (a very common shrub farther south), as well as mountain laurel, fly poison, turkeybeard, starflower and wild bleeding heart, all blooming in late May. *Note:* The Riprap Hollow/Wildcat Ridge trails are heavily visited. Legal campsites in Riprap Hollow are limited. Backpackers wishing to stay overnight in the hollow should allow extra time to locate sites that meet the Backcountry Camping Regulations.

A *circuit hike* of 9.5 mi. makes use of the Wildcat Ridge Trail, most of the Riprap Trail and the section of *AT* between them.

Access: To reach northern end of Riprap Trail, park at Riprap Trail Parking Area, SDMP 90.0, take short spur trail to *AT* and turn right. Follow *AT* north 0.4 mi. to start of Riprap Trail.

To reach southern terminus, turn east from US 340 onto SR 612 at Crimora and drive about 1.7 mi., nearly to end of state maintenance. Follow Black Bear Road left for 1 mi. Large boulders at trailhead block trail to vehicles.

Trail Description: Skyline Drive to Park boundary
0.0-4.5 Junction with *AT* at a point on *AT* 0.4 mi. north of short spur trail leading to Riprap Trail Parking Area, SDMP 90.0 (and 2.9 mi. south of Blackrock Gap via *AT*).
1.0-3.5 Path leads right 15 ft. to cliffs, good overlook, near Calvary Rocks.
1.2-3.3 Trail turns sharply left. Spur trail leads right 75 ft. to edge of cliffs, Chimney Rock, with fine views north.
1.8-2.7 Turn sharply left from ridge down into Cold

Spring Hollow.

2.8-1.7 Trail descends steeply through a rocky chasm. Route here is very spectacular.

3.0-1.5 Cross to east of stream.

3.1-1.4 Recross stream. Deep pool at base of sloping falls makes excellent swimming hole. Considerable amounts of pink Catawba rhododendron near run.

3.6-0.9 Junction with Wildcat Ridge Trail which goes east (left), climbing 2.7 mi. to Skyline Drive, SDMP, 92.1.

4.5-0.0 Park boundary.

WILDCAT RIDGE TRAIL
2.7 miles — blue-blazed

This lovely trail starts at the Wildcat Ridge Parking Area on Skyline Drive, SDMP 92.1. It crosses the *AT* in 0.1 mi., continues west following Wildcat Ridge, then descends into Riprap Hollow to end on the Riprap Trail. It is used along with the Riprap Trail and the *AT* for an exceptionally beautiful *circuit hike* of about 9.5 mi. *Note:* The Riprap Hollow/Wildcat Ridge trails are heavily visited. Legal campsites in Riprap Hollow are limited. Backpackers wishing to stay overnight in the hollow should allow extra time to locate sites that meet the Backcountry Camping Regulations.

Trail Description: Skyline Drive to Riprap Trail

0.0-2.7 Junction with Skyline Drive at Wildcat Ridge Parking Area, SDMP 92.1.

0.1-2.6 Intersection with *AT*. (To right, via *AT*, it is 2.8 mi. to Riprap Trail Parking Area and 3.1 mi. to northern end of Riprap Trail. To left it is 0.3 mi. to next *AT* crossing of Drive and 2.3 mi. to Turk Gap.) From here, trail descends gradually along Wildcat Ridge.

1.0-1.7 Cross over knob (2,514 ft.), then continue descent along ridge. Occasional good views south. In winter one may be able to glimpse Crimora Lake in Dorsey

Hanger Hollow below trail.

1.5-1.2 Come into sag.

1.8-0.9 In another sag, trail turns sharply to right, leaves ridge crest and descends steeply.

2.1-0.6 Cross a run, then turn sharply left, descending along it and recrossing it farther down.

2.6-0.1 To right, across run, short spur trail leads to a conspicuous cave at base of cliffs.

2.7-0.0 Junction with Riprap Trail. (To left it is 0.9 mi. to Park boundary. To right it is 3.6 mi. to *AT*.)

TURK GAP TRAIL
1.6 miles — yellow-blazed

This former fire road, blocked to vehicles, runs from Turk Gap on Skyline Drive, SDMP 94.1, down the west side of the Blue Ridge, reaching the Park boundary just above the muddy ponds of the old Crimora mine. Public access outside the Park is closed.

The Crimora Manganese Mine was formerly one of the largest manganese mining operations in the country. The operations commenced in 1867 and extended, through various mining methods, periodically to 1947; operations resumed in 1949, but the mines are now closed. The manganese was mined out of clay deposits in a syncline of Cambrian quartzite. Crimora Lake, an artificial lake, furnished water power for mining operations. Visitors will find this area more interesting if they have read the detailed history of the mines, "The Crimora Manganese Mine" by Samuel V. Moore, in the October 1947 PATC *Bulletin*.

TURK MOUNTAIN TRAIL
0.9 mile — blue-blazed

This short trail is highly recommended. It starts from the *AT* 0.2 mi. south of Turk Gap and heads west, following a ridge. In about 0.4 mi., where the Sawmill Ridge goes off to left, the Turk Mtn. Trail continues straight ahead and begins to climb Turk Mtn. (2,981 ft.). The view from the summit is outstanding. As on several of the other peaks of the Park which are west of the main Blue Ridge crest, the rock is a type of sandstone full of fossil wormholes, giving it a distinctive striated appearance. In early June, turkeybeard, a member of the lily family, can be found blooming here.

MOORMANS RIVER FIRE ROAD AND NORTH FORK MOORMANS RIVER TRAIL
9.5 miles — yellow-blazed

This was the original route of the Appalachian Trail between Blackrock Gap and Jarman Gap. From Blackrock Gap the road leads southeast, then south, following down the tumbling North Fork of Moormans River to SR 614. From here the fire road fords the North Fork a short distance above the Charlottesville Reservoir (wading may be required during the wetter seasons or during periods of heavy rain). It then climbs southwestward to Jarman Gap, following up the South Fork of Moormans River. The fire road is gated at both ends and at the Park boundaries.

During the evening of June 27, 1995, an intense rainstorm triggered nearly 100 landslides in the area of about five square miles within the drainage of the North Fork of the Moormans River. Many of the landslides, or debris flows, with tons of soil, rock and thousands of trees, reached the river and were carried away in the flood waters. Although the natural revegetation of the denuded hillsides and streambed has begun, evidence of this "2000-year flood event" will be evident for decades to come. In 1997, after the flood debris settled, what remained of the lower three miles of the North Fork Moormans River Road in SNP was reconstructed as a foot and horse trail, North Fork Moormans River Trail. The upper half of the North Fork Moormans River Road and the entire South Fork

Moormans River Road were relatively unaffected by the flood of 1995. The flood of 1995 has made this a fascinating area to explore, but hikers are encouraged to use caution when hiking or camping near debris piles.

A long *circuit hike* can be made by following the fire road in one direction and the *AT* in the other. For *shorter circuits* a portion of the fire road can be used, along with the Turk Branch Trail and *AT*. From Blackrock Gap a circuit using the fire road, Turk Branch Trail and the *AT* is about 18 mi.; from Jarman Gap a circuit using the southern portion of the fire road, the Turk Branch Trail and the *AT* is only 8 mi. in length.

Access: Northern end of fire road is on Skyline Drive, SDMP 87.4, at Blackrock Gap. Southern end is at Jarman Gap, SDMP 96.7.

To reach fire road from valley follow SR 810 from Crozet to White Hall (about 4.5 mi.). Follow SR 614 west 5.8 mi. to its end just beyond Charlottesville Reservoir. Junction with fire road is here.

Trail Description: Blackrock Gap to Jarman Gap

0.0-9.5 From Skyline Drive at Blackrock Gap, SDMP 87.4 (2,321 ft.), road leads southeast, immediately crossing *AT*.

1.4-8.1 Take right fork and cross stream. (Old road to left leads up valley through overgrown fields to Via Gap.) Continue downstream, heading almost due south.

1.6-7.9 To left, an old road leads uphill to Pasture Fence Mtn.

2.2-7.3 Re-enter Park at Park gate. North Fork Moormans River Road becomes North Fork Moormans River Trail for next 3 mi. as it passes through flood-impacted area from flood of 1995.

3.7-5.8 To right, a side trail leads 0.1 mi. up Big Branch to series of cascades, highest of which has a free fall of about 50 ft.

5.2-4.3 Pass Park gate and bulletin board. North Fork Moormans River Trail ends. Continue on North Fork Moormans River Road.

5.5-4.0 Cross SR 614 at end of that road. In 0.1 mi. ford North Fork of Moormans River. Ford (1,000 ft.) is a few hundred feet below former highway bridge, foundations of which are still visible, and a few hundred feet upriver from Charlottesville Reservoir. Fire road continues south to South Fork of Moormans River, then climbs along it, crossing stream several times.

7.6-1.9 Turk Branch Trail leads right up mountain 2.1 mi. to Skyline Drive, joining it at Turk Gap, SDMP 94.1.

9.3-0.2 Intersection with *AT* 0.2 mi. north of Bucks Elbow Mtn. Fire Road.

9.5-0.0 Junction with Skyline Drive and Bucks Elbow Mtn. Fire Road at Jarman Gap, SDMP 96.7 (2,173 ft.)

TURK BRANCH TRAIL
2.1 miles — yellow-blazed

This is a pretty trail and not a difficult one to follow. From Skyline Drive and *AT* at Turk Gap, SDMP 94.1 (2,600 ft.), the trail follows an old road down the east side of the Blue Ridge. Its lower end is on the Moormans River Fire Road (1,440 ft.) at a point on fire road 1.9 mi. north of Jarman Gap.

A *circuit hike* of 7.5 mi. can be made by descending the Turk Branch Trail to Moormans River Fire Road, following up the fire road (south) to the *AT* just below Jarman Gap, and then taking the *AT* north to Turk Gap. (Starting the circuit at Jarman Gap the hike would be 0.3 mi. longer as one would first have to hike down the Moormans River Fire Road to its intersection with the *AT*.) A *longer circuit*, 18 mi., can be made by following the fire road north to Blackrock Gap and returning to Turk Gap via the *AT*.

BUCKS ELBOW MOUNTAIN FIRE ROAD
0.6 mile in Park — not blazed

From Skyline Drive and its junction with the Moormans River Fire Road at Jarman Gap, SDMP 96.7, the Bucks Elbow Mtn. Fire Road leads east, uphill, winding its way up to the top of Bucks Elbow Mtn. (outside Park) to an FAA installation. Road is gated near Skyline Drive. It intersects the *AT* 0.1 mi. from the Drive.

GASLINE ROAD
2.0 miles — yellow-blazed

From Skyline Drive, SDMP 96.2, the Gasline Road leads down the west slopes of the Blue Ridge to the Park boundary. It was constructed to give access to the gas pipeline and is of little interest to hikers. Like the fire roads, it is gated at Skyline Drive.

Corbin Cabin *PATC photo*

DESCRIPTION OF CABINS

For more information see PATC publication, *Cabins*, which includes complete descriptions and photos of all cabins.

Following is a listing and brief history of cabins in and around the Park. As noted, some cabins are open to the general public and others are available to PATC members only. Information on all 38 cabins maintained by PATC, including descriptions, locations and rental procedures, can also be obtained on the PATC website at *www.patc.net*.

NOTE: Although each cabin has a natural source of water (spring or stream) this water has not been tested and its purity cannot be guaranteed. Boiling is recommended.

PUBLIC CABINS WITHIN THE PARK
(north to south)

Range View (PATC Map # 9)
North District; Primitive; Sleeps 8 persons

This one-room stone structure was built by PATC in 1933, but title went to SNP when the Park was established. The cabin looks out on a cleared grassy area with a view of the valley on the eastern slopes of the Blue Ridge and the top of Old Rag Mtn. in the distance.

Corbin Cabin (PATC Map # 10)
Central District; Primitive; Sleeps 12 persons

This two-story mountaineer's cabin was built by George Corbin in 1910 and was his home until it was bought by the state in 1938 for inclusion in SNP. It's listed on the National Registry of Historic Places. In 1954 PATC took over stewardship of the cabin and maintains it for rental. It is situated in Nicholson Hollow about 6.5 miles south of Thornton Gap, and 1.5 miles east of and 1,100 ft. below the Skyline Drive. It has a fireplace in the living room and a stove in the kitchen. Being situated near the Hughes River, it offers cool dips in the summer time and fishing opportunities (as regulated by SNP catch-and-release rules) throughout the year.

Rock Spring Cabin (PATC Map # 10)
Central District; Primitive; Sleeps 12 persons

This log cabin lies on the western slope of Hawksbill Mtn. and looks out across Page Valley to Massanutten Mtn. It was built by the Park in 1936 with squared logs. Like all the other cabins in the Park, except for Corbin and Jones Mtn. cabins, it has an outdoor fireplace under the overhanging roof, as well as a stove inside, both usable for cooking. The highest peak in the Park (4,049 ft.) is at the summit of Hawksbill Mountain and is a favorite goal for hikers leaving from this cabin.

Jones Mountain Cabin (PATC Map # 10)
Central District; Primitive; Sleeps 10 persons

Jones Mtn. Cabin is a two-story log cabin situated near Bear Church Rock on Jones Mtn., an eastward-trending arm of SNP's Central District. Before it became part of SNP in the mid-1930s, it was the home of mountaineer Harvey Nichols, known widely for his apple brandy. It was rehabilitated by PATC between 1969 and 1974. The cabin is located near the head of a hollow with a view to the southeast. Much of the hike in, via the approach from the east, follows the Staunton River, which has wading pools. (Water should not be assumed safe to drink.) Like several other cabins constructed or rehabilitated by the Club, Jones Mtn. Cabin has a loft that only partly covers the first floor, and a skylight that makes the cabin light inside, even in cloudy weather. The cabin has a large covered porch on the downhill side, which may be a hazard for small children.

Pocosin Cabin (PATC Map # 10)
Central District; Primitive; Sleeps 12 persons

Pocosin, pronounced poh-COH-sin in PATC, is an Indian name generally connoting a marsh, swamp, or tract of low land subject to flooding but is used in soil science in southeastern Virginia for a relatively high, un-drained flat area. This one-room cabin looks eastward from 3,200 ft. elevation over a forested valley and the Piedmont, and little fits the name, which is taken from the Upper Pocosin Mission, founded in 1904. This is one of the coziest cabins and was built by the Park in 1937, using squared logs.

Doyles River Cabin (PATC Map # 11)
South District; Primitive; Sleeps 12 persons

Architects of the National Park Service prepared the plans for this one-room cabin in June 1935. It was constructed in 1936 entirely by artisans and through facilities of the Civilian Conservation Corps. The walls are of timbers sawed 10 inches square from seasoned chestnut logs, with the surfaces chipped to simulate rough dressing and with the four edges beveled. It is in the South Section of the Park, 15.4 miles southward on Skyline Drive from Swift Run Gap From its elevation of about 2,800 feet at the head of Doyles River, the cabin looks southeastward down a picturesque valley and across to Cedar Mountain and Via Gap. The steep drop in front of the cabin may be dangerous for small children.

Mutton Top Cabin   *PATC photo*

MEMBER-ONLY CABINS ADJACENT TO
SHENANDOAH NATIONAL PARK:

Vining Tract Cabins (PATC Map #11)
South District

Mutton Top, Morris, Conley, Wineberry, and Johnson cabins are located above Lydia, Virginia, on PATC property bordering the east side of SNP. The site is part of a tract obtained by donation and purchase from Dr. and Mrs. Rutledge Vining, who wished to preserve the many vestiges of this Appalachian settlement occupied from the mid-nineteenth century until the 1940s. These include cabins and outbuildings, cemeteries, split rail and stone fences, foundations, terraces and orchards. Former residents and their descendants, many of whom live nearby, occasionally visit the area. Members of the local community also use the dirt road bisecting the property, collect nuts and mushrooms, and hunt on the property with permits issued by a Club member living in Mutton Hollow. Neighborly contact with these people and continuation of their traditional activities will help to promote and maintain the good relations with the community that are essential to the success of the Club's activity in the area.

Morris Cabin
Primitive; Sleeps 12 persons

This four-room cabin includes a kitchen, a living/dining room, two bunkrooms, and two porches. It has a view of the Virginia Piedmont below.

Waymond Morris started building the cabin in 1927 on land that had been his mother's. He grew corn on fields that were then open down to Conley Cabin and raised horses on pasture land now grown up with trees, except for the meadow surrounding Mutton Top Cabin, about 275 yards uphill. In 1957 he built a horse barn of logs salvaged from the building that once surrounded the two-story stone chimney just above the barn. Among Dr. Vining's improvements was the bathtub at the spring. According to his son Joe, "T. S. Eliot, W. H. Auden, Winston Churchill, and Bertrand Russell have bathed in it when it was at its original location" at the University of Virginia Guest House.

Mutton Top Cabin
Primitive; Sleeps 9 persons

Mutton Top Cabin, donated to PATC by the William Craddock family in 1983, was originally a board-and-batten structure that was destroyed by fire in 1989. Following the plans of architect and Club member Roberto Pena, Club members rebuilt it between 1989 and 1992. The square-cut logs framing the building came from a dismantled cabin. It has a kitchen alcove with a cookstove, a sitting area with a heating stove, and bunks along the back and side walls. There are covered porches on two sides, with an outdoor cook area. The deck and picture windows offer an exceptional panoramic view of the surrounding terrain and of the Virginia Piedmont to the east.

Conley Cabin
Primitive; Sleeps 8 persons

Conley Cabin was built by Elijah Conley. The south porch and open yard offer an exceptional view of the surrounding area. It is a one-room cabin sectioned off to give a kitchen/eating area and a sitting/sleeping area. The sitting area has a wood-burning Franklin stove, which gives heat, at the same time offering a fireplace atmosphere. The kitchen area is equipped with a small wood-burning cook stove. Windows almost surrounding the cabin make it light and airy in the summer months, yet the cabin stays warm and toasty in the winter months. A wraparound porch has a south view porch swing that adds to the relaxed nature of this cabin.

Wineberry Cabin
Primitive; Sleeps 8 persons

Wineberry Cabin is located above Lydia, Virginia, on PATC property bordering the east side of SNP. The site is part of a tract obtained by donation and purchase from Dr. and Mrs. Rutledge Vining, who wished to preserve the many vestiges of this Appalachian settlement occupied from the mid-nineteenth century until the 1940s.

Not much is known about who built Wineberry Cabin or when it was built. All we really know is that they picked a secluded location next to a spring that flows year-round. Most of the logs and the roof are original. Club volunteers have replaced five logs, installed a new floor and windows and added decks on two sides of the cabin. The one-room cabin has a wood-burning stove for heating and warming food (not recommended for cooking), a sink for washing dishes, two Adirondack chairs for relaxing on the deck,

Wineberry Cabin

PATC photo

and an outdoor grill for cooking. The spring is located just a few yards from the cabin

Johnson Cabin
Primitive; Sleeps 4 persons

Located along the western edge of the Vining Tract, Johnson Cabin was built in the 1980s by family members as a hunting camp. It is solidly constructed of logs salvaged from various out-buildings that had been part of the Morris farm. Efficient use of the small 7' x 15' interior provides space for beds, a heating/cooking stove, a table, four chairs and a Hoosier cabinet. A detached cook shed, with counter space, a cooking grill and a picnic table, was added in 2005.

Vining Cabin   *PATC photo*

Vining Cabin (PATC Map #11)
Modern; Sleeps 6 persons

PATC leases the 675-acre Daniel Vining family farm in Greene County, VA. The farm, previously owned by Daniel Vining's parents, Dr. and Mrs. Rutledge Vining, adjoins PATC's Vining Tract, which was obtained by purchase and grant from the Vinings in early 1980. It is a classic example of a 19th century Appalachian farm, containing a log cabin, numerous barns and other out-buildings, and pastures surrounded by stone and rail fences. The farm (known as Mutton Hollow Farm) is located at the end of Mattie's Run Road (SR 653) in a valley at the base of High Top Mtn. and Daniels Mtn. The cabin consists of the original chestnut log structure, estimated to be more than 100 years old, and a stone addition constructed by Dr. Vining. The first floor contains two large sitting rooms, a kitchen, and a bathroom. A large bedroom is above the sitting room in the log portion of the house. The cabin has electricity and fireplaces to provide additional heating. Well water is pumped into the house.

MEMBER-ONLY CABINS IN VICINITY OF SHENANDOAH VALLEY

Tulip Tree Cabin (PATC Map #10)
Central District; Primitive; Sleeps 8 persons

Located on the western slopes just outside of SNP, Tulip Tree Cabin was constructed by volunteer PATC members using native materials and primitive hand tools, much as our pioneer forefathers would have done. For a mountain cabin it is bright, cheerful and airy in summer. When closed up in winter it can be kept toasty warm with the wood-heating stove. It also has a fireplace.

Lambert Cabin (PATC Map #10)
Central District; Modern; Sleeps 8 persons

Lambert Cabin near Luray, Virginia is located in Shaver Hollow. It is the former home of Darwin Lambert, long-time PATC member, conservationist, editor, and first park employee of SNP. The old mountain road that leads from Jewell Hollow Road to Lambert Cabin is the continuation of Crusher Ridge Trail, which intersects the AT in SNP. The cabin is 0.2 mi. from the Tulip Tree Cabin. The log structure dates to the Revolutionary War and now has two frame additions. Inside are a living room, library, parlor, two upstairs bedrooms and a bunkroom, bathroom with lavatory, toilet, bathtub and a work room. There is a modern kitchen equipped with electric refrigerator, an electric cooking range and a dining area. The water source for the cabin is well water. An outside moldering privy can also be used for sanitation.

Cliff's House (PATC Map #10)
Central District; Modern; Sleeps 8 persons

Cliff's House has living space upstairs and a workshop area downstairs. The living area has large sliding glass doors and picture windows. There are sliding barn doors to cover the windows. The cabin is well insulated and little heat is needed to keep it cozy. It has electricity and running water.

Cliff's House *PATC photo*

Weaver Cabin (PATC Map #10)
Central District; Semi-Primitive; Sleeps 10 persons

Weaver Cabin is a two-story structure, but only the downstairs is being used. It is about 115 years old and was the Joe Lam family homestead. Cliff Firestone lived in this cabin while his house was being constructed. The cabin supports upstairs are made with "tongue & groove" junctions put together with wooden pegs (no nails). On the outside, the wood used was from the property and what was available. It has a wood-burning stove for heat, and propane-driven lights and cook stove.

Meadows Cabin (PATC Map #10)
Central District; Semi-Primitive; Sleeps 12 persons

In 1913 Edgar Meadows moved from the old home-stead, located just over the ridge immediately in front of the cabin, and built Meadows Cabin on the present site. He raised five children, a few of whom attended the Hoover Community School several miles west of the cabin. The cabin stayed in the Meadows family until 1981, when PATC purchased it and 94 acres of land. This two-story frame cabin is located adjacent to the east side of SNP and provides access to some of the finest trails in the Park.

John's Rest Cabin (Map #10)
Central District; Primitive; Sleeps 6 persons

This cabin was partially built in West Virginia, using logs salvaged from old buildings in the area. It was bought by PATC, taken down, and rebuilt at its present site. It has a main room, upstairs loft and side porch overlooking Entry Run.

J. Frank Schairer Trail Center (PATC Map #11)
South District; Semi-Primitive; Sleeps 12 persons

The Trail Center is on a ridge providing spectacular views of Rocky Mount and Massanutten Mtn. to the west and Bush Mtn. to the east. The large main room has a stone fireplace and a wood-burning stove for heat. A deck with picnic tables offers views of the valley and distant mountains. Access is from Skyline Drive.

Argow Cabin (PATC Map #11)
South District; Semi-private; Sleeps 8 persons

Argow Cabin is an 1850's chestnut log home formerly owned by Samuel Eaton (1828-1896). It is a 2-story structure with a basement. The cabin sits on the 200-acre Firestone tract dedicated to Cliff Firestone, a long-time

PATC member who left PATC his property (where Cliff's House and Weaver currently sit) and a sizable donation that greatly enhanced the club's endowment. The Frank Schairer Trail Center is also located on this tract, which is adjacent to SNP. The surrounding land to the west is owned by Honorary Life Member Keith Argow. In keeping with the club's philosophy of preservation and conservation, Keith suggested that the club restore this historic chestnut log cabin located about a mile from the Schairer Trail Center and offered a generous donation to begin the restoration. The cabin was dedicated on October 23, 2010 and offers a superb view to the west.

Argow Cabin   *Photo by Jeff Testerman*

INDEX OF PLACE NAMES
(Trails in **bold face**)

PATC MAPS AND GUIDE BOOKS

The following maps and guides are available from the PATC. In addition, PATC publishes books of historic interest, including several on the people and land of the SNP. To learn more, or to place an order, visit *www.patc.net* or call PATC at 703-242-0693 Monday through Wednesday 7 p.m. to 9 p.m. or Thursday or Friday, noon to 2 p.m.

Maps:
- Appalachian Trail, Cumberland Valley, Pennsylvania (Susquehanna River to Route 94)
- Appalachian Trail, Michaux State Forest, Pennsylvania (Route 94 to Route 30)
- Appalachian Trail, Michaux State Forest, Pennsylvania (Route 30 to Pennsylvania-MD State Line)
- Appalachian Trail, Maryland
- Appalachian Trail, Northern Virginia (Potomac River to Snickers Gap)
- Appalachian Trail, Shenandoah National Park (North District)
- Appalachian Trail, Shenandoah National Park (Central District)
- Appalachian Trail, Shenandoah National Park (South District)
- Appalachian Trail, George Washington National Forest—Pedlar District (Rockfish Gap to Tye River)
- Appalachian Trail, George Washington National Forest—Pedlar District (Tye River to James River)
- Potomac River Gorge Area and Cabin John Trail
- Great North Mountain—North Half (Virginia/West Virginia)
- Massanutten Mountain—North Half (Signal Knob to New Market Gap)
- Massanutten Mountain—South Half (New Market Gap to Massanutten Peak)

• Tuscarora Trail—Appalachian Trail in Pennsylvania to Pennsylvania Route 641

• Tuscarora Trail—Pennsylvania Route 641 to Hancock, Maryland

• Tuscarora Trail—Hancock, Maryland, to Capon Springs, West Virginia including Cacapon State Park

• Rock Creek Park Area, District of Columbia

Guidebooks:

• *Appalachian Trail Guide Book—Maryland and Northern Virginia*

• *Appalachian Trail Guide Book—Shenandoah National Park*

• *Circuit Hikes in Shenandoah National Park*

• *Circuit Hikes in Virginia, West Virginia, Maryland, and Pennsylvania*

• *Hikes in Western Maryland*

• *The Tuscarora Trail North (Guide to Maryland and Pennsylvania)*

• *The Tuscarora Trail South (Guide to West Virginia and Virginia)*

• *Hikes in the Washington Region: Part A—Montgomery and Frederick Counties, Maryland*

• *Hikes in the Washington Region: Part B—Arlington, Fairfax, Loudon and Prince William Counties, Virginia*

• *Hikes in the Washington Region: Part C—District of Columbia and Calvert, Charles, Prince George's, Carroll, Howard, Baltimore and Harford Counties, Maryland*

• *Guide to Massanutten Mountain Hiking Trails*

• *Hiking Guide to the Pedlar District, George Washington National Forest*

• *Guide to Great North Mountain Trails*